D0375961

THE SECOND ADMINISTRATION

OF

THOMAS JEFFERSON

1805—1809

HISTORY OF THE UNITED STATES.

BY

HENRY ADAMS.

HISTORY

OF THE

UNITED STATES OF AMERICA

DURING THE SECOND ADMINISTRATION OF

THOMAS JEFFERSON

BY HENRY ADAMS

VOL. II.

ANTIQUARIAN PRESS LTD.
New York
1962

First Published
1891-1896
by
Charles Scribner's Sons

Reprinted 1962
by
Antiquarian Press, Ltd.
New York, N.Y.

Edition Limited to 750 Sets

Library of Congress Catalog Card Number: 61-8054

Printed in the U.S.A.

NOBLE OFFSET PRINTERS, INC.
NEW YORK 3, N.Y.

CONTENTS OF VOL. II.

HISTORY OF THE UNITED STATES.

CHAPTER I.

June 22, 1807, while Jefferson at Washington was fuming over Chief-Justice Marshall's subpœna, and while the grand jury at Richmond were on the point of finding their indictment against Burr, an event occurred at sea, off the entrance to Chesapeake Bay, which threw the country into violent excitement, distracting attention from Burr, and putting to a supreme test the theories of Jefferson's statesmanship.

That the accident which then happened should not have happened long before was matter for wonder, considering the arbitrary character of British naval officers and their small regard for neutral rights. For many years the open encouragement offered to the desertion of British seamen in American ports had caused extreme annoyance to the royal navy; and nowhere had this trouble been more serious than at Norfolk. Early in 1807 a British squadron happened to be lying within the Capes watching for some French frigates which had taken refuge at Annapolis.

One or more of these British ships lay occasionally in Hampton Roads, or came to the navy-yard at Gosport for necessary repairs. Desertions were of course numerous; even the American ships-of-war had much difficulty from loss of men, — and March 7 a whole boat's crew of the British sixteen-gun sloop "Halifax" made off with the jolly-boat and escaped to Norfolk. The commander of the "Halifax" was informed that these men had enlisted in the American frigate "Chesapeake," then under orders for the Mediterranean. He complained to the British consul and to Captain Decatur, but could get no redress. He met two of the deserters in the streets of Norfolk, and asked them why they did not return. One of them, Jenkin Ratford by name, replied, with abuse and oaths, that he was in the land of liberty and would do as he liked. The British minister at Washington also made complaint that three deserters from the "Melampus" frigate had enlisted on the "Chesapeake." The Secretary of the Navy ordered an inquiry, which proved that the three men in question, one of whom was a negro, were in fact on board the "Chesapeake," but that they were native Americans who had been improperly impressed by the "Melampus," and therefore were not subjects for reclamation by the British government. The nationality was admitted, and so far as these men were concerned the answer was final; but the presence of Jenkin Ratford, an Englishman, on board the "Chesapeake" under the name of Wilson escaped notice.

The admiral in command of the British ships on the North American station was George Cranfield Berkeley, a brother of the Earl of Berkeley. To him, at Halifax, the British officers in Chesapeake Bay reported their grievances; and Admiral Berkeley, without waiting for authority from England, issued the following orders, addressed to all the ships under his command:—

"Whereas many seamen, subjects of his Britannic Majesty, and serving in his ships and vessels as per margin ["Bellona," "Belleisle," "Triumph," "Chichester," "Halifax," "Zenobia"], while at anchor in the Chesapeake, deserted and entered on board the United States frigate called the 'Chesapeake,' and openly paraded the streets of Norfolk, in sight of their officers, under the American flag, protected by the magistrates of the town and the recruiting officer belonging to the above-mentioned American frigate, which magistrates and naval officer refused giving them up, although demanded by his Britannic Majesty's consul, as well as the captains of the ships from which the said men had deserted:

"The captains and commanders of his Majesty's ships and vessels under my command are therefore hereby required and directed, in case of meeting with the American frigate 'Chesapeake' at sea, and without the limits of the United States, to show to the captain of her this order, and to require to search his ship for the deserters from the before-mentioned ships, and to proceed and search for the same; and if a similar demand should be made by the American, he is to be permitted to search for any deserters from their service, according to the customs and usage of civilized nations on terms of peace and amity with each other."

The admiral's conception of the "customs and usage of civilized nations" did not expressly require the use of force; and any captain or commander who received this circular must at once have asked whether, in case the American captain should refuse to allow a search, — as was certain, — force should be employed. The order, dated June 1, 1807, was sent to Chesapeake Bay by the frigate "Leopard," commanded by Captain S. P. Humphreys; and since the "Leopard" was the admiral's flagship, Captain Humphreys was probably acquainted with the meaning of his instructions. The "Leopard" arrived at Lynnhaven on the morning of June 21; and Captain Humphreys reported his arrival and orders to Captain John Erskine Douglas of the "Bellona," a line-of-battle ship, then lying with the "Melampus" frigate in Lynnhaven Bay, enjoying the hospitality of the American government. Apparently Captain Douglas carried verbal explanations of the order from Captain Humphreys, for he made no attempt to qualify its extremest meaning. The "Leopard" remained twenty-four hours with the "Bellona," while the two commanders were in consultation. The next morning, June 22, at 4 A. M., the "Leopard" made sail,[1] and two hours later re-anchored a few miles to the eastward, and about three miles north of Cape Henry Lighthouse.

The "Chesapeake," during the difficulties at Norfolk and afterward, lay in the Eastern Branch at Wash-

[1] James's Naval History, iv. 329.

ington. The inefficiency of the Government in doing those duties which governments had hitherto been created to perform, was shown even more strikingly in the story of the "Chesapeake" than in the conspiracy of Burr. The frigate "Constitution" had sailed for the Mediterranean in August, 1803. The Government knew that her crew were entitled to their discharge, and that the President had no right to withhold it. The country was at peace; no emergency of any kind existed. A single ship of about one thousand tons burden needed to be fitted for sea at a date fixed three years beforehand; yet when the time came and the "Constitution" ought to have reached home, the "Chesapeake" had not so much as begun preparation. Captain James Barron was selected to command her as commodore of the Mediterranean squadron; Captain Charles Gordon—a native of the eastern shore of Maryland, the youngest master-commandant on the list—was appointed as her captain. Both were good officers and seamen; but Gordon received his orders only February 22, and could not take command until May 1,—long after he should have reached Gibraltar. Such was the inefficiency of the navy-yard at Washington that although the Secretary of the Navy had the "Chesapeake" under his eye and was most anxious to fit her out, and although Gordon fretted incessantly, making bitter complaints of delay, the frigate still remained in the mechanics' hands until the month of May. According to Commodore Barron the Washington navy-yard was more than incompetent.[1] "I have long known," he claimed to have written, "the perverse disposition of the rulers of that establishment." Yet he urged Gordon to complete his outfit at Washington, because the Norfolk yard was worse.[2] "I would by no means advise your leaving the navy-yard with any unfinished work and depend on Norfolk. You will experience more difficulty and trouble than you can imagine." As Burr's trial showed that the army was honeycombed by incompetence and conspiracy, so Barron's court-martial proved that nothing in naval administration could be depended upon.

For much of this, Congress and the people were responsible, and they accepted their own feebleness as the necessary consequence of a system which acted through other agencies than force; but much was also due to the Administration and to the President's instincts, which held him aloof from direct contact with both services. Jefferson did not love the deck of a man-of-war or enjoy the sound of a boatswain's whistle. The ocean was not his element; and his appetite for knowledge never led him to criticise the management of his frigates or his regiments so long as he could shut his eyes to their shortcomings. Thus while Wilkinson was left at his own pleasure to create or to stifle a rebellion at New Orleans, the crew of the "Constitution" were in a state of mutiny

[1] Barron's Court-martial, p. 241.

[2] Barron to Gordon, May 1, 1807; Court-martial, p. 239.

in the Mediterranean, and the officers of the "Chesapeake" were helpless under the control of the navy-yard at Washington.

At length, in the earliest days of June, Gordon dropped down the Potomac. The "Chesapeake" was to carry on this cruise an armament of forty guns,—twenty-eight 18-pounders and twelve 32-pound carronades; but owing to the shoals in the river she took but twelve guns on board at Washington, the rest waiting her arrival at Norfolk. With these twelve guns Gordon tried to fire the customary salute in passing Mount Vernon; and he wrote to the secretary in exasperation at the result of this first experience:[1]—

"Had we been engaged in an active war I should suspect the officers of the yard with having a design on my character; but fortunately Mount Vernon drew our attention to the guns before we could apprehend any danger from an enemy. In the act of saluting that place I was struck with astonishment when the first lieutenant reported to me that neither the sponges nor cartridges would go in the guns. I immediately arrested my gunner; but on his satisfying me that he had received them from the gunner of the yard I released him, and hold Mr. Stevenson responsible."

The mistakes were easily corrected, and the ship arrived in Hampton Roads without further incident. Commodore Barron, who first came aboard June 6,

[1] Captain Gordon to the Secretary of the Navy, June 22, 1807; Court-martial, p. 259.

wrote[1] at once to the secretary, "that from the extreme cleanliness and order in which I found her I am convinced that Captain Gordon and his officers must have used great exertions. Captain Gordon speaks in high terms of his lieutenants. The state of the ship proves the justice of his encomiums."

Nevertheless much remained to be done, and in spite of the secretary's urgency the ship was still delayed in Hampton Roads. From June 6 to June 19, notwithstanding bad weather, the whole ship's company were hard worked. The guns were taken on board and fitted; water was got in; spars and rigging had to be overhauled, and stores for four hundred men on a three-years cruise were shipped. June 19 the guns were all fitted, and the crew could for the first time be assigned to their stations at quarters. According to the custom of the service, the guns were charged with powder and shot. They had no locks, and were fired by the old-fashioned slow-match, or by loggerheads kept in the magazine and heated red-hot in the galley fire whenever need for them arose.

June 19 Captain Gordon considered the ship ready for sea, and wrote to the commodore on shore,[2] "We are unmoored and ready for weighing the first fair wind." Both Captain Gordon and Commodore Barron were aware that the decks were more or less

[1] Barron to the Secretary of the Navy, June 6, 1807; Court-martial, p. 371.

[2] Gordon to Barron, June 19, 1807, p. 367.

encumbered, and that the crew had not been exercised at the guns; but they were not warranted in detaining her on that account, especially since the guns could be better exercised at sea, and the ship was already four months behind time. Accordingly, June 21, Commodore Barron came on board, and at four o'clock in the afternoon the "Chesapeake" weighed anchor and stood down the Roads; at six o'clock she came to, dropped anchor, called all hands to quarters, and prepared to start for sea the next morning. From Lynnhaven Bay the "Leopard," which had arrived from Halifax only a few hours before, could watch every movement of the American frigate.

At a quarter-past seven o'clock on the morning of June 22 the "Chesapeake" got under way with a fair breeze. Her ship's company numbered three hundred and seventy-five men and boys, all told, but, as was not uncommon in leaving port, much sickness prevailed among the crew, and by the doctor's order the sick seamen were allowed to lie in the sun and air on the upper deck. The gun-deck between the guns was encumbered with lumber of one sort or another; the cables were not yet stowed away; four of the guns did not fit quite perfectly to their carriages, and needed a few blows with a maul to drive the trunnions home, but this defect escaped the eye; in the magazine the gunner had reported the powder-horns, used in priming the guns, as filled, whereas only five were in fact filled. Otherwise the ship, except for the freshness of her crew, was in fair condition.

At nine o'clock, passing Lynnhaven Bay, the officers on deck noticed the "Bellona" and "Melampus" at anchor. The "Leopard" lay farther out, and the "Bellona" was observed to be signalling. A story had been circulated at Norfolk that the captain of the "Melampus" threatened to take his deserters out of the "Chesapeake;" but rumors of this sort roused so little attention that no one on board the American frigate gave special notice to the British squadron. The "Melampus" lay quietly at anchor. Had Barron been able to read the "Bellona's" signals he would have suspected nothing, for they contained merely an order to the "Leopard" to weigh and reconnoitre in the southeast by east.[1] The British squadron was in the habit of keeping a cruiser outside to overhaul merchant-vessels; and when the "Leopard" stood out to sea, the officers of the "Chesapeake" naturally supposed that this was her errand.

At noon Cape Henry bore southwest by south, distant one or two miles. The day was fine; but the breeze then shifted to the south-southeast, and began to blow fresh. The change of wind brought the "Leopard" to windward. At about a quarter-past two the "Chesapeake" tacked in shore to wait for the pilot-boat which was to take off the pilot. The "Leopard" tacked also, about a mile distant. At the same time dinner was served at the commodore's

[1] James's Naval History, iv. 329.

table, and Barron, Gordon, Captain Hall of the marines, Dr. Bullus and his wife sat down to it. Captain Gordon afterward testified that as they were dining Commodore Barron noticed the British frigate through the larboard forward port of the cabin, and made the remark "that her movements appeared suspicious, but she could have nothing to do with us."[1] Barron positively denied ever having made the remark; but whether he said it or not, nothing more than a passing doubt occurred to him or to any other person on board. Gordon returned to his work; the crew began to stow away the cable; and at a quarter before three o'clock, the pilot-boat nearing, the "Chesapeake" again stood out to sea, the "Leopard" immediately following her tack.

At about half-past three o'clock, both ships being eight or ten miles southeast by east of Cape Henry, the "Leopard" came down before the wind, and rounding to, about half a cable's length to windward, hailed, and said she had despatches for the commodore. Barron returned the hail and replied, "We will heave to and you can send your boat on board of us." British ships-of-war on distant stations not infrequently sent despatches by the courtesy of American officers, and such a request implied no hostile purpose. British ships also arrogated a sort of right to the windward; and the "Leopard's" manœuvre, although one which no commander except an Englishman would naturally have made, roused no pecu-

[1] Court-martial, p. 101.

liar attention. The "Leopard's" ports were seen to be triced up; but the season was midsummer, the weather was fine and warm, and the frigate was in sight of her anchorage. Doubtless Barron ought not to have allowed a foreign ship-of-war to come alongside without calling his crew to quarters, — such was the general rule of the service; but the condition of the ship made it inconvenient to clear the guns, and the idea of an attack was so extravagant that, as Barron afterward said, he might as well have expected one when at anchor in Hampton Roads. After the event several officers, including Captain Gordon, affirmed that they felt suspicions; but they showed none at the time, and neither Gordon nor any one else suggested, either to the commodore or to each other, that it would be well to order the crew to quarters.

Barron went to his cabin to receive the British officer, whose boat came alongside. At a quarter before four o'clock Lieutenant Meade from the "Leopard" arrived on board, and was shown by Captain Gordon to the commodore's cabin. He delivered the following note: —

"The captain of his Britannic Majesty's ship 'Leopard' has the honor to enclose the captain of the United States ship 'Chesapeake' an order from the Honorable Vice-Admiral Berkeley, commander-in-chief of his Majesty's ships on the North American station, respecting some deserters from the ships (therein mentioned) under his command, and supposed to be now serving as part of the crew of the 'Chesapeake.'

"The captain of the 'Leopard' will not presume to say anything in addition to what the commander-in-chief has stated, more than to express a hope that every circumstance respecting them may be adjusted in a manner that the harmony subsisting between the two countries may remain undisturbed."

Having read Captain Humphrey's note, Commodore Barron took up the enclosed order signed by Admiral Berkeley. This order, as the note mentioned, designated deserters from certain ships. Barron knew that he had on board three deserters from the "Melampus," and that these three men had been the only deserters officially and regularly demanded by the British minister. His first thought was to look for the "Melampus" in the admiral's list; and on seeing that Berkeley had omitted it, Barron inferred that his own assurance would satisfy Captain Humphreys, and that the demand of search, being meant as a mere formality, would not be pressed. He explained to the British lieutenant the circumstances relating to the three men from the "Melampus," and after some consultation with Dr. Bullus, who was going out as consul to the Mediterranean, he wrote to Captain Humphreys the following reply: —

"I know of no such men as you describe. The officers that were on the recruiting service for this ship were particularly instructed by the Government, through me, not to enter any deserters from his Britannic Majesty's ships, nor do I know of any being here. I am also instructed never to permit the crew of any ship that I command to be mustered by any other but their own officers. It is my disposition to preserve harmony, and I hope this answer to your despatch will prove satisfactory."

Such an answer to such a demand was little suited to check the energy of a British officer in carrying out his positive orders. If Barron had wished to invite an attack, he could have done nothing more to the purpose than by receiving Berkeley's orders without a movement of self-defence.

Meanwhile, at a quarter-past four the officer of the deck sent down word that the British frigate had a signal flying. The lieutenant understood it for a signal of recall, as he had been half an hour away, and as soon as the letter could be written he hurried with it to his boat. No sooner had he left the cabin than Barron sent for Gordon and showed him the letters which had passed. Although the commodore hoped that the matter was disposed of, and assumed that Captain Humphreys would give some notice in case of further action, he could not but feel a show of energy to be proper, and he directed Gordon to order the gun-deck to be cleared. Instantly the officers began to prepare the ship for action.

Had the British admiral sent the "Bellona" or some other seventy-four on this ugly errand, Barron's error would have been less serious; for the captain of a seventy-four would have felt himself strong enough to allow delay. Sending the "Leopard" was arrogance of a kind that the British navy at that time frequently displayed. In 1804, when the Spanish treasure-ships were seized, the bitterest complaint of Spain was not that she had been made the unsuspecting victim of piracy, but that her squadron had been waylaid by one of only equal force, and could not in honor yield without a massacre which cost four ships and three hundred lives, besides the disgrace of submission to an enemy of not superior strength. The "Leopard" did indeed carry fifty-two guns, while the "Chesapeake" on this cruise carried only forty; but the "Chesapeake's" twelve carronades threw heavier shot than the "Leopard's" heaviest, and her broadside weighed 444 pounds, while that of the "Leopard" weighed 447. In tonnage the "Chesapeake" was a stronger ship and carried a larger crew than the "Leopard;" and a battle on fair terms would have been no certain victory. That Captain Humphreys felt it necessary to gain and retain every possible advantage was evident from his conduct. He could not afford to run the risk of defeat in such an undertaking; and knowing that the "Chesapeake" needed time to prepare for battle, he felt not strong enough to disregard her power of resistance, as he might have done had he commanded a ship of the line. To carry out his orders with as little loss as possible was his duty; for the consequences, not he but his admiral was to blame. Without a moment of delay, edging nearer, he hailed and cried: "Commodore Barron, you must be aware of the necessity I am under of complying with the orders of my commander-in-chief."

Hardly more than five minutes passed between the moment when the British officer left Commodore Barron's cabin and the time when Barron was hailed. To get the ship ready for action required fully half an hour. Barron, after giving the order to clear the guns, had come on deck and was standing in the gangway watching the "Leopard" with rapidly increasing anxiety, as he saw that the tompions were out of her guns and that her crew were evidently at quarters. He instantly repeated the order to prepare for battle, and told Gordon to hurry the men to their stations quietly without drum-beat. Gordon hastened down to the gun-deck with the keys of the magazine; the crew sprang to their quarters as soon as they understood the order. Barron, aware that his only chance was to gain time, remained at the gangway and replied through his trumpet: "I do not hear what you say." Captain Humphreys repeated his hail, and Barron again replied that he did not understand. The "Leopard" immediately fired a shot across the "Chesapeake's" bow;[1] a minute later another shot followed; and in two minutes more, at half-past four o'clock, the "Leopard" poured her whole broadside of solid shot and canister, at the distance of one hundred and fifty or two hundred feet, point-blank into the helpless American frigate. Before the gunner of the "Chesapeake" got to his magazine he heard the first gun from the "Leopard;" just as he opened and entered the magazine the "Leopard's" broadside was fired.

[1] James's Naval History, iv. 330.

No situation could be more trying to officers and crew than to be thus stationed at their guns without a chance to return a fire. The guns of the "Chesapeake" were loaded, but could not be discharged for want of lighted matches or heated loggerheads; and even if discharged, they could not be reloaded until ammunition should be handed from the magazine. Time was required both to clear the guns and to fire them; but the "Leopard's" first broadside was thrown just as the crew were beginning to clear the deck. The crew were fresh and untrained; but no complaint was made on this account,—all were willing enough to fight. The confusion was little greater than might have occurred under the same circumstances in the best-drilled crew afloat; and the harshest subsequent scrutiny discovered no want of discipline, except that toward the end a few men left their guns, declaring that they were ready to fight but not to be shot down like sheep. About the magazine the confusion was greatest, for a crowd of men and boys were clamoring for matches, powder-flasks, and loggerheads, while the gunner and his mates were doing their utmost to pass up what was needed; but in reasonable time all wants could have been supplied. On the upper deck both officers and men behaved well. Barron, though naturally much excited, showed both sense and courage. Standing in the open gangway fully exposed to the "Leopard's" guns, he was wounded by the first broadside, but remained either there or on the quarter-deck without noticing his wound, while he repeatedly hailed the "Leopard" in the hope of gaining a moment's time, and sent officer after officer below to hurry the men at the guns. Neither among the officers nor among the crew was courage the resource that failed them. Many of the men on the upper deck exposed themselves unnecessarily to the flying grapeshot by standing on the guns and looking over the hammocks, till Barron ordered them down. Careful subsequent inquiry could detect no lack of gallantry except in the pilot, who when questioned as to the commodore's behavior had the manliness to confess his alarm, — "I was too bad scared myself to observe him very particularly."

The British account, which was very exact, said that the "Leopard's" fire lasted fifteen minutes, — from 4.30 to 4.45 P.M., — during which time three full broadsides were discharged without return. No one could demand that Commodore Barron should subject his crew and ship to a longer trial when he had no hope of success. The time in which the "Leopard" could have sunk the "Chesapeake" might be a matter of doubt; but in the next battle between similar ships, five years afterward, the "Constitution," with about the "Leopard's" armament, totally disabled the "Guerriere" in less than thirty minutes, so that she sank within twenty-four hours, — though at the time of the action a heavy sea was running, and the "Guerriere" fought desperately with her whole broadside of twenty-five guns. June 22, 1807, the sea was calm; the "Leopard" lay quietly within pistol-shot; the

"Chesapeake" could not injure her; and if the "Leopard" was as well fought as the "Constitution" she should have done at least equal damage. If she did not succeed, it was not for want of trying. The official survey, taken the next day, showed twenty-two round-shot in the "Chesapeake's" hull, ten shot-holes in the sails, all three masts badly injured, the rigging much cut by grape, three men killed, eight severely and ten slightly wounded, including Commodore Barron, — which proved that of the seventy or eighty discharges from the "Leopard's" guns a large proportion took effect.

After enduring this massacre for fifteen minutes, while trying to fire back at least one gun for the honor of the ship, Commodore Barron ordered the flag to be struck. It was hauled down; and as it touched the taffrail one gun was discharged from the gun-deck sending a shot into the "Leopard." This single gun was fired by the third lieutenant, Allen, by means of a live coal which he brought in his fingers from the galley.

The boats of the "Leopard" then came on board, bringing several British officers, who mustered the ship's company. They selected the three Americans who had deserted from the "Melampus," and were therefore not included in Berkeley's order. Twelve or fifteen others were pointed out as English deserters, but these men were not taken. After a search of the ship, Jenkin Ratford was dragged out of the coal-hole; and this discovery alone saved Captain

Humphreys from the blame of committing an outrage not only lawless but purposeless. At about seven o'clock the British officers left the ship, taking with them the three Americans and Jenkin Ratford. Immediately afterward Commodore Barron sent Lieutenant Allen on board the "Leopard" with a brief letter to Captain Humphreys: —

"I consider the frigate 'Chesapeake' your prize, and am ready to deliver her to any officer authorized to receive her. By the return of the boat I shall expect your answer."

The British captain immediately replied as follows:

"Having to the utmost of my power fulfilled the instructions of my commander-in-chief, I have nothing more to desire, and must in consequence proceed to join the remainder of the squadron, — repeating that I am ready to give you every assistance in my power, and do most sincerely deplore that any lives should have been lost in the execution of a service which might have been adjusted more amicably, not only with respect to ourselves but the nations to which we respectively belong."

At eight o'clock Barron called a council of officers to consider what was best to be done with the ship, and it was unanimously decided to return to the Roads and wait orders. Disgraced, degraded, with officers and crew smarting under a humiliation that was never forgotten or forgiven, the unlucky "Chesapeake" dragged her way back to Norfolk.

There she lay for many months. Barron's wrong was in the nature of a crime. His brother officers made severe comments on his conduct; and Captain Gordon and some of his fellow-sufferers joined in the cry. One of his harshest critics was Stephen Decatur. Public sentiment required a victim. A court of inquiry which sat at Norfolk in October reported strongly against the commodore. He was charged with neglect of duty, with having failed to prepare his ship for action, with having surrendered prematurely, with having discouraged his men; but beneath all these charges lay an unjust belief in his want of courage. After six months delay, Barron was brought before a court-martial Jan. 4, 1808, and allowed to make his defence.

The court-martial took place at Norfolk, on board the "Chesapeake," — his own ship, which recalled at every moment his disgrace. The judges were his juniors, with the single exception of Captain John Rodgers, who was president of the court. Among them sat Stephen Decatur, — a brilliant officer, but one who had still to undergo the experience of striking his flag and of hearing the world suspect his surrender to be premature. Decatur held strong opinions against Barron, and not only expressed them strongly, but also notified Barron of them in order that he might, if he pleased, exercise the privilege of challenging. Barron made no objection, and Decatur unwillingly kept his place. In other respects Barron was still more hardly treated by fortune; the first lieutenant of the "Chesapeake" had died in the interval; Dr. Bullus, whose evidence was of the utmost importance, could not appear; Captain Gordon turned against him, and expressed the free opinion that Barron had never meant to resist; Captains Murray, Hull, and Chauncey, on the court of inquiry, had already made a hostile report; and the government prosecutor pressed every charge with a persistency that, as coming from the Department, seemed almost vindictive.

From January 4 to February 8 the court-martial tried charges against Barron, after which it continued until February 22 trying Captain Gordon, Captain Hall of the marines, and William Hook the gunner. The result of this long, searching, and severe investigation was remarkable, for it ended in a very elaborate decision [1] that Barron was blameless in every particular except one. He had not been negligent of his duty; he was not to blame for omitting to call the crew to quarters before he received Captain Humphreys' letter; he did well in getting the men to quarters secretly without drum-beat; he did not discourage his men; he had shown coolness, reflection, and personal courage under the most trying circumstances; he was right in striking his flag when he did, — but he was wrong in failing to prepare for action instantly on reading Admiral Berkeley's order; and for this mistake he was condemned to suspension for five years from the service, without pay or emoluments.

Barron had argued that although his judgment on

[1] Court-martial, pp. 337–350.

this point proved to be mistaken, it was reasonable, and in accord with his instructions. He produced the orders of the Secretary of the Navy, dated May 15, 1807, written with full knowledge that the deserters from the "Melampus" had been claimed by the British minister, and that a British squadron was lying in Chesapeake Bay. "Our interest as well as good faith requires," said the secretary, ". . . that we should cautiously avoid whatever may have a tendency to bring us into collision with any other Power." Barron urged that if he had given the order to prepare for battle as required by the court-martial, he must have detained by force the British lieutenant and his boat's crew, which would have had a direct "tendency to bring us into collision," or he must have let them go, which would have hurried the collision. He said that he had tried to gain time by keeping the appearances of confidence and good-will. He admitted that he had failed, but claimed that the failure was due to no fault which could have been corrected at that moment by those means.

The defence was open to criticism, especially because Barron himself could claim to have made no use of the time he gained. Yet perhaps, on the whole, the court-martial might have done better to punish Barron for his want of caution in permitting the British frigate to approach. This was his first error, which could not be retrieved; and Barron could hardly have complained of his punishment, even though every officer in the service knew that the rule of going to quarters in such cases was seldom strictly observed. The President and the Secretary of the Navy could alone say whether Barron had understood their orders correctly, and whether his plea, founded on the secretary's instructions, was sound. In the light of Jefferson's diplomacy, Barron's course accorded with his instructions; and perhaps, had the President claimed his own share in the "Chesapeake's" disaster, he would have refused to degrade a faithful, able, and gallant seaman for obeying the spirit and letter of his orders. Unfortunately such an interference would have ruined the navy; and so it happened that what Jefferson had so long foreseen took place. He had maintained that the frigates were a mere invitation to attack; that they created the dangers they were built to resist, and tempted the aggressions of Great Britain, which would, but for these ships, find no object to covet; and when the prediction turned true, he was still obliged to maintain the character of the service. He approved the sentence of the court-martial.

So far as the service was concerned, Barron's punishment was not likely to stimulate its caution, for no American captain, unless he wished to be hung by his own crew at his own yard-arm, was likely ever again to let a British frigate come within gunshot without taking such precautions as he would have taken against a pirate; but though the degradation could do little for the service, it cost Barron his honor, and ended by costing Decatur his life.

Meanwhile, Captain Humphreys reported to Captain Douglas on the "Bellona," and Captain Douglas reported the whole affair to Admiral Berkeley at Halifax, who received at the same time accounts from American sources. The admiral immediately wrote to approve the manner in which his orders had been carried out. "As far as I am enabled to judge," he said[1] in a letter to Captain Humphreys, dated July 4, "you have conducted yourself most properly." The inevitable touch of unconscious comedy was not wanting in the British admiral, whose character recalled Smollett's novels and memories of Commodore Hawser Trunnion. "I hope you mind the public accounts which have been published of this affair as little as I do," he continued; "we must make allowances for the heated state of the populace in a country where law and every tie, both civil and religious, is treated so lightly." No broader humor could be found in "Peregrine Pickle" than in one breath to approve an act so lawless that no man of common-sense even in England ventured to defend it as lawful, and in the next to read the Americans a moral lecture on their want of law and religion; yet grotesque as this old-fashioned naval morality might be, no man in England noticed either its humor or its absurdity.

As though to show that he meant no humor by it, the admiral, August 25, called a court-martial, which the next day sentenced Jenkin Ratford to be hanged,

[1] Marshall's Naval Biography, iv. 895.

and the three American deserters from the "Melampus" to receive five hundred lashes each. The last part of the sentence was not carried out, and the three Americans remained quietly in prison; but August 31, Jenkin Ratford was duly hanged from the foreyard-arm of his own ship, the "Halifax."

CHAPTER II.

FOR the first time in their history the people of the United States learned, in June, 1807, the feeling of a true national emotion. Hitherto every public passion had been more or less partial and one-sided; even the death of Washington had been ostentatiously mourned in the interests and to the profit of party: but the outrage committed on the "Chesapeake" stung through hide-bound prejudices, and made democrat and aristocrat writhe alike. The brand seethed and hissed like the glowing olive-stake of Ulysses in the Cyclops' eye, until the whole American people, like Cyclops, roared with pain and stood frantic on the shore, hurling abuse at their enemy, who taunted them from his safe ships. The mob at Norfolk, furious at the sight of their dead and wounded comrades from the "Chesapeake," ran riot, and in the want of a better object of attack destroyed the water-casks of the British squadron. July 29 the town forbade communication with the ships in Lynnhaven Bay, which caused Captain Douglas to write to the Mayor of Norfolk a letter much in the tone of Admiral Berkeley.

"You must be perfectly aware," said he, "that the British flag never has been, nor will be, insulted with impunity. You must also be aware that it has been, and still is, in my power to obstruct the whole trade of the Chesapeake since the late circumstance; which I desisted from, trusting that general unanimity would be restored. . . . Agreeably to my intentions, I have proceeded to Hampton Roads, with the squadron under my command, to await your answer, which I trust you will favor me with without delay."

He demanded that the prohibition of intercourse should be "immediately annulled." The Mayor sent Littleton Tazewell to carry an answer to this warlike demand from the "Bellona," and Tazewell was somewhat surprised to find Captain Douglas highly conciliatory, and unable to see what the people of Norfolk could have found in his letter which could be regarded as "menacing;" but meanwhile all Virginia was aroused, an attack on Norfolk was generally expected, the coast was patrolled by an armed force, and the British men-of-war were threatened by mounted militia.

In the Northern States the feeling was little less violent. Public meetings were everywhere held. At New York, July 2, the citizens, at a meeting over which De Witt Clinton presided, denounced "the dastardly and unprovoked attack" on the "Chesapeake," and pledged themselves to support the government "in whatever measures it may deem necessary to adopt in the present crisis of affairs." At Boston, where the town government was wholly Federalist, a moment of hesitation occurred.[1] The principal Federalists consulted with each other, and decided not to call a town-meeting. July 10 an informal meeting was called by the Republicans, over which Elbridge Gerry presided, and which Senator J. Q. Adams alone among the prominent Federalists attended. There also a resolution was adopted, pledging cheerful co-operation "in any measures, however serious," which the Administration might deem necessary for the safety and honor of the country. In a few days public opinion compelled the Federalists to change their tone. A town-meeting was held at Faneuil Hall July 16, and Senator Adams again reported resolutions, which were unanimously adopted, pledging effectual support to the government. Yet the Essex Junto held aloof; neither George Cabot, Theophilus Parsons, nor Timothy Pickering would take part in such proceedings, and the Federalist newspaper which was supposed to represent their opinions went so far as to assert that Admiral Berkeley's doctrine was correct, and that British men-of-war had a right to take deserters from the national vessels of the United States. In private, this opinion was hotly maintained; in public, its expression was generally thought unwise in face of popular excitement.

President Jefferson was at Washington June 25, the day when news of the outrage arrived; but his

[1] New England Federalism, p. 182.

Cabinet was widely scattered, and some time passed before its members could be reassembled. Gallatin was last to arrive; but July 2, at a full meeting, the President read the draft of a proclamation, which was approved, and the proclamation issued on the same day. It rehearsed the story of American injuries and forbearance, and of British aggressions upon neutral rights; and so moderate was its tone as to convey rather the idea of deprecation than of anger: —

"Hospitality under such circumstances ceases to be a duty; and a continuance of it, with such uncontrolled abuses, would tend only, by multiplying injuries and irritations, to bring on a rupture between the two nations. This extreme resort is equally opposed to the interests of both, as it is to assurances of the most friendly dispositions on the part of the British government, in the midst of which this outrage has been committed. In this light the subject cannot but present itself to that government, and strengthen the motives to an honorable reparation of the wrong which has been done, and to that effectual control of its naval commanders which alone can justify the government of the United States in the exercise of those hospitalities it is now constrained to discontinue."

With this preamble the proclamation required all armed vessels of Great Britain to depart from American waters; and in case of their failing to do so, the President forbade intercourse with them, and prohibited supplies to be furnished them.

At the same Cabinet meeting, according to Jefferson's memoranda,[1] other measures were taken. The gunboats were ordered to points where attack might be feared. The President was to "recall all our vessels from the Mediterranean, by a vessel to be sent express, and send the 'Revenge' to England with despatches to our minister demanding satisfaction for the attack on the 'Chesapeake;' in which must be included — (1) a disavowal of the act and of the principle of searching a public armed vessel; (2) a restoration of the men taken; (3) a recall of Admiral Berkeley. Communicate the incident which has happened to Russia." Two days afterward, at another Cabinet meeting, it was "agreed that a call of Congress shall issue the fourth Monday of August (24), to meet the fourth Monday in October (26), unless new occurrences should render an earlier call necessary. Robert Smith wished an earlier call." He was not alone in this wish. Gallatin wrote privately to his wife that he wanted an immediate call, and that the chief objection to it, which would not be openly avowed, was the unhealthiness of Washington city.[2]

The news of Captain Douglas's threatening conduct and language at Norfolk produced further measures. July 5 "it was agreed to call on the governors of the States to have their quotas of one hundred thousand militia in readiness. The object is to have the portions on the sea-coast ready for any emergency; and

[1] Cabinet Memoranda, Jefferson MSS.

[2] Adams's Gallatin, p. 358.

for those in the North we may look to a winter expedition against Canada." July 7 it was "agreed to desire the Governor of Virginia to order such portion of militia into actual service as may be necessary for defence of Norfolk and of the gunboats at Hampton and in Matthews County." Little by little Jefferson was drawn into preparations for actual war.

Even among earnest Republicans the tone of Jefferson's proclamation and the character of his measures were at first denounced as tame. John Randolph called the proclamation an "apology;" Joseph Nicholson wrote to Gallatin a remonstrance.

> "But one feeling pervades the nation," said he;[1] "all distinctions of Federalism and Democracy are vanished. The people are ready to submit to any deprivation; and if we withdraw ourselves within our own shell, and turn loose some thousands of privateers, we shall obtain in a little time an absolute renunciation of the right of search for the purposes of impressment. A parley will prove fatal; for the merchants will begin to calculate. They rule us, and we should take them before their resentment is superseded by considerations of profit and loss. I trust in God the 'Revenge' is going out to bring Monroe and Pinkney home."

Gallatin, who had hitherto thrown all his influence on the side of peace, was then devoting all his energies to provision for war. He answered Nicholson that the tone of Government, though he thought

[1] Nicholson to Gallatin, July 14, 1807; Adams's Gallatin, p. 360.

it correct, was of little consequence, for in any case the result would be the same; he was confident that England would give neither satisfaction nor security.[1]

"I will, however, acknowledge that on that particular point I have not bestowed much thought; for having considered from the first moment war was a necessary result, and the preliminaries appearing to me but matters of form, my faculties have been exclusively applied to the preparations necessary to meet the times. And although I am not very sanguine as to the brilliancy of our exploits, the field where we can act without a navy being very limited, and perfectly aware that a war, in a great degree passive, and consisting of privations, will become very irksome to the people, I feel no apprehension of the immediate result. We will be poorer both as a nation and as a government, our debt and taxes will increase, and our progress in every respect be interrupted; but all those evils are not only not to be put in competition with the independence and honor of the nation, they are moreover temporary, and a very few years of peace will obliterate their effects. Nor do I know whether the awakening of nobler feelings and habits than avarice and luxury might not be necessary to prevent our degenerating, like the Hollanders, into a nation of mere calculators."

Jefferson followed without protest the impulse toward war; but his leading thought was to avoid it. Peace was still his passion, and his scheme of peace-

[1] Gallatin to Nicholson, July 17, 1807; Adams's Gallatin, p. 361.

ful coercion had not yet been tried. Even while the nation was aflame with warlike enthusiasm, his own mind always reverted to another thought. The tone of the proclamation showed it; his unwillingness to call Congress proved it; his letters dwelt upon it.

"We have acted on these principles," he wrote in regard to England,[1] — "(1) to give that Government an opportunity to disavow and make reparation; (2) to give ourselves time to get in the vessels, property, and seamen now spread over the ocean; (3) to do no act which might compromit Congress in their choice between war, non-intercourse, or any other measure."

To Vice-President Clinton he wrote,[2] that since the power of declaring war was with the Legislature, the Executive should do nothing necessarily committing them to decide for war in preference to non-intercourse, "which will be preferred by a great many." Every letter[3] written by the President during the crisis contained some allusion to non-intercourse, which he still called the "peaceable means of repressing injustice, by making it the interest of the aggressor to do what is just, and abstain from future wrong." As the war fever grew stronger he talked more boldly about hostilities, and became silent about

[1] Jefferson to Bidwell, July 11, 1807; Works, v. 125.

[2] Jefferson to the Vice-President, July 6, 1807; Works, v. 115.

[3] Jefferson to Governor Cabell, June 29, 1807, Works, v. 114; to Mr. Bowdoin, July 10, 1807, Works, v. 123; to M. Dupont, July 14, 1807, Works, v. 127; to Lafayette, July 14, 1807, Works, v. 129.

non-intercourse;[1] but the delay in calling Congress was certain to work as he wished, and to prevent a committal to the policy of war.

To no one was this working of Jefferson's mind more evident than to General Turreau, whose keen eyes made the President uneasy under the sense of being watched and criticised. Turreau, who had left Washington for the summer, hurried back on hearing of the "Chesapeake" disaster. On arriving, he went the same evening to the White House, "where there had been a dinner of twenty covers, composed, they say, of new friends of the Government, to whom Mr. Madison had given a first representation two days before. Indeed, I knew none of the guests except the Ambassador of England and his secretary of legation. The President received me even better than usual, but left me, presently, to follow with the British minister a conversation that my entrance had interrupted."[2]

Then came a touch of nature which Turreau thought strikingly characteristic. No strong power of imagination is needed to see the White House parlor, on the warm summer night, with Jefferson, as Senator Maclay described him, sitting in a lounging manner on one hip, with his loose, long figure, and his clothes that seemed too small for him, talking, without a break, in his rambling, disjointed way,

[1] Jefferson to Colonel Taylor, Aug. 1, 1807; Works, v. 148.

[2] Turreau to Talleyrand, July 18, 1808; Archives des Aff. Étr. MSS.

showing deep excitement under an affectation of coolness, and at every word and look betraying himself to the prying eyes of Talleyrand's suspicious agent. What Jefferson said, and how he said it, can be told only in Turreau's version; but perhaps the few words used by the prejudiced Frenchman gave a clearer idea of American politics than could be got from all other sources together: —

"This conversation with the British minister having been brought to an end, Mr. Jefferson came and sat down by my side; and after all the American guests had successively retired, Mr. Erskine, who had held out longest, — in the hope, perhaps, that I should quit the ground, — went away also. The President spoke to me about the 'Chesapeake' affair, and said: 'If the English do not give us the satisfaction we demand, we will take Canada, which wants to enter the Union; and when, together with Canada, we shall have the Floridas, we shall no longer have any difficulties with our neighbors; and it is the only way of preventing them. I expected that the Emperor would return sooner to Paris, — and then this affair of the Floridas would be ended.' Then, changing the subject, he asked me what were the means to employ in order to be able to defend the American harbors and coasts. I answered that the choice of means depended on local conditions, and that his officers, after an exact reconnoissance, ought to pronounce on the application of suitable means of defence. — 'We have no officers!' — He treated twenty-seven different subjects in a conversation of half an hour; and as he showed, as usual, no sort of distrust, this conversation of fits and starts (*à bâtons rompus*) makes me infer that the event would embarrass him much, — and Mr. Madison seemed to me to share this embarrassment. . . . Once for all, whatever may be the disposition of mind here, though every one is lashing himself (*se batte les flancs*) to take a warlike attitude, I can assure your Highness that the President does not want war, and that Mr. Madison dreads it still more. I am convinced that these two personages will do everything that is possible to avoid it, and that if Congress, which will be called together only when an answer shall have arrived from England, should think itself bound, as organ of public opinion, to determine on war, its intention will be crossed by powerful intrigues, because the actual Administration has nothing to gain and everything to lose by war."

Turreau was not the only observer who saw beneath the surface of American politics. The young British minister, Erskine, who enlivened his despatches by no such lightness of touch as was usual with his French colleague, wrote to the new Foreign Secretary of England, George Canning, only brief and dry accounts of the situation at Washington, but showed almost a flash of genius in the far-reaching policy he struck out.

"The ferment in the public mind," he wrote July 21,[1] "has not yet subsided, and I am confirmed in the opinion . . . that this country will engage in war rather than submit to their national armed ships being forcibly searched on the high seas. . . . Should his Majesty think fit to cause an apology to be offered to these States on ac-

[1] Erskine to Canning, July 21, 1807; MSS. British Archives.

count of the attack of his Majesty's ship 'Leopard' on the United States frigate 'Chesapeake,' it would have the most powerful effect not only on the minds of the people of this country, but would render it impossible for the Congress to bring on a war upon the other points of difference between his Majesty and the United States at present under discussion."

A single blow, however violent, could not weld a nation. Every one saw that the very violence of temper which made the month of July, 1807, a moment without a parallel in American history since the battle of Lexington, would be followed by a long reaction of doubt and discord. If the President, the Secretary of State, and great numbers of their stanchest friends hesitated to fight when a foreign nation, after robbing their commerce, fired into their ships of war, and slaughtered or carried off their fellow-citizens, — if they preferred "peaceable means of repressing injustice" at the moment when every nerve would naturally have been strung to recklessness with the impulse to strike back, — it was in the highest degree unlikely that they would be more earnest for war when time had deadened the sense of wrong. Neither England, France, nor Spain could fail to see that the moment when aggression ceased to be safe had not yet arrived.

The people were deeply excited, commerce for the moment was paralyzed, no merchant dared send out a ship, and the country resounded with cries of war when the "Revenge" sailed, bearing instructions to

Monroe to demand reparation from the British government. These instructions, dated July 6, 1807, were framed in the spirit which seemed to characterize Madison's diplomatic acts. Specific redress for a specific wrong appeared an easy demand. That the attack on the "Chesapeake" should be disavowed; that the men who had been seized should be restored; that punctilious exactness of form should mark the apology and retribution, — was matter of course; but that this special outrage, which stood on special ground, should be kept apart, and that its atonement should precede the consideration of every other disputed point, was the natural method of dealing with it if either party was serious in wishing for peace. Such a wound, left open to fester and smart, was certain to make war in the end inevitable. Both the President and Madison wanted peace; yet their instructions to Monroe made a settlement of the "Chesapeake" outrage impracticable by binding it to a settlement of the wider dispute as to impressments from merchant vessels.

"As a security for the future," wrote Madison,[1] "an entire abolition of impressments from vessels under the flag of the United States, if not already arranged, is also to make an indispensable part of the satisfaction."

Among the many impossibilities which had been required of Monroe during the last four years, this was one of the plainest. The demand was prelimi-

[1] Madison to Monroe, July 6, 1807; State Papers, iii. 183.

nary, in ordinary diplomatic usage, to a declaration of war; and nothing in Jefferson's Presidency was more surprising than that he should have thought such a policy of accumulating unsettled causes for war consistent with his policy of peace.

While the "Revenge" was slowly working across the Atlantic, Monroe in London was exposed to the full rigor of the fresh storm. News of the "Chesapeake" affair reached London July 25; and before it could become public Canning wrote to Monroe a private note,[1] cautiously worded, announcing that a "transaction" had taken place "off the coast of America," the particulars of which he was not at present enabled to communicate, and was anxious to receive from Monroe: —

> "But whatever the real merits and character of the transaction may turn out to be, Mr. Canning could not forbear expressing without delay the sincere concern and sorrow which he feels at its unfortunate result, and assuring the American minister, both from himself and on the behalf of his Majesty's government, that if the British officers should prove to have been culpable, the most prompt and effectual reparation shall be afforded to the government of the United States."

When on Monday morning, July 27, Monroe read in the newspapers the account of what had taken place, and realized that Canning, while giving out that he knew not the particulars, must have had Admiral Berkeley's official report within his reach

[1] Canning to Monroe, July 25, 1807; State Papers, iii. 187.

if not on his table, the American minister could not but feel that the British secretary might have spoken with more frankness. In truth ministers were waiting to consult the law, and to learn whether Berkeley could be sustained. The extreme Tories, who wanted a quarrel with the United States; the reckless, who were delighted with every act of violence, which they called energy; the mountebanks, represented by Cobbett, who talked at random according to personal prejudices, — all approved Berkeley's conduct. The Ministry, not yet accustomed to office, and disposed to assert the power they held, could not easily reconcile themselves to disavowing a British admiral whose popular support came from the ranks of their own party. Seeing this, Monroe became more and more alarmed.

The tone of the press was extravagant enough to warrant despair. July 27 the "Morning Post," which was apt to draw its inspiration from the Foreign Office, contained a diatribe on the "Chesapeake" affair.

"America," it said, "is not contented with striking at the very vitals of our commercial existence; she must also, by humbling our naval greatness and disputing our supremacy, not only lessen us in our own estimation, but degrade us in the eyes of Europe and of the world. . . . It will never be permitted to be said that the 'Royal Sovereign' has struck her flag to a Yankee cockboat."

In the whole press of England, the "Morning Chronicle" alone deprecated an American war or blamed Berkeley's act; and the "Morning Chronicle" was the organ of opposition.

Monroe waited two days, and heard no more from Canning. July 29, by a previous appointment, he went to the Foreign Office on other business.[1] He found the Foreign Secretary still reticent, admitting or yielding nothing, but willing to satisfy the American government that Berkeley's order had not been the result of instructions from the Tory ministry. Monroe said he would send a note on the subject, and Canning acquiesced. Monroe on the same day sent his letter, which called attention to the outrage that had been committed and to its unjustifiable nature, expressing at the same time full confidence that the British government would at once disavow and punish the offending officer. The tone of the note, though strong, was excellent, but on one point did not quite accord with the instructions on their way from Washington.

"I might state," said Monroe, "other examples of great indignity and outrage, many of which are of recent date; . . . but it is improper to mingle them with the present more serious cause of complaint."

Monday, August 3, Canning sent a brief reply. Since Monroe's complaint was not founded on official knowledge, said Canning, the King's government was not bound to do more than to express readiness to

[1] Monroe to Madison, Aug. 4, 1807; State Papers, iii. 186.

make reparation if such reparation should prove to be due:[1] —

"Of the existence of such a disposition on the part of the British government you, sir, cannot be ignorant. I have already assured you of it, though in an unofficial form, by the letter which I addressed to you on the first receipt of the intelligence of this unfortunate transaction; and I may perhaps be permitted to express my surprise, after such an assurance, at the tone of that representation which I have just had the honor to receive from you. But the earnest desire of his Majesty to evince in the most satisfactory manner the principles of justice and moderation by which he is uniformly actuated, has not permitted him to hesitate in commanding me to assure you that his Majesty neither does nor has at any time maintained the pretension of a right to search ships of war in the national service of any State for deserters."

If it should prove that Berkeley's order rested on no other ground than the simple and unqualified pretension to such a right, the King had no difficulty in disavowing it, and would have none in showing his displeasure at it.

Although Monroe thought this reply to be "addressed in rather a harsh tone," as was certainly the case, he considered it intended to concede the essential point, and he decided to say no more without instructions. He might well be satisfied, for Canning's "surprise" was a mild expression of public feeling.

[1] Canning to Monroe, Aug. 3, 1807; American State Papers, iii. 188.

Hitherto the British press had shown no marked signs of the insanity which sometimes seized a people under the strain of great excitement, but the "Chesapeake" affair revealed the whole madness of the time. August 6, three days after Canning had disavowed pretension to search national vessels, the "Morning Post" published an article strongly in favor of Berkeley and war. "Three weeks blockade of the Delaware, the Chesapeake, and Boston Harbor would make our presumptuous rivals repent of their puerile conduct." August 5 the "Times" declared itself for Berkeley, and approved not only his order, but also its mode of execution. The "Courier" from the first defended Berkeley. Cobbett's peculiar powers of mischief were never more skilfully exerted: —

"I do not pretend to say that we may not in this instance have been in the wrong, because there is nothing authentic upon the subject; nor am I prepared to say that our right of search, *in all cases*, extends to ships of war. But of this I am certain, that if the laws of nations do not allow you to search for deserters in a friend's territory, neither do they allow that friend to inveigle away your troops or your seamen, to do which is an act of hostility; and I ask for no better proof of inveigling than the enlisting and refusing to give up such troops or seamen."

Owing to his long residence in the United States, Cobbett was considered a high authority on American affairs; and he boldly averred that America could not go to war without destroying herself as a political body. More than half the people of America, he said, were already disgusted with the French bias of their government.

In the face of a popular frenzy so general, Monroe might feel happy to have already secured from Canning an express disavowal of the pretension to search ships of war. He was satisfied to let the newspapers say what they would while he waited his instructions. A month passed before these arrived. September 3 Monroe had his next interview, and explained the President's expectations, — that the men taken from the "Chesapeake" should be restored, the offenders punished, a special mission sent to America to announce the reparation, and the practice of impressment from merchant-vessels suppressed.[1] Canning listened with civility, for he took pride in tempering the sternness of his policy by the courtesy of his manner. He made no serious objection to the President's demands so far as they concerned the "Chesapeake;" but when Monroe came to the abandonment of impressment from merchant-vessels, he civilly declined to admit it into the discussion.

Monroe wrote the next day a note,[2] founded on his instructions, in which he insisted on the proposition which he had expressly discarded in his note of July 29, that the outrages rising from impressment in general ought to be considered as a part of the

[1] Monroe to Madison, Oct. 10, 1807; State Papers, iii. 191.
[2] Monroe to Canning, Sept. 7, 1807; State Papers, iii. 189.

"Chesapeake" affair; and he concluded his argument by saying that his Government looked on this complete adjustment as indispensably necessary to heal the deep wound which had been inflicted on the national honor of the United States. After the severity with which Monroe had been rebuked for disregarding his instructions on this point barely a few months before, he had no choice but to obey his orders without the change of a letter; but he doubtless knew in advance that this course left Canning master of the situation. The British government was too well acquainted with the affairs of America to be deceived by words. That the United States would fight to protect their national vessels was possible; but every one knew that no party in Congress could be induced to make war for the protection of merchant seamen. In rejecting such a demand, not only was Canning safe, but he was also sure of placing the President at odds with his own followers and friends.

A fortnight was allowed to pass before the British government replied. Then, September 23, Canning sent to the American legation an answer.[1] He began by requesting to know whether the President's proclamation was authentic, and whether it would be withdrawn on a disavowal of the act which led to it; because, as an act of retaliation, it must be taken into account in adjusting the reparation due. He insisted that the nationality of the men seized must

[1] Canning to Monroe, Sept. 23, 1807; State Papers, iii. 199.

also be taken into account, not as warranting their unauthorized seizure, but as a question of redress between government and government. In respect to the general question of impressment in connection with the specific grievance of the "Chesapeake," he explained at some length the different ground on which the two disputes rested; and while professing his willingness to discuss the regulation of the practice, he affirmed the rights of England, which, he said,—

"existed in their fullest force for ages previous to the establishment of the United States of America as an independent government; and it would be difficult to contend that the recognition of that independence can have operated any change in this respect, unless it can be shown that in acknowledging the government of the United States, Great Britain virtually abdicated her own rights as a naval Power, or unless there were any express stipulations by which the ancient and prescriptive usages of Great Britain, founded in the soundest principles of natural law, though still enforced against other independent nations of the world, were to be suspended whenever they might come in contact with the interests or the feelings of the American people."

After disposing of the matter with this sneer, Canning closed by earnestly recommending Monroe to consider whether his instructions might not leave him at liberty to adjust the case of the "Chesapeake" by itself:—

"If your instructions leave you no discretion, I cannot press you to act in contradiction to them. In that case there can be no advantage in pursuing a discussion which you are not authorized to conclude; and I shall have only to regret that the disposition of his Majesty to terminate that difference amicably and satisfactorily is for the present rendered unavailing.

"In that case his Majesty, in pursuance of the disposition of which he has given such signal proofs, will lose no time in sending a minister to America, furnished with the necessary instructions and powers for bringing this unfortunate dispute to a conclusion consistent with the harmony subsisting between Great Britain and the United States; but in order to avoid the inconvenience which has arisen from the mixed nature of your instructions, that minister will not be empowered to entertain, as connected with this subject, any proposition respecting the search of merchant-vessels."

Monroe replied,[1] September 29, that his instructions were explicit, and that he could not separate the two questions. He closed by saying that Canning's disposition and sentiments had been such as inspired him with great confidence that they should soon have been able to bring the dispute to an honorable and satisfactory conclusion. With this letter so far as concerned Monroe, the "Chesapeake" incident came to its end in failure of redress.

One more subject remained for Monroe to finish. His unfortunate treaty returned by Madison with a long list of changes and omissions, had been made by Monroe and Pinkney the subject of a letter to Can-

[1] Monroe to Canning, Sept. 29, 1807; State Papers, iii. 201.

ning as early as July 24;[1] but the affair of the "Chesapeake" intervened, and Canning declined to touch any other subject until this was adjusted. No sooner did he succeed in referring the "Chesapeake" negotiation to Washington than he turned to the treaty. That a measure which had been the most unpopular act of an unpopular Whig ministry could expect no mercy at Canning's hands, was to be expected; but some interest attached to the manner of rejection which he might prefer. In a formal note, dated October 22, Canning addressed the American government in a tone which no one but himself could so happily use,—a tone of mingled condescension and derision.[2] He began by saying that his Majesty could not profess to be satisfied that the American government had taken effectual steps in regard to the Berlin Decree; but the King had nevertheless decided, in case the President should ratify Monroe's treaty, to ratify it in his turn, "reserving to himself the right of taking, in consequence of that decree, and of the omission of any effectual interposition on the part of neutral nations to obtain its revocation, such measures of retaliation as his Majesty might judge expedient." Without stopping to explain what value a ratification under such conditions would have, Canning continued that the President had thought

[1] Monroe and Pinkney to Canning, July 24, 1807; State Papers, iii. 194.

[2] Canning to Monroe and Pinkney, Oct. 22, 1807; State Papers, iii. 198.

proper to propose alterations in the body of the treaty: —

"The undersigned is commanded distinctly to protest against a practice altogether unusual in the political transactions of States, by which the American government assumes to itself the privilege of revising and altering agreements concluded and signed on its behalf by its agents duly authorized for that purpose, of retaining so much of those agreements as may be favorable to its own views, and of rejecting such stipulations, or such parts of stipulations, as are conceived to be not sufficiently beneficial to America."

Without discussing the correctness of Canning's assertion that the practice was "altogether unusual in the political transactions of States," Monroe and Pinkney might have replied that every European treaty was negotiated, step by step, under the eye of the respective governments, and that probably no extant treaty had been signed by a British agent in Europe without first receiving at every stage the approval of the King. No American agent could consult his government. Canning was officially aware that Monroe and Pinkney, in signing their treaty, had done so at their own risk, in violation of the President's orders. The requirement that the President of the United States should follow European rules was unreasonable; but in the actual instance Canning's tone was something more than unreasonable. His own note assumed for the British government "the privilege of revising and altering" whatever provisions of the treaty it pleased; and after a condition so absolute, he violated reciprocity in rejecting conditions made by the President because they were "unusual in the political transactions of States:" —

> "The undersigned is therefore commanded to apprise the American commissioners that, although his Majesty will be at all times ready to listen to any suggestions for arranging, in an amicable and advantageous manner, the respective interests of the two countries, the proposal of the President of the United States for proceeding to negotiate anew upon the basis of a treaty already solemnly concluded and signed, is a proposal wholly inadmissible."

With this denial of the right of others to exercise arbitrary methods, Canning declared the field open for the British government to give full range to its arbitrary will. A week afterward Monroe left London forever. He had taken his audience of leave October 7, and resigned the legation to Pinkney. October 29 he started for Portsmouth to take ship for Virginia. His diplomatic career in Europe was at an end; but these last failures left him in a state of mind easy to imagine, in which his irritation with Jefferson and Madison, the authors of his incessant misfortunes, outran his suspicions of Canning, whose pretence of friendship had been dignified and smooth.

For reasons to be given hereafter, the Ministry decided to disavow Admiral Berkeley's attack on the "Chesapeake;" but in order to provide against the reproach of surrendering British rights, a proclamation[1] almost as offensive to the United States as Admiral Berkeley's order was issued, October 16. Beginning with the assertion that great numbers of British seamen "have been enticed to enter the service of foreign States, and are now actually serving as well on board the ships of war belonging to the said foreign States as on board the merchant-vessels belonging to their subjects," the proclamation ordered such seamen to return home, and commanded all naval officers to seize them, without unnecessary violence, in any foreign merchant-vessels where they might be found, and to demand them from the captains of foreign ships of war, in order to furnish government with the necessary evidence for claiming redress from the government which had detained the British seamen. Further, the proclamation gave warning that naturalization would not be regarded as relieving British subjects of their duties, but that, while such naturalized persons would be pardoned if they returned immediately to their allegiance, all such as should serve on ships-of-war belonging to any State at enmity with England would be guilty of high treason, and would be punished with the utmost severity of the law.

That the British public, even after the battle of Trafalgar and the firing upon the "Chesapeake," might have felt its pride sufficiently flattered by such a proclamation seemed only reasonable; for in truth this proclamation forced war upon a government which

[1] American State Papers, iii. 25.

wished only to escape it, and which cowered for years in submission rather than fight for what it claimed as its due; but although to American ears the proclamation sounded like a sentence of slavery, the British public denounced it as a surrender of British rights. The "Morning Post," October 20 and 22, gave way to a paroxysm of wrath against ministers for disavowing and recalling Berkeley. "With feelings most poignantly afflicting," it broke into a rhapsody of unrestrained self-will. The next day, October 23, the same newspaper — then the most influential in the kingdom — pursued the subject more mildly: —

"Though the British government, from perhaps too rigid an adherence to the law of nations, outraged as they are by the common enemy, may, however irritated by her conduct, display a magnanimous forbearance toward so insignificant a Power as America, they will not, we are persuaded, suffer our proud sovereignty of the ocean to be mutilated by any invasion of its just rights and prerogatives. Though the right, tacitly abandoned for the last century, may be suffered to continue dormant, the Americans must not flatter themselves that the principle will be permitted to have any further extent. In the mildness of our sway we must not suffer our sovereignty to be rebelled against or insulted with impunity. . . . The sovereignty of the seas in the hands of Great Britain is an established, legitimate sovereignty, — a sovereignty which has been exercised on principles so equitable, and swayed with a spirit so mild, that the most humble of the maritime Powers have been treated as if they were on a perfect equality with us."

The same lofty note ran through all the "Morning Post's" allusions to American affairs: —

"A few short months of war," said a leading article, October 24, "would convince these desperate politicians of the folly of measuring the strength of a rising, but still infant and puny, nation with the colossal power of the British empire."

The "Times" declared that the Americans could not even send an ambassador to France, — could hardly pass to Staten Island, — without British permission.[1] "Right is power sanctioned by custom," said the "Times;" and October 20 and 22 it joined the "Morning Post" in denouncing the disavowal of Berkeley. The "Morning Chronicle" alone resisted the torrent which was sweeping away the traditions of English honor.

"Our Government," it said,[2] in support of its enemy, Canning, "in acting with prudence and wisdom, have to resist the pressure of a spirit not popular, like that in America, but as violent and as ignorant, with the addition of being in the highest degree selfish and sordid."

In the case of the "Chesapeake" the Ministry resisted that "selfish and sordid" interest; but Americans soon learned that the favor, such as it was, had been purchased at a price beyond its value. Canning's most brilliant stroke was for the moment only half revealed.

[1] The Times, Aug. 26, 1807.

[2] The Morning Chronicle, Aug. 6, 1807.

CHAPTER III.

THE new Ministry which succeeded "All the Talents" and took seat in Parliament April 8, 1807, represented everything in English society that was most impervious to reason. In its origin a creature of royal bigotry trembling on the verge of insanity, before it had been a few short weeks in office every liberal or tolerant Englishman was shocked to find that this band of Tories, whose prejudices were such as modern society could scarcely understand, and who had been forced into office by the personal will of an almost imbecile King, did in reality represent a great reaction of the English people against tolerant principles, and reflected the true sense of the nation as it had never been reflected by Grenville or Fox. Parliament was dissolved April 27, though only four months old; and June 22, when the "Leopard" was firing into the "Chesapeake," the new Parliament met at Westminster Hall, with a ministerial majority of more than two hundred country squires, elected on the cry that the Church was in danger.

From its nominal head, this Ministry was called the Portland administration; but its leader was Spencer Perceval, the Chancellor of the Exchequer, and its mouthpiece was George Canning, the Foreign Secretary. These two commoners — men of no special family connection, of no estates, and little so-called "stake in the country" — guided the aristocratic and conservative society of England, and exaggerated its tendencies. In modern days little is remembered of Spencer Perceval except that he became at last one of the long list of victims to lunatic assassins; but for a whole generation no English Liberal mentioned the name of the murdered prime minister without recalling the portrait drawn by Sydney Smith in the wittiest and keenest of his writings,[1] in which Perceval was figured as living at Hampstead upon stewed meats and claret, and walking to church every Sunday before eleven young gentlemen of his own begetting, with their faces washed and their hair pleasingly combed.

In Sydney Smith's caricature there was little exaggeration. Spencer Perceval was forty-five years old, a lawyer of the best character, devoted to his family, his church, and sovereign; a man after Lord Eldon's heart, who brought to the Treasury Bench the legal knowledge and mental habits of a leader at the Chancery Bar and the political morality of a lawyer's brief. The criticism was not less revolting than remarkable, that many of the men whose want of political morality was most conspicuous in this story were, both in England and in America, models of private respectability and fanatical haters of vice. That

[1] Peter Plymley's Letters, ix.

Timothy Pickering and Roger Griswold should join hands with Aaron Burr was less wonderful than that Spencer Perceval and his friend James Stephen, the author of "War in Disguise," should adopt the violence of Napoleon as the measure of their own morals, and avow that they meant to respect no other standard. With the same voice Spencer Perceval expressed fear lest calling Parliament on a Monday should lead members into Sunday travel, and justified the bombardment of Copenhagen and the robbery of American commerce.

The Whigs thought little of his abilities. Sydney Smith, who delighted to ridicule him, said that he had the head of a country parson and the tongue of an Old Bailey lawyer.[1] The Tories admired and followed him as readily as they had once followed Pitt; but to an American, necessarily prejudiced, Sydney Smith's estimate seemed just. Every American critic placed Perceval in an order of intelligence not only below the Whigs, but below Lord Sidmouth. When confronted with the dulness of Spencer Perceval, Americans could even feel relief in the sarcasm of George Canning, which, unlike Perceval's speeches, had at least the merit of rhetoric.

Of George Canning, who passed so rapidly across the scene, and yet left so sharp an impression on the memory of America, something must be said, if only to explain how a man so gifted, and in later life so different in influence, should have thought it worth

[1] Peter Plymley's Letters, i.

his while to challenge the hatred of a people whose future he, unlike his colleague Perceval, had imagination enough to foresee. George Canning was thirty-seven years old when he took charge of the Foreign office. His father, who came from a very respectable but in no way eminent family, died in 1771; his mother having no means of support became a provincial actress, and the boy was adopted by an uncle, who sent him to Eton and Oxford. He left Oxford at the time when the French Revolution promised a new birth to Europe, and Canning was then a warm Republican from sympathy and conviction. The political reaction which followed swept the young man to the opposite extreme; and his vehemence for monarchy and the Tories gave point to a Whig sarcasm, — that men had often been known to turn their coats, but this was the first time that a boy had turned his jacket. In consequence of his conversion Pitt brought him into Parliament in 1793, and placed him in office in 1796. In the hotbed of Pitt's personal favor [1] Canning's natural faults were stimulated, until the irritation caused by his sarcastic wit and by what the stolid gentry thought his flippancy roused a sort of insurrection against him. Few men were more admired, and none was more feared or hated; for it was impossible to say what time-honored monument he might overthrow in defending.

No man in England flung himself more violently

[1] Malmesbury's Diary, iv. 376.

into the reaction against Republican ideas than this young Republican of 1789. Canning's contempt was unbounded for everything that savored of liberal principles; and in following the impulses of his passion he lost whatever political morality he had possessed. If one act in Bonaparte's career concentrated more than another the treason and violence of a lifetime, it was the *coup d'état* of the 18th Brumaire, in 1799, when he drove the Legislature at the point of the bayonet from the hall at St. Cloud, and annihilated French liberty, as he hoped, forever; yet this act, which might have been applauded by some English statesmen whose heads paid on Tower Hill the penalty for such treason to the liberties of their own country, threw Canning into paroxysms of delight.

"Huzza! huzza! huzza!" he wrote[1] on hearing the news; "for no language but that of violent and tumultuous and triumphant exclamation can sufficiently describe the joy and satisfaction which I feel at this complete overthrow and extinction of all the hopes of the proselytes to new principles. . . . It is the lasting ridicule thrown upon all systems of democratic equality, — it is the galling conviction carried home to the minds of all the brawlers for freedom in this and every other country, — that there never was, nor will be, nor can be, a leader of a mob faction who does not mean to be the lord and not the servant of the people. It is this that makes the name of Bonaparte dear to me. . . . Hence-

[1] Canning to Boringdon, Nov. 19, 1799; Stapleton's Canning, p. 43.

forth, with regard to France and the principles of France, or to any country similarly circumstanced as to extent, population, manners, etc., *Republican* and *fool* are synonymous terms."

Canning had several qualities in common with Bonaparte, and one of them was the habit of classifying under the head of fools persons whose opinions he did not fancy, — from the man who believed in a republic to the man who liked dry champagne. In his mouth such persons were either fools or liars; and Americans, with few exceptions, came under one or the other of these heads. After the 18th Brumaire the world contained but one leader of a mob faction, brawling for liberty; but he was President of the United States. No miraculous sagacity was needed to foretell what treatment he was likely to receive at the hands of two men like Canning and Bonaparte, should the empire of the world ever be divided between them. To throw lasting ridicule upon all systems of democratic equality was Canning's most passionate wish, and his success was marvellous. Even his squibs exploded like rockets. In literature, his "Needy Knife-grinder" was a harmless piece of clever satire, but in the "Anti-Jacobin" it was a political event.

In Parliament Canning's influence was not yet very great. He relied too much on wit, and what was then called quizzing, or he imitated Pitt's oratory too closely; but even in the House of Commons he steadily won ground, and while Burke, Pitt,

Fox, Windham, and Sheridan, one after another, disappeared or were thrown into the shade, Canning's figure became more prominent on the Treasury Bench between two such foils as Spencer Perceval and Lord Castlereagh. Although his mind ripened slowly, and was still far from maturity, he was already a master in choice of language; he always excelled in clearness of statement and skill of illustration; and if his taste had been as pure as his English, he would have taken rank with the greatest English orators. Some of his metaphors survived, with those of Burke and Sheridan. When Napoleon was forced back to the Elbe, "the mighty deluge, by which the Continent had been overwhelmed, began to subside; the limits of nations were again visible; and the spires and turrets of ancient establishments began to reappear above the subsiding wave." In addressing the people at Plymouth, he likened England to a line-of-battle ship; "one of those stupendous masses now reposing on their shadows in perfect stillness," but ready at a sign to ruffle, as it were, its swelling plumage, to awaken its dormant thunder. Such eloquence recalled Burke at his less philosophical moments. It contained more rhetoric than thought; but Canning was there at his best. At his worst, as Americans commonly saw him, his natural tones seemed artificial, and only his imitations seemed natural. To Americans Canning never showed himself except as an actor. As an instance of his taste, Americans could best appreciate the climax with which he once electrified the House of Commons in speaking of the Spanish American Republics: "I called the new world into existence to redress the balance of the old." The House cheered to the echo, while America stood open-mouthed in astonishment at the success of such extravagant egoism.

In the new Ministry of 1807, the lead was to the strongest; and Canning, who treated with almost open contempt his rival Lord Castlereagh, a man intellectually his inferior, could count upon a great destiny. Less scrupulous or less broad than Pitt, he held that Napoleon's course had absolved England from ordinary rules of morals. To fight Bonaparte with his own weapons had become the duty of Englishmen; and the first act of the new Administration showed what meaning was to be put on this favorite phrase.

February 8, Napoleon fought the desperate battle of Eylau, which closely resembled a defeat. His position was critical; but before Canning could fairly get control of events, Napoleon, June 14, again attacked the Russians at Friedland and won a decisive victory. June 25 Napoleon and Alexander held an interview on an island in the Niemen. The chief point in question was whether Alexander would abandon England; and this he was almost glad to do, for England had abandoned him. Alexander yielded to the force and flattery of Napoleon, and signed July 7 the treaty of Tilsit. By a private understanding the remaining neutrals were left to Napoleon to be dealt with as he pleased. Denmark was the only neutral power the control of which was necessary for the success of Napoleon's system, and August 2 he sent orders to Bernadotte, who was to command at Hamburg: "If England does not accept the mediation of Russia, Denmark must declare war upon her, or I will declare war on Denmark."[1] Finding that the Prince Royal hesitated, Napoleon, August 17, sent orders[2] to Bernadotte to hold himself ready with all his troops to march into Denmark either as ally or enemy, according to the issue of the pending negotiation. Threatened by this overwhelming danger, the Prince Royal of Denmark alternately promised and evaded the declaration of war; when suddenly his doubts were brought to an end by the diplomacy of Canning.

The British ministry had been secretly informed of what took place at Tilsit, and even without secret information could not have doubted the fate of Denmark. Vigor was necessary; and as early as July 19, before news had arrived of the formal signature of the Tilsit treaty, the Cabinet decided on sending to Copenhagen a large naval expedition which had been collected for a different purpose. July 26 the expedition, commanded by Lord Gambier, sailed from the Downs. It consisted of some twenty ships of the line, forty frigates, and transports containing twenty-seven

[1] Correspondance, xv. 467.

[2] Napoleon to Berthier, Aug. 17, 1807; Correspondance, xv. 504.

thousand troops commanded by Lord Cathcart; and it carried a diplomatic agent with instructions to require from the Prince Royal of Denmark the delivery of the Danish fleet, as a temporary security for the safety of England.

The man whom Canning charged with this unpleasant duty was the same Jackson whose appointment as Minister to the United States had been opposed by Rufus King, and who had subsequently gone as British minister to Berlin. Jackson's dogmatic temper and overbearing manners made him obnoxious even to the clerks of the Foreign Office;[1] but he was a favorite with Lord Malmesbury, who since Pitt's death had become Canning's political mentor, and Lord Malmesbury's influence was freely used in Jackson's behalf. Obeying his instructions, the British envoy went to Kiel and had an interview with the Prince Royal early in August, at about the time when Napoleon issued his first orders to Bernadotte. The Prince could only refuse with indignation Jackson's demand, and sent orders to Copenhagen to prepare for attack. He was in the situation of Barron on the "Chesapeake." Copenhagen had hardly a gun in position, and no troops to use in defence.

The British demand was in itself insulting enough, but Jackson's way of presenting it was said to have been peculiarly offensive, and London soon rang with stories of his behavior to the unfortunate Prince

[1] Malmesbury's Diary, iv. 392.

Royal.[1] Even the King of England seemed to think that his agent needed rebuke. Lord Eldon, who was one of the advisers and most strenuous supporters of the attack on Copenhagen, — although he said in private that the story made his heart ache and his blood run cold, — used to relate,[2] on the authority of old King George himself, that when Jackson was presented at Court on his return from Copenhagen the King abruptly asked him, "Was the Prince Royal upstairs or down, when he received you?" "He was on the ground floor," replied Jackson. "I am glad of it! I am glad of it!" rejoined the old King; "for if he had half the spirit of his uncle George III., he would infallibly have kicked you downstairs." The Prince did not kick Mr. Jackson, though the world believed he had reason to do so, but he declined to accept the British envoy's remark that in war the weak must submit to the strong; and Lord Gambier landed twenty thousand men, established batteries, and for three days and nights, from September 1 to September 5, bombarded Copenhagen. The city was neither invested nor assaulted nor intended to be occupied; it was merely destroyed, little by little, — as a bandit would cut off first an ear, then the nose, then a finger of his victim, to hasten payment of a ransom. At the end of the third day's bombardment, when at last the Danish ships were delivered, the bodies of near two thousand

[1] Morning Chronicle, Oct. 7, 1807.

[2] Campbell's Lord Chancellors, ix. 288, *n.*

non-combatants lay buried in the smoking ruins of about one half the city. At the same time all the Danish merchant-vessels in English waters, with their cargoes, to the value of ten million dollars, were seized and confiscated; while the Danish factory in Bengal was, without warning, swept into England's pouch.

At the news of the awful tragedy at Copenhagen, Europe, gorged as for fifteen years she had been with varied horrors, shuddered from St. Petersburg to Cadiz. A long wail of pity and despair rose on the Continent, was echoed back from America, and found noble expression in the British Parliament. The attack upon the "Chesapeake" was a caress of affection compared with this bloody and brutal deed. As in 1804 Bonaparte — then only First Consul, but about to make himself a bastard Emperor — flung before the feet of Europe the bloody corpse of the Duc d'Enghien, so George Canning in 1807, about to meet Bonaparte on his own field with his own weapons, called the world to gaze at his handiwork in Copenhagen; and the world then contained but a single nation to which the fate of Copenhagen spoke in accents of direct and instant menace. The annihilation of Denmark left America almost the only neutral, as she had long been the only Republican State. In both characters her offences against Canning and Perceval, Castlereagh and Eldon, had been more serious than those of Denmark, and had roused to exasperation the temper of England. A single ship of the line, supported by one or two frigates, could without a moment's notice repeat at New York the tragedy which had required a vast armament at Copenhagen; and the assault on the "Chesapeake" had given warning of what the British navy stood ready to do. Other emphatic omens were not wanting.

About July 27 — the day after Lord Gambier's fleet sailed from the Downs, and the day when Monroe first saw in the newspapers an account of the "Leopard's" attack on the "Chesapeake" — the American minister might have read a report made by a committee of the House of Commons on the commercial state of the West Indian Islands. The main evil, said the committee,[1] was the very unfavorable state of the foreign market, in which the British merchant formerly enjoyed nearly a monopoly. "The result of all their inquiries on this most important part of the subject has brought before their eyes one grand and primary evil from which all the others are easily to be deduced; namely, the facility of intercourse between the hostile colonies and Europe under the American neutral flag, by means of which not only the whole of their produce is carried to a market, but at charges little exceeding those of peace, while the British planter is burdened with all the inconvenience, risk, and expense resulting from a state of war." To correct this evil, a block-

[1] Cobbett's Debates, ix., Appendix lxxx.; Atcheson's American Encroachments, Appendix No. viii. 114.

ade of the enemies' colonies had been suggested; "and such a measure, if it could be strictly enforced, would undoubtedly afford relief to our export trade. But a measure of more permanent and certain advantage would be the enforcement of those restrictions on the trade between neutrals and the enemies' colonies which were formerly maintained by Great Britain, and from the relaxation of which the enemies' colonies obtain indirectly, during war, all the advantages of peace."

In its way this West Indian Report was stamped with the same Napoleonic character as the bombardment of Copenhagen or the assault on the "Chesapeake;" in a parliamentary manner it admitted that England, with all her navy, could not enforce a blockade by lawful means, and therefore it had become "a matter of evident and imperious necessity" that she should turn pirate. The true sense of the recommendation was neither doubted nor disputed in England, except as matter of parliamentary form. That the attempt to cut off the supply of French and Spanish sugar from Europe, either by proclaiming a paper blockade or the Rule of 1756, might result in war with the United States was conceded, and no one in private denied that America in such a case had just cause for war. The evidence upon which the Report founded its conclusion largely dealt with the probable effect on the colonies of a war with the United States; and the Report itself, in language only so far veiled as to be decent, intimated that although war would be essentially detrimental to the islands it would not be fatal, and would be better than their actual condition. The excuse for what every reasonable Englishman frankly avowed to be "a system of piracy,"[1] was that the West Indian colonies must perish without it, and England must share their fate. In vain did less terrified men, like Alexander Baring or William Spence, preach patience, explaining that the true difficulty with the West Indies was an overproduction of sugar, with which the Americans had nothing to do.

"To charge the distresses of the West Indian planters upon the American carriers," said Spence,[2] "is almost as absurd as it would be for the assassin to lay the blame of murder upon the arsenic which he had purposely placed in the sugar-dish of his friend."

Thus Parliament, Ministry, navy, colonies, the shipping and the landed interest of England had wrought public opinion to the point of war with the United States at the moment when Lord Gambier bombarded Copenhagen and the "Leopard" fired into the "Chesapeake." The tornado of prejudice and purposeless rage which broke into expression on the announcement that a British frigate had fired into an American, surpassed all experience. The English newspapers for the year that followed the "Chesapeake" affair seemed irrational, the drunkenness of power incredible. The Americans, according to the "Morn-

[1] The Radical Cause, etc., by William Spence, 1808, p. 43.

[2] The Radical Cause, etc., by William Spence, 1808, p. 19.

ing Post" of Jan. 14, 1808, "possess all the vices of their Indian neighbors without their virtues;" and two days afterward the same newspaper — which gave tone to the country press — declared that England was irresistible: "Our vigor and energy have just reached that sublime pitch from which their weight must crush all opposition."

No one could say for how much of this extravagance Canning was directly responsible; but the tone of the press was certainly an echo of the tone he had so long taken, and which he stimulated. That he was really so reckless as he seemed need not be imagined; although eighteen months afterward, Lord Grenville with the utmost emphasis said in the House of Lords,[1] "I do firmly believe that it is the object of his Majesty's ministers to do everything in their power to force America into hostility with this country." Lord Grenville occasionally exaggerated, and he was probably mistaken in this instance; but he found it possible to believe ministers capable of acting with the motive he charged on them. In truth he had strong ground for the opinion he held, which was by no means peculiar to him. As early as July 27, 1807, the "Morning Chronicle," in announcing the first news of the "Chesapeake" affair, added: —

"We trust it is of a nature to be adjusted without that most ruinous of all follies yet left us to be guilty of, — an American war. We have rather more fear than hope

[1] Cobbett's Debates (Feb. 17, 1809), xii. 776.

however on the subject, when we reflect that the present ministers are of those who consider an American war as rather desirable."

Within a short time the "Morning Post" avowed and proclaimed, in articles evidently inspired by Government, the wish for war with America:[1] —

"A war of a very few months, without creating to us the expense of a single additional ship, would be sufficient to convince her of her folly by a necessary chastisement of her insolence and audacity."

In January, 1808, the same newspaper spoke even more plainly:[2] —

"For us, we have always been of the opinion that in the present temper of the American government no relations of amity can be maintained with that nation unless at the expense of our dearest rights and most essential interests."

Perhaps this tone was taken partly with the idea of terrifying the Americans into obedience; but beyond question a strong party leaned to violence. Monroe, who had the best means of knowing, felt no doubts on this point, and warned the President of the danger to the United States.

"There has been," he wrote Aug. 4, 1807,[3] "at all times since the commencement of the present war, a strong party here for extending its ravages to them. This party is composed of the shipowners, the navy, the

[1] The Morning Post, Nov. 12, 1807.
[2] The Morning Post, Jan. 13, 1808.
[3] Monroe to Madison, Aug. 4, 1807; State Papers, iii. 186.

East and West India merchants, and certain political characters of great consideration in the State. So powerful is this combination that it is most certain that nothing can be obtained of the government on any point but what may be extorted by necessity."

Insane as such a policy might seem, Lord Grenville's charge against ministers had solid ground.

Special interests were commonly blind to the general good. That the navy, the mercantile marine, and the colonies should have favored war with America was not surprising; but that the mania should have seized upon the English nation at large was a phenomenon to be explained only by general causes. The true explanation was not far to seek; the secret, if secret it could be called, was the inevitable result of Jefferson's passion for peace, — social and political contempt. This feeling was unbounded, pervading all parties and all classes, and finding expression in the most gross as in the simplest and least intentional forms.

"Hatred of America," said one of the numerous British pamphleteers of the time,[1] "seems a prevailing sentiment in this country. Whether it be that they have no crown and nobility, and are on this account not quite a *genteel* Power; or that their manners are less polished than our own; or that we grudge their independence, and hanker after our old monopoly of their trade; or that they closely resemble us in language, character, and

[1] Orders in Council; or, An Examination of the Justice, Legality, and Policy of the New System, etc. (London, 1808), p. 61.

laws; or finally, that it is more our interest to live well with them than with any other nation in the world, — the fact is undeniable that the bulk of the people would fain be at war with them."

The Somersetshire squire and the chancery barrister in Westminster Hall — the extremes of national obtuseness and professional keenness — agreed in despising America. The pompous Lord Sidmouth, the tedious Lord Sheffield, the vivacious Canning, the religious Perceval, and the merry-andrew Cobbett — whose genius was peculiar in thinking itself popular — joined hands in spreading libels against a people three thousand miles away, who according to their own theory were too contemptible to be dangerous. Except a few Whig noblemen, a number of Yorkshire and Lancashire manufacturers and a great mass of the laboring people, or American merchants like the Barings, and one or two Scotch Liberals who wrote in the "Edinburgh Review," the English public had but one voice against Americans. Young Henry Brougham, not yet thirty years old, whose restless mind persistently asked questions which parsons and squires thought absurd or impious, speculated much upon the causes of this prejudice. Was it because the New York dinners were less elegant than those of London, or because the Yankees talked with an accent, or because their manners were vulgar? No doubt a prejudice might seize on any justification, however small; but a prejudice so general and so deep became respectable, and needed a correct explanation. The British nation was sometimes slow-witted, and often narrow-minded, but was not insane.

For a thousand years every step in the progress of England had been gained by sheer force of hand and will. In the struggle for existence the English people, favored by situation, had grown into a new human type, — which might be brutal, but was not weak; which had little regard for theory, but an immense and just respect for facts. America considered herself to be a serious fact, and expected England to take her at her own estimate of her own value; but this was more than could reasonably be asked. England required America to prove by acts what virtue existed in her conduct or character which should exempt her from the common lot of humanity, or should entitle her to escape the tests of manhood, — the trials, miseries, and martyrdoms through which the character of mankind had thus far in human history taken, for good or bad, its vigorous development. England had never learned to strike soft in battle. She expected her antagonists to fight; and if they would not fight, she took them to be cowardly or mean. Jefferson and his government had shown over and over again that no provocation would make them fight; and from the moment that this attitude was understood, America became fair prey. Jefferson had chosen his own methods of attack and defence; but he could not require England or France to respect them before they had been tried.

Contempt for America was founded on belief in American cowardice; but beneath the disdain lurked an uneasy doubt which gave to contempt the virulence of fear. The English nation, and especially the aristocracy, believed that America was biding her time; that she expected to become a giant; and that if she succeeded, she would use her strength as every other giant in the world's history had done before her. The navy foresaw a day when American fleets might cover the ocean. The merchant dreaded competition with Yankee shrewdness, for he well knew the antiquated processes, the time-honored percentages, the gross absurdities of English trade, the abuses of the custom-house, the clumsiness and extravagance of government. The shipowners had even more cause for alarm. Already the American ship was far in advance of the British model, — a swifter and more economical sailer, more heavily sparred and more daringly handled. In peace competition had become difficult, until the British shipowner cried for war; yet he already felt, without acknowledging it even to himself, that in war he was likely to enjoy little profit or pleasure on the day when the long, low, black hull of the Yankee privateer, with her tapering, bending spars, her long-range gun, and her sharp-faced captain, should appear on the western horizon, and suddenly, at sight of the heavy lumbering British merchantman, should fling out her white wings of canvas and fly down on her prey.

Contempt, mingled with vague alarm, was at the bottom of England's conduct toward America; and whatever the swarm of newspaper statesmen might say or think, the element of alarm was so great that the Tory ministers, although they might expect war, did not want it, and hoped to prevent it by the very boldness of their policy. Even Canning was cautious enough to prefer not to give America occasion for learning her strength. He meant to clip her wings only so far as she would submit to have her wings clipped; and he not only astonished but disgusted the over-zealous politicians who applauded Admiral Berkeley, by disavowing the admiral's doctrines of international law and recalling the admiral himself. The war faction broke into a paroxysm of rage [1] when this decision became known, and for a time Canning seemed likely to be devoured by his own hounds, so vociferous was their outcry. Monroe and Pinkney were loud in praise of Canning's and Perceval's temperate and candid behavior.[2]

Canning was obliged to defend himself, and under his promptings a long reply to his critics was written for the "Morning Post," [3] — a newspaper version of the instructions carried by his special minister to Washington. He excused his treatment of Admiral

[1] Brougham to Lord Howick, Nov. 7, 1807; Brougham's Memoirs, i. 386.

[2] Brougham to Lord Howick, Nov. 7, 1807; Brougham's Memoirs, i. 383.

[3] The Morning Post, Oct. 23, 1807.

Berkeley on the ground that lawyers recognized no right of search in national ships. The excuse was evidently feeble. The law, or at least the lawyers, of England had hitherto justified every act which the government had chosen to commit, — the seizure of the Spanish treasure-ships in 1804, accompanied by the unnecessary destruction of hundreds of lives; the secret seizure of the larger part of American commerce in 1805, by collusion with the Admiralty judges; the paper blockade of Charles James Fox in 1806; the Order in Council of January, 1807, by which Lord Howick cut off another main branch of neutral commerce with which England had no legal right to interfere; finally, the lawyers justified the bombardment of Copenhagen as an act of necessary defence, and were about to justify a general control of all neutral commerce as an act of retaliation. To suppose that law so elastic, or lawyers with minds so fertile, could discover no warrant for Berkeley's act was preposterous. To neutral commerce England had no legal right; yet she took it, and her lawyers invented a title. To her citizens and seamen she actually had a legal right, recognized by every court in Christendom; and if after a fair demand on the neutral government she found that her right could be satisfied only by violating neutral jurisdiction, the lawyers, in view of all their other decisions, must hold that such violation was a matter of expediency and not of law. Canning's critics in reply to his assertion that the lawyers would recognize no right of search in national ships, could fairly say that he was alone to blame, — he should have ordered them to find it. George Canning could not seriously propose to sacrifice a vital English interest in obedience to the scrupulous legal morality of Spencer Perceval, Lord Eldon, Sir William Scott, and Sir Vicary Gibbs.

In truth, Canning had reasons more forcible. With a character not unlike that which Dryden ascribed to Lord Shaftesbury, he was pleased with the danger when the waves ran high; and if he steered too near the shoals in order to prove his wit, he did not wish to run the vessel ashore. He disavowed Admiral Berkeley, not because the lawyers were unable to prove whatever the government required, but because the right of searching foreign ships-of-war was not worth asserting, and would cost more than it could ever bring in return. Besides this obvious reason, he was guided by another motive which would alone have turned the scale. Perceval had invented a scheme for regulating neutral commerce. This measure had begun to take a character so stern that even its author expected it to produce war with the United States; and if war could be avoided at all, it could be avoided only by following Erskine's advice, and by sending to America, before the new Orders in Council, an apology for the attack on the "Chesapeake."

CHAPTER IV.

THE Orders in Council of Nov. 11, 1807, gave an impulse so energetic to the history of the United States; they worked so effectually to drive America into a new path, and to break the power and blot out the memory of Virginia and Massachusetts principles, — that every detail of their history was important. Englishmen were little likely to dwell on acts of which even at the time England was at heart ashamed, and which she afterward remembered with astonishment. To Americans alone the statesmanship of Spencer Perceval and George Canning was a matter of so much interest as to deserve study.

At the close of the year 1806 American merchants might, as always before, send cargoes of West Indian produce to any port on the continent not blockaded, provided they could satisfy British cruisers and courts that the cargo was in good faith neutral, — not French or Spanish property disguised. Jan. 7, 1807, Lord Howick issued the Order in Council which, under pretence of retaliation for Napoleon's Berlin Decree, cut off the coasting rights of neutrals. After that time the American merchant might still send a ship to Bordeaux; but if the ship, finding no market at Bordeaux, should resume her voyage, and make for Amsterdam or the Mediterranean, she became fair prize. Something has been already said[1] upon the character of Lord Howick's order, and on the subsequent debate in Parliament, when, February 4, Spencer Perceval attacked the Whig ministry for not carrying the principle of retaliation far enough. Two objects were to be gained, said Perceval[2] from the opposition bench: the first and greatest was to counteract the enemy's measures and protect English trade; the second was to distress France. Howick's order neither did nor could effect either object; and Perceval called for a measure which should shut out colonial produce from France and Spain altogether, unless it came from England and had paid a duty at a British customhouse to enhance the price. If Lord Howick's principle of retaliation was good for anything, Perceval contended it was good to this extent; and as for neutrals, there was no necessity for consulting them, — all they could reasonably expect was a notice.

The Whigs naturally replied to Perceval that before further punishing America for the acts of France, America should be allowed time to assert her own rights. This suggestion called out Lord Castlereagh, who frequently spoke the truth in ways inconvenient to his colleagues and amusing to his enemies. In this instance he admitted and even accented a point

[1] See vol. iii. p. 416.

[2] Cobbett's Debates, Feb. 4, 1807, viii. 620–656.

which became afterward the strongest part of the American argument. He ridiculed the idea of waiting for America to act, because notoriously the Berlin Decree had not been enforced against American commerce: —

"This is one ground why we should look upon America with jealousy. It is an aggravation that she has, by a secret understanding with the French government, contrived to take her shipping out of the operation of the decree, that was at first general, and placed herself in a situation of connivance with the French government."

A few weeks afterward Perceval and Castlereagh took office. One of their first acts set on foot a parliamentary inquiry into the state of West Indian commerce. The report of this committee, presented to the House July 27, was ordered to be printed August 8. August 10 the House voted to take it into consideration early in the next session; and four days afterward Parliament was prorogued, leaving ministers to deal at their leisure with the "Chesapeake" affair, the Danish fleet, and Napoleon's attempts to exclude English manufactures and commerce from Europe.

Napoleon's Berlin Decree of Nov. 21, 1806, had remained till then almost a dead letter. The underwriters at Lloyds, alarmed at first by the seizures made under that decree, recovered courage between April and August, 1807, so far as to insure at low rates neutral vessels bound to Holland and Hamburg. This commerce attracted Napoleon's notice.

August 19 he threatened his brother Louis, King of Holland, to send thirty thousand troops into his kingdom if the ports were not shut;[1] August 24 he sent positive orders[2] that his decree of Berlin should be executed in Holland; and in the last days of August news reached London that a general seizure of neutral vessels had taken place at Amsterdam.[3] From that moment no ship could obtain insurance, and trade with the Continent ceased. Soon afterward the American ship "Horizon" was condemned by the French courts under the Berlin Decree, and no one could longer doubt that the favor hitherto extended to American commerce had also ceased.

These dates were important, because upon them hung the popular defence of Perceval's subsequent Orders in Council. No argument in favor of these orders carried so much weight in England as the assertion that America had acquiesced in Napoleon's Berlin Decree. The President had in fact submitted to the announcement of Napoleon's blockade, as he had submitted to Sir William Scott's decisions, Lord Howick's Order in Council, the blockade of New York, and the custom of impressment, without effectual protest; but the Berlin Decree was not enforced against American commerce until about Sept. 1, 1807,

[1] Napoleon to Champagny, Aug. 19, 1807; Correspondance, xv. 509.

[2] Same to Same, Aug. 24, 1807; Ibid., p. 542.

[3] Parliamentary Inquiry, 1808; Evidence of Robert Shedden and Mr. Hadley.

and no one in America knew of the enforcement, or could have acted upon it, before the British government took the law into its own hands.

The month of September passed, and the British ministry was sufficiently busy with the bombardment of Copenhagen and the assault on the "Chesapeake," without touching neutral trade; but October 1 Lord Castlereagh wrote a letter[1] to Perceval, urging retaliation upon France in order to make her feel that Napoleon's anti-commercial system was useless, and in order to assert for future guidance the general principle that England would reject any peace which did not bring commerce with it. The idea presented by Castlereagh was clear and straightforward, — the double-or-quits of a gambler; and however open to the charge of ignorance or violence, it was not mean or dishonest.

In reply Perceval drew up a paper of suggestions[2] for the use of the Cabinet, dealing first with the justice, next with the policy of retaliation. Of its justice as against France he thought there could be no doubt, while Lord Howick's order had already asserted the principle as against neutrals, even before it could be known whether neutrals would retaliate on their own account; but apart from this precedent, "the injury which neutrals sustain is consequential; the measure

[1] Castlereagh to Perceval, Oct. 1, 1807; Castlereagh Correspondence, viii. 87.

[2] Original Suggestions to the Cabinet, Oct. 12, 1807; Perceval MSS.

is not adopted with a view to injure the neutrals, but to injure the enemy." Perhaps Perceval felt that this argument might lead too far, and that on such a doctrine England might appropriate the world on every declaration of war; for in the next paragraph he pleaded the particular war in which England was actually engaged as his warranty: —

"When an enemy arises who declares to all the world that he will trample upon the law of nations, and hold at nought all the privileges of neutral nations when they do not suit his belligerent interests; and when by the great extent of his power he is enabled in great measure to act up to his declaration, — it is evident that if those Powers with which he is at war should continue to hold themselves bound to rules and obligations of which he will not acknowledge the force, they cannot carry on the contest on equal terms. And the neutral who would control their hostility by those rules and laws which their enemy refuses to recognize, and which such neutral does not compel that enemy to observe, ceases to be a neutral by ceasing to observe that impartiality which is the very life and soul of neutrality."

This allegation differed from the first. Perceval began by maintaining that England possessed a right, if she chose, to suppress the existence of America or of any other neutral, provided the suppression were consequential on an intent to injure France. He next argued that the existence of America might be equally suppressed because she had not yet succeeded in compelling France to observe neutral privileges, which so far as she was concerned had not been violated. If these two propositions were worth making, they should have settled the question. Yet Perceval was not satisfied; he took a third ground:—

"This question, however, need not now be argued to the extent which was necessary to justify the assertion of the late Government; because whatever might be the doubts upon it when the decree of France first issued, and before it was known to what extent neutrals would resist or acquiesce in it, since those neutrals have acquiesced in it, or at least have not resisted or resented it to the extent of obtaining a formal recall of the decree and an open renunciation of the principle which dictated it, nor the abandonment of the practices which flow from it, —they by their acquiescence and submission have given to Great Britain a right to expect from them (when her interests require the exertion of measures of correspondent efficacy) a forbearance similar to that which they have shown toward her enemy."

If Perceval's two opening premises gave a strange idea of English statesmanship, his third was little creditable to the English bar. He took the ground that England might do what she would with American commerce, because America, whatever effort she might have made, had not already forced Napoleon to recall a decree from the application of which the United States notoriously had till within six weeks been exempted. Lord Castlereagh's doctrine that America's exemption aggravated her offence was a wide-minded argument by the side of Perceval's assertion that America's acquiescence was proved by the

French decree itself. Considering that America had in this sense acquiesced in Sir William Scott's decisions and the wholesale confiscation of her commerce, in the impressment of her native citizens and their compulsory service in the British navy, in the blockade of New York, in Fox's paper blockade of the German coast, in Lord Howick's Order in Council, and perhaps even in the "Chesapeake" outrage,— Perceval's argument must have seemed convincing to Napoleon, if not to President Jefferson. If the law of nations thus laid down was sound, the continued presence of American citizens in British ships of war was alone sufficient proof of American acquiescence in impressment to warrant Napoleon in acting without regard to neutral rights. From a neutral or French point of view Perceval's reasoning not only conceded the legality of the Berlin Decree, but barred his own right of retaliation, since England, as the first and worst offender, could not properly profit by her own misdeeds.

There Perceval rested his case, so far as concerned the law. His three grounds were — (1) That as a neutral the United States could complain of no retaliation between belligerents, unless this retaliation was avowedly adopted with a view to injure neutrals; (2) That America ceased to be a neutral from the moment that she wished England to observe rules which France refused to recognize, and which America did not at once compel France to recognize; and (3) That the continued existence and recent enforcement of the Berlin Decree were sufficient proof of the neutral's acquiescence.

Thus a measure of vital consequence to England was proposed to the Cabinet on grounds which would hardly have been sufficient to warrant an injunction to restrain a private nuisance. So far as argument was concerned, Perceval had no more to say. Having in his opinion established his legal right to do what he pleased with American commerce, he next discussed the policy and extent of the proposed interference. His first idea was comparatively moderate.

"If we actually prohibit all intercourse between neutrals and the enemies' colonies," he continued, "or between neutrals and the enemies' continental possessions, it would be such a severe blow upon the trade of America as might make it no unreasonable choice on her part to prefer the dangers and chances of war to such a restriction upon her trade. I should therefore wish to leave such advantages still to neutral trade as to make it quite clear to be the policy of America, if she is wise, to prefer the neutral trade that will be left to her to the total stoppage of her trade with the enemy and with ourselves which a war might occasion. . . . With this view, therefore, I would recommend to relax thus far in the rigor of our retaliatory prohibitions as to leave to neutral nations the right of trading *directly* in articles of their own growth, produce, and manufacture exported in their own vessels to enemies' countries, and of importing from the enemies' countries for their own use articles the growth, produce, and manufacture of such enemies' countries; that is, leaving to them free the *direct* trade between the enemy and themselves in articles of their respective growth, etc., but to prohibit the re-exportation of any articles the growth, etc., of the enemies' countries or their colonies, or the carriage of them to any other country but their own."

Perceval's first suggestion was far from being so radical as the measure at last adopted. He proposed to cut off France from her colonies and force all trade between those colonies and Europe to pass through British hands; but an American ship laden with American cotton or wheat might still sail from the United States direct to France and return to the United States, or might carry provisions and lumber to Martinique and Cuba, carrying French or Spanish sugar back to New York. This so-called "direct" trade was to be untouched; the "indirect" or carrying trade between the West Indies and the continent of Europe was to be permitted only under special licenses to be issued by British authorities.

In this shape Perceval sent his suggestions to the Prime Minister, the Duke of Portland, who gave his entire approval to the principle of retaliation as against France, but wished to retaliate against France alone:[1] "Considering the unpopularity which, it cannot be denied, we are held in throughout the Continent, I very much doubt whether we should limit this intercourse beyond the actual dominions of

[1] Opinion of the Duke of Portland; Perceval MSS.

France. I am well aware that by admitting the intercourse with Holland and Spain, France will obtain circuitously those supplies which she will stand in want of."

This disadvantage, the Duke thought, could be largely compensated by a rigid observance of the navigation laws. The Duke's opinion was very short, and barely hinted at the American question.

John Fane, Earl of Westmoreland, Lord Privy Seal, — *Sot Privé*, or Privy Fool, as Canning afterward nicknamed him by a pun on the French word *sceau*,[1] — gave next his written opinion on the subject.[2] Going beyond either Perceval or Portland, he urged the expediency of stopping all trade with the enemy except through the medium of England, — "the effect of which must be either to distress them to such a degree as to induce a relaxation of their decrees, or to cause a great trade from this country. Its effect in case of an extension of hostility can certainly not be ascertained; but I am disposed to think that we cannot carry on war allowing our enemy advantages of commerce as in peace, and that if we only do what is right we must take our chance for the consequences."

The next opinion was apparently that of Lord Hawkesbury, the Home Secretary, who was also clear that Perceval's plan wanted energy. While supporting the Duke of Portland in narrowing its scope

[1] Stapleton's Canning, p. 411.

[2] Opinion of the Earl of Westmoreland; Perceval MSS.

to France, or at the utmost to Holland, he favored harsher treatment of America:[1]

"I incline strongly to the opinion that it is expedient to put an end, as far as in us lies, to all intercourse by sea between neutrals and the continental dominions of France, and possibly of Holland. I am satisfied that the measure of retaliation as proposed in the enclosed paper would have no other effect than to raise the price of colonial produce in France to a small degree. It would offend neutrals, particularly the Americans, and inflict no adequate injury upon the enemy. But if we should determine to prevent all intercourse whatever with the ports of France except by British license, we should have it in our power to destroy at once all the remaining commerce of France, which by means of neutrals is not inconsiderable, and to strike a most important blow against her agriculture by preventing the exportation of her wines."

Lord Hawkesbury kept in view the retaliatory character of the measure as a punishment of France. Lord Castlereagh, the Secretary for War, was not quite so careful.[2] He acquiesced in Perceval's scheme, provided it should reserve the right to extend its own application whenever the balance of advantage should favor the extension; but he added, —

"I am of opinion that some decisive measure, in vindication of our own commerce and in counteraction of the unsocial system of France, — the principle of which is not the growth of this war, but was acted upon by

[1] Opinion of Lord Hawkesbury; Perceval MSS.
[2] Opinion of Lord Castlereagh; Perceval MSS.

her throughout the late short peace, — is become indispensable, not merely as a measure of commercial policy, but in order to put the contest in which we are engaged upon its true grounds in the view of our own people and of the world. It is no longer a struggle for territory or for a point of honor, but whether the existence of England as a naval power is compatible with that of France."

Avowing that a commercial transaction was his object, and that the punishment of France was secondary to a "vindication of our own commerce," Castlereagh assumed that punishment of France and "vindication" of English commerce were both belligerent rights, as though the right to kill an adversary in a duel implied the right to pick a bystander's pocket. His colleague and rival Canning was not so confused, for Canning's duties obliged him to defend the new policy against neutral objections. Carefully as the other ministers mingled the ideas of retaliation and of commerce, the double motive of Perceval's measure had never been concealed; the intention to permit a licensed trade with France was avowed. Perceval and Castlereagh wanted, not to take commerce from France, but to force commerce upon her; and none of their colleagues could detect this inconsistency so readily as Canning, whose duties would oblige him to assert before the world that retaliation alone was the object of a measure which he privately knew to have no motive but that of commercial rivalry. Canning's written opinion, beginning by affirming in strong terms the right and justice of retaliation, continued as follows: [1] —

"The question of policy is all that remains; and in this view I should think all such modifications as go to lighten the burden imposed upon neutrals, and as are obviously intended for that purpose, more advisable than any direct reservations for our own interest and advantage. For this reason I would rather confine the measure to a part of the countries in the occupation of the enemy (a large part to be sure, — France and Holland, for instance), and apply it in all its rigor to that part, than extend it to the whole and relax it generally by complicated exceptions and regulations. And I would keep out of sight the exceptions in favor of ships going from this country, the benefit of which might be equally obtained by licenses; but the *publication* of that exception would give to the measure the air of a commercial rather than a political transaction."

By the end of October all the Cabinet opinions were in Perceval's hands, and he began the task of drafting the proposed orders. His original draft [2] contained an elaborate preamble, asserting that Napoleon's decrees violated the laws of nations, which Perceval broadly maintained were binding on one belligerent only when the obligation was reciprocally acknowledged by the other; that neutrals had not resented and resisted the outrage, "nor interposed with effect for obtaining the revocation of those orders, but on the con-

[1] Opinion of Mr. Canning; Perceval MSS.

[2] First Draft of Orders in Council, with remarks by Earl Bathurst; Perceval MSS.

trary the same have been recently reinforced;" that Lord Howick's retaliatory order had served only to encourage Napoleon's attempts; that his Majesty had a right to declare all the dominions of France and her allies in a state of blockade; but "not forgetting the interests of neutral nations, and still desirous of retaliating upon the commerce of his enemies with as little prejudice to those interests" as was consistent with his purpose, he would for the present prohibit only trade which neutrals might be disposed to pursue in submission to the French decrees, and require that such trade should pass to or from some British port.

Then followed the order, which prohibited all neutral trade with the whole European sea-coast from Copenhagen to Trieste, leaving only the Baltic open. No American vessel should be allowed to enter any port in Europe from which British vessels were excluded, unless the American should clear from some British port under regulations to be prescribed at a future time.

This draft was completed in the first days of November, and was sent to Lord Bathurst, President of the Board of Trade, who mercilessly criticised the preamble, and treated his colleague's law with as little respect as though Bathurst were an American.

"I wish the principle of retaliation," wrote Lord Bathurst, "not to be unqualifiedly advanced, for which I think there is no necessity. May it not be said that in a contest with an unprincipled enemy the doctrine of retaliation is one dangerous to admit without qualifications? I own I do not like the word. If my enemy commits an act of injustice, I am not therefore justified in committing the same, except so far as may be necessary, in consequence of his act, either to protect myself from injury, or prevent a recurrence to, or continuance in, such acts of injustice. All operations of war are justified only on the principle of defence. Retaliation seems to admit something of a vindictive spirit."

The Board of Trade was not usually scrupulous in dealing with American commerce; but in this instance Earl Bathurst let it be plainly seen that he wished to have no share of responsibility for Perceval's casuistry. The longer he studied the proposed order the less he liked it; and in the end he wrote an opinion contrary to his first. He withdrew his assent to the order altogether, and hinted some unpleasant truths in regard to it.

"Our ability to continue the war," he said,[1] "depends on our commerce; for if our revenues fail from a diminution of our commerce, additional imports will only add to the evil. The enemy forms one great military empire. The extent of country he covers does not render him so dependent on an export and import trade. The whole of that trade might perish and he could still continue the war. If one third of ours were to fail we should be soon reduced to peace."

The proposed order, Bathurst argued, not only restricted the neutral trade still further than had

[1] Opinion of Lord Bathurst in dissent to the Principle of Mr. Perceval's proposed Order; Perceval MSS.

been done by Napoleon, but risked war with Russia and America, without materially hurting France; he added an argument which struck at the foundation of Perceval's policy: —

"The object of the proposed order, though general, is in fact nothing but the colonial trade carried on through America; and by making it general we unite Russia in defence of a trade with which she has no concern or any interest to defend. As far as America is concerned, it must be expected she will resist it; and an American war would be severely felt by our manufacturers, and even by the very class of merchants now so eager for some measure of relief. We might therefore have to fight for a rule of war, new, the policy of which would be questionable, to support an interest which would be the first to suffer by the war, — against two countries, one of which the order unnecessarily mixes in the question, and with both of which we have great commercial relations."

Bathurst closed by expressing a preference for the Rule of 1756, or for a blockade of the West Indian Islands, — which, if the Admiralty thought it practicable, Bathurst considered as the best of all the measures proposed; but besides this radical change, he demanded certain alarming reforms. He complained to Perceval that already, even under the existing orders, such abuses prevailed that in order to prevent a public parliamentary inquiry he had been obliged by the general clamor of merchants to investigate their grievances:[1] —

[1] Lord Bathurst to Spencer Perceval, Nov. 5, 1807; Perceval MSS.

"The result of the examination established the truth of the vexations to which the trade is now subject by privateers, who are enabled to persevere in them in consequence of the commercial restrictions and the proceedings of the Court of Admiralty. In a communication I had with Sir William Scott, who had been very angry with the inquiry, I proposed some regulations which, indeed, I knew would be unsatisfactory unless there were some alterations in the proceedings of his Court, — a subject which I did not venture to touch."

Lord Bathurst's well-meant efforts for reform, gentle as they were, showed him the fortresses in which corruption was already entrenched. Sir William Scott, like his brother Lord Eldon, never relaxed his grasp on a profitable abuse. He gave cogent reasons for rejecting Lord Bathurst's suggestions, and could afford to disregard the danger of interference, for Spencer Perceval was completely under the influence of Lord Eldon. Bathurst urged Perceval to reform the license-system, so that at least the license should give complete protection to the cargo, no matter to whom the cargo might belong; and he hoped that this reform would put an end to the abuses of the Admiralty Court. "But," he added, "I did not venture to give this as my reason before Sir John Nichol [advocate-general], for you must be aware that both his profits and those of Sir William Scott depend much on privateers and the litigations which, it is my hope, will by this alteration be considerably diminished."

Many members of the British government and nearly the whole British navy were growing rich on the plunder of American commerce. From King George downward, mighty influences were involved in maintaining a system which corrupted law officers, judges, admirals, and even the King himself. Spencer Perceval's proposed Order in Council extended these abuses over whatever branches of commerce had hitherto been exempt; turned a new torrent of corruption into the government; and polluted the sources of British honor. In the light of Lord Bathurst's protest, and his significant avowal that the object of the proposed order, though general in form, was in fact nothing but the colonial trade carried on through America, Canning might well wish to *publish* nothing that would draw attention to what he called the "commercial" side of the affair. Jefferson's measures of peaceful coercion bore unexpected results, reacting upon foreign nations by stimulating every mean and sordid motive. No possible war could have so degraded England.

As the Cabinet came closer to the point, the political, or retaliatory, object of the new order disappeared, and its commercial character was exclusively set forth. In a letter written about November 30, by Spencer Perceval to Charles Abbot, Speaker of the House of Commons, not a word was said of retaliation, or of any political motive in this process of "recasting the law of trade and navigation, as far as belligerent principles are concerned, for the whole world."

"The short principle is," said Perceval,[1] "that trade in British produce and manufactures, and trade either from a British port or with a British destination, is to be protected as much as possible. For this purpose all the countries where French influence prevails to exclude the British flag shall have no trade but to or from this country, or from its allies. All other countries, the few that remain strictly neutral (with the exception of the colonial trade, which backward and forward direct they may carry on), cannot trade but through this being done as an ally with any of the countries connected with France. If therefore we can accomplish our purpose, it will come to this, — that either those countries will have no trade, or they must be content to accept it through us. This is a formidable and tremendous state of the world; but all the part of it which is particularly harassing to English interests was existing through the new severity with which Bonaparte's decrees of exclusion against our trade were called into action. Our proceeding does not aggravate our distress from it. If he can keep out our trade he will; and he would do so if he could, independent of our orders. Our orders only add this circumstance: they say to the enemy, 'If you will not have *our* trade, as far as we can help it you shall have *none;* and as to so much of any trade as you can carry on yourselves, or others carry on with you through us, if you admit it you shall pay for it. The only trade, cheap and untaxed, which you shall have shall be either

[1] Spencer Perceval to Speaker Abbot; Diary and Correspondence of Lord Colchester, ii. 134.

direct from us, in our own produce and manufactures, or from our allies, whose increased prosperity will be an advantage to us.'"

These private expressions implied that retaliation upon France for her offence against international law was a pretence on the part of Perceval and Canning, under the cover of which they intended to force British commerce upon France contrary to French wishes. The act of Napoleon in excluding British produce from French dominions violated no rule of international law, and warranted no retaliation except an exclusion of French produce from British dominions. The rejoinder, "If you will not have *our* trade you shall have *none*," was not good law, if law could be disputed when affirmed by men like Lord Eldon and Lord Stowell, echoed by courts, parliaments, and press, — not only in private, but in public; not only in 1807, but for long years afterward; and not only at moments, but without interruption.

Thus Canning, although he warned Perceval against betraying the commercial object of his orders, instructed[1] Erskine at Washington to point out that American ships might still bring colonial produce to England, under certain regulations, for re-export to France. "The object of these regulations will be the establishment of such a protecting duty as shall prevent the enemy from obtaining the produce of his own colonies at a cheaper rate than that of the colonies of Great Britain." Not to distress France,

[1] Erskine to Madison, Feb. 23, 1808; State Papers, iii. 209.

but to encourage British trade, was, according to Canning, the object of this "political" weapon.

Thus Perceval, in the debate of Feb. 5, 1808, in discussing the policy of his order, affirmed that the British navy had been "rendered useless by neutral ships carrying to France all that it was important for France to obtain."[1] The Rule of 1756, he said, would not have counteracted this result, — a much stronger measure was necessary; and it was sound policy "to endeavor to force a market." Lord Bathurst, a few days afterward, very frankly told[2] the House that "the object of these orders was to regulate that which could not be prohibited, — the circuitous trade through this country," — in order that the produce of enemies' colonies might "be subjected to a duty sufficiently high to prevent its having the advantage over our own colonial produce;" and Lord Hawkesbury, in the same debate, complained[3] that neutrals supplied colonial produce to France at a much less rate than the English paid for it. "To prevent this," he said, "was the great object of the Orders in Council." James Stephen's frequent arguments[4] in favor of the orders turned upon the commercial value of the policy as against neutrals; while George Rose, Vice-President of the Board of

[1] Cobbett's Debates, x. 328.

[2] Debate of Feb. 15, 1808; Cobbett's Debates, x. 471.

[3] Debate of Feb. 15, 1808; Cobbett's Debates, x. 485.

[4] Speech of James Stephen, March 6, 1809; Cobbett's Debates, xiii., Appendix lxxvi.

Trade, went still further, and not only avowed, in the face of Parliament, the hope that these Orders in Council would make England the emporium of all trade in the world, but even asserted, in an unguarded moment of candor, that it was a mistake to call the orders retaliatory, — they were a system of self-defence, a plan to protect British commerce.[1]

Thus, too, the orders themselves, while licensing the export through England to France of all other American produce, imposed a prohibitive duty on the export of cotton, on the ground — as Canning officially informed[2] the American government — that France had pushed her cotton manufactures to such an extent as to make it expedient for England to embarrass them.

According to the public and private avowals of all the Ministry, the true object of Perceval's orders was, not to force a withdrawal of the Berlin Decree so far as it violated international law, but to protect British trade from competition. Perceval did not wish to famish France, but to feed her. His object was commercial, not political; his policy aimed at checking the commerce of America in order to stimulate the commerce of England. The pretence that this measure had retaliation for its object and the vindication of international law for its end was a legal fiction, made to meet the objections of America

1 Debate of March 3, 1812; report in Times and Morning Chronicle of March 4, 1812.

2 Erskine to Madison, Feb. 23, 1808; State Papers, iii. 209.

and to help Canning in maintaining a position which he knew to be weak.

After this long discussion, and after conferences not only with his colleagues in the Cabinet, but also with George Rose, Vice-President of the Board of Trade, with James Stephen, who was in truth the author of the war on neutrals, and with a body of merchants from the city, — at last, Nov. 11, 1807, Spencer Perceval succeeded in getting his General Order approved in Council. In its final shape this famous document differed greatly from the original draft. In deference to Lord Bathurst's objections, the sweeping doctrine of retaliation was omitted, so that hardly an allusion to it was left in the text; the assertion that neutrals had acquiesced in the Berlin Decree was struck out; the preamble was reduced, by Lord Eldon's advice, to a mere mention of the French pretended blockade, and of Napoleon's real prohibition of British commerce, followed by a few short paragraphs reciting that Lord Howick's order of Jan. 7, 1807, had "not answered the desired purpose either of compelling the enemy to recall those orders or of inducing neutral nations to interpose with effect to obtain their revocation, but on the contrary the same have been recently enforced with increased rigor;" and then, with the blunt assertion that "his Majesty, under these circumstances, finds himself compelled to take further measures for asserting and vindicating his just rights," Perceval, without more apology, ordered in effect that all American commerce, except that to Sweden and the West Indies, should pass through some British port and take out a British license.

The exceptions, the qualifications, and the verbiage of the British Orders need no notice. The ablest British merchants gave up in despair the attempt to understand them; and as one order followed rapidly upon another, explaining, correcting, and developing Perceval's not too lucid style, the angry Liberals declared their belief that he intended no man to understand them without paying two guineas for a legal opinion, with the benefit of a chance to get a directly contrary opinion for the sum of two guineas more.[1] Besides the express provisions contained in the Order of November 11, it was understood that American commerce with the enemies of England must not only pass through British ports with British license, but that colonial produce would be made to pay a tax to the British Treasury to enhance its price, while cotton would not be allowed to enter France.

The general intention, however confused, was simple. After November 11, 1807, any American vessel carrying any cargo was liable to capture if it sailed for any port in Europe from which the British flag was excluded. In other words, American commerce was made English.

This measure completed, diplomacy was to resume its work. Even Canning's audacity might be stag-

[1] Baring's Inquiry, pp. 14, 15.

gered to explain how the government of the United States could evade war after it should fairly understand the impressment Proclamation of October 17, the Order in Council of November 11, and the Instructions of George Henry Rose, — who was selected by Canning as his special envoy for the adjustment of the "Leopard's" attack on the "Chesapeake," and who carried orders which made adjustment impossible. Such outrages could be perpetrated only upon a helpless people. Even in England, where Jefferson's pacific policy was well understood, few men believed that peace could be longer preserved.

CHAPTER V.

THE curtain was about to rise upon a new tragedy, — the martyrdom of Spain. At this dramatic spectacle the United States government and people might have looked with composure and without regret, for they hardly felt so deep an interest in history, literature, or art as to care greatly what was to become of the land which had once produced Cortes, Cervantes, and Murillo; but in the actual condition of European politics their own interests were closely entwined with those of Spain, and as the vast designs of Napoleon were developed, the fortunes of the Spanish empire more and more deeply affected those of the American Union.

General Armstrong waited impatiently at Paris while Napoleon carried on his desperate struggle with the Emperor Alexander amid the ice and snows of Prussia. After the battle of Eylau the American minister became so restless that in May, 1807, he demanded passports for Napoleon's headquarters, but was refused. Had he gone as he wished, he might have seen the great battle of Friedland, June 14, and witnessed the peace of Tilsit, signed July 7, which swept away the last obstacle to Napoleon's schemes against Spain and America. After the peace of Tilsit, Armstrong could foresee that he should have to wait but a short time for the explanations so mysteriously delayed.

Except Denmark and Portugal, every State on the coast of Europe from St. Petersburg to Trieste acknowledged Napoleon's domination. England held out; and experience proved that England could not be reached by arms. The next step in the Emperor's system was to effect her ruin by closing the whole world to her trade. He began with Portugal. From Dresden, July 19, he issued orders[1] that the Portuguese ports should be closed by September 1 against English commerce, or the kingdom of Portugal would be occupied by a combined French and Spanish army. July 29 he was again in Paris. July 31 he ordered Talleyrand to warn the Prince Royal of Denmark that he must choose between war with England and war with France. That the turn would next come to the United States was evident; and Armstrong was warned by many signs of the impending storm. August 2, at the diplomatic audience, the brunt of Napoleon's displeasure fell on Dreyer, the Danish minister, and on his colleague from Portugal; but Armstrong could see that he was himself expected to profit by the lesson. He wrote instantly to the Secretary of State.[2]

[1] Napoleon to Talleyrand, July 19, 1807; Correspondance, xv. 433.

[2] Armstrong to Madison, Aug. 3, 1807; State Papers, iii. 243.

"We had yesterday our first audience of the Emperor since his return to Paris. Happening to stand near the minister of Denmark, I overheard his Majesty say to that minister: 'So, M. Baron, the Baltic has been violated!' The minister's answer was not audible to me; nor did it appear to be satisfactory to the Emperor, who repeated, in a tone of voice somewhat raised and peremptory, 'But, sir, the Baltic has been violated!' From M. Dreyer he passed to myself and others, and lastly to the ambassador of Portugal, to whom, it is said, he read a very severe lecture on the conduct of his Court. These circumstances go far to justify the whispers that begin to circulate, that an army is organizing to the south for the purpose of taking possession of Portugal, and another to the north for a similar purpose with regard to Denmark; and generally, that, having settled the business of belligerents, with the exception of England, very much to his own liking, he is now on the point of settling that of neutrals in the same way. It was perhaps under the influence of this suggestion that M. Dreyer, taking me aside, inquired whether any application had been made to me with regard to a projected union of all commercial States against Great Britain, and on my answering in the negative, he replied: 'You are much favored, but it will not last!'"

A few days afterward another rumor ran through Paris. The Prince of Benevento was no longer Minister of Foreign Affairs, and his successor was to be M. de Champagny, hitherto Minister of the Interior. At first Armstrong would not believe in Talleyrand's disgrace. "It is not probable that this is very serious, or that it will be very durable," he wrote.[1] "A trifling cause cannot alienate such a master from such a minister; and a grave one could not fail to break up all connections between them." Reasonable as this theory seemed, it was superficial. The master and the minister had not only separated, but had agreed to differ and to remain outwardly friends. Their paths could no longer lie together; and the overwhelming power of Bonaparte — who controlled a million soldiers with no enemy to fight — made cabals and Cabinet opposition not only useless but ridiculous. Yet with all this, Talleyrand stood in silent and cold disapproval of the Emperor's course; and since Talleyrand represented intelligent conservatism, it was natural to suppose that the Emperor meant to be even more violent in the future than in the past. The new minister, Champagny, neither suggested a policy of his own, nor presumed, as Talleyrand sometimes dared, to argue or remonstrate with his master.

Toward the end of August Dreyer's prophecy became true. Napoleon's orders forced the King of Denmark and King Louis of Holland to seize neutral commerce and close the Danish and Dutch ports. The question immediately rose whether United States ships and property were still to be treated as exempt from the operation of the Berlin Decree by virtue of the treaty of 1800; and the Emperor promptly decided against them.

[1] Armstrong to Madison, Aug. 11, 1807; MSS. State Department Archives.

"In actual circumstances," he wrote to Decrès,[1] "navigation offers all sorts of difficulties. France cannot regard as neutral flags which enjoy no consideration. That of America, however exposed it may be to the insults of the English, has a sort of existence, since the English still keep some measure in regard to it, and it imposes on them. That of Portugal and that of Denmark exist no longer."

This opinion was written before the British ministry touched the Orders in Council; and the "sort of existence" which Napoleon conceded to the United States was already so vague as to be not easily known from the extinction which had fallen upon Portugal and Denmark. A few days afterward General Armstrong received officially an order[2] from the Emperor which expressly declared that the Berlin Decree admitted of no exception in favor of American vessels; and this step was followed by a letter[3] from Champagny, dated October 7, to the same effect. At the same time the Council of Prizes pronounced judgment in the case of the American ship "Horizon," wrecked some six months before near Morlaix. The Court decreed that such part of the cargo as was not of English origin should be restored to its owners; but that the merchandise which was acknowledged to be of English manufacture or to come from English

[1] Napoleon to Decrès, Sept. 9, 1807; Correspondance, xvi. 20.

[2] M. Regnier to the Procureur Général, Sept. 18, 1807; State Papers, iii. 244.

[3] Champagny to Armstrong, Oct. 7, 1807; State Papers, iii. 245.

territory should be confiscated under the Berlin Decree. To this decision Armstrong immediately responded in a strong note[1] of protest to Champagny, which called out an answer from the Emperor himself.

"Reply to the American minister," wrote Napoleon[2] to Champagny November 15, "that since America suffers her vessels to be searched, she adopts the principle that the flag does not cover the goods. Since she recognizes the absurd blockades laid by England, consents to having her vessels incessantly stopped, sent to England, and so turned aside from their course, why should the Americans not suffer the blockade laid by France? Certainly France is no more blockaded by England than England by France. Why should Americans not equally suffer their vessels to be searched by French ships? Certainly France recognizes that these measures are unjust, illegal, and subversive of national sovereignty; but it is the duty of nations to resort to force, and to declare themselves against things which dishonor them and disgrace their independence."

Champagny wrote this message to Armstrong November 24, taking the ground that America must submit to the Berlin Decree because she submitted to impressments and search.[3]

As a matter of relative wrong, Napoleon's argu-

[1] Armstrong to Champagny, Nov. 12, 1807; State Papers, iii. 245.

[2] Napoleon to Champagny, Nov. 15, 1807; Correspondance, xvi. 165.

[3] Champagny to Armstrong, Nov. 24, 1807; State Papers, iii. 247.

ment was more respectable than that of Spencer Perceval and George Canning. He could say with truth that the injury he did to America was wholly consequential on the injury he meant to inflict on England. He had no hidden plan of suppressing American commerce in order to develop the commerce of France; as yet he was not trying to make money by theft. His Berlin Decree interfered in no way with the introduction of American products directly into France; it merely forbade the introduction of English produce or the reception of ships which came from England. Outrageous as its provisions were, "unjust, illegal, and subversive of national sovereignty," as Napoleon himself admitted and avowed, they bore their character and purpose upon their face, and in that sense were legitimate. He had no secrets on this point. In a famous diplomatic audience at Fontainebleau October 14, Armstrong witnessed a melodramatic scene, in which the Emperor proclaimed to the world that his will was to be law.[1] "The House of Braganza shall reign no more," said he to the Portuguese minister; then turning to the representative of the Queen of Etruria, — the same Spanish princess on whose head he had five years before placed the shadowy crown of Tuscany, —

"Your mistress," he said, "has her secret attachments to Great Britain, — as you, Messieurs Deputies of the Hanse Towns are also said to have; but I will put an

[1] Armstrong to Madison, Oct. 15, 1807; MSS. State Department Archives.

end to this. Great Britain shall be destroyed. I have the means of doing it, and they shall be employed. I have three hundred thousand men devoted to this object, and an ally who has three hundred thousand to support them. I will permit no nation to receive a minister from Great Britain until she shall have renounced her maritime usages and tyranny; and I desire you, gentlemen, to convey this determination to your respective sovereigns."

Armstrong obeyed the order; and in doing so he might easily have pointed out the machinery by which Napoleon expected to insure the co-operation of America in securing the destruction of England. He could combine the Berlin Decree with the baffled negotiations for Florida, and could understand why the Emperor at one moment dangled the tempting bait before Jefferson's eyes, and the next snatched it away. This diplomatic game was one which Napoleon played with every victim he wished to ensnare, and the victim never showed enough force of character to resist temptation. German, Italian, Russian, Spaniard, American, had all been lured by this decoy; one after another had been caught and devoured, but the next victim never saw the trap, or profited by the cries of the last unfortunate. Armstrong knew that whenever Napoleon felt the United States slipping through his fingers, Florida would again be offered to keep Jefferson quiet; yet even Armstrong, man of the world as he was, tried to persuade himself that Napoleon did not know his own mind. One of his despatches at this crisis related a curious story, which he evidently believed to be true, and to prove the vacillating temper of Napoleon's Florida negotiation.

November 15 Armstrong wrote that the Emperor had left Fontainebleau for Italy; that great changes were predicted, among which it was rumored "that Portugal, taken from the Braganzas, may be lent to the children of the Toscan House, and that the Bourbons of Spain are at last to make way for Lucien Bonaparte, who, in atonement or from policy, is to marry the Queen Regent of Etruria." That the American minister should at that early day have been so well informed about projects as yet carefully concealed, was creditable to his diplomacy. Not till nearly a month later did Lucien himself, in his Italian banishment, receive notice of the splendid bribe intended for him.

In the same despatch of November 15 Armstrong discussed the Emperor's plans in their bearing on Florida. "We are, it seems, to be invited to make common cause against England, and to take the guaranty of the Continent for a maritime peace which shall establish the principle of 'free ships, free goods.'" Armstrong argued that it was wiser to act alone, even in case of war with England; in regard to Florida, France had done all that was to be expected from her, and had latterly become sparing even of promises. Finally, he told the anecdote already alluded to: —

"The fact appears to be, which I communicate with the most intimate conviction of its truth, that some sycophant, entering into the weakness of the Emperor, and perceiving that he was only happy in giving a little more circumference to the bubble, seized the moment of Izquierdo's nomination, and pointing to the United States, said: 'These are destined to form the last labor of the modern Hercules. The triumph over England cannot be complete so long as the commerce and republicanism of this country be permitted to exist. Will it then be wise to insulate it, — to divest yourselves or your allies of those points which would place you at once in the midst of it? With what view was it that after selling Louisiana, attempts were made by France to buy the Floridas from Spain? Was it not in the anticipation of events which may make necessary to you a place in the neighborhood of these States, — a point on which to rest your political lever? Remember that Archimedes could not move the world without previously finding a resting-place for his screw. Instead, therefore, of parting with the Floridas, I would suggest whether we should not make the repossession of Canada a condition of a peace with England.' The conception itself, and the manner in which it was presented, struck the Emperor forcibly. He mused a moment upon it, and then in the most peremptory manner ordered that the negotiation should not go on."

Armstrong regarded this anecdote as important. Perhaps he had it, directly or indirectly, from Talleyrand, who used more freedom of speech than was permitted to any other man in France; but the task of penetrating the depths of Napoleon's mind was one which even Talleyrand attempted in vain. From the first, Florida had been used by Napoleon as a means of controlling President Jefferson. "To enlarge the circumference of his bubble" was a phrase keen and terse enough to have come from Talleyrand himself; but this was not the purpose for which Florida had hitherto been used in Napoleon's diplomacy, and in ordering that the negotiation should be stopped, the Emperor might well have other motives, which he preferred keeping to himself.

An observer far less intelligent than Armstrong might have seen that in face of the great changes which his despatch announced for Italy, Portugal, and Spain, the time when Napoleon would need support from the United States had not yet come. The critical moment was still in the future. Perhaps America might be forced into war by the "Chesapeake" outrage; at all events, she was further than ever from alliance with England, and the Emperor could safely wait for her adhesion to the continental system until his plans for consolidating his empire were more mature. For the present, Don Carlos IV. and the Prince of Peace were the chief objects of French diplomacy.

The story of Toussaint and St. Domingo was about to be repeated in Spain. Even while Armstrong wrote these despatches, the throne of Don Carlos IV. crumbled, almost without need of a touch from without. France had drawn from Spain everything she once possessed, — her navy, sacrificed at Trafalgar to Napoleon's orders; her army, nearly half of which was in Denmark; her treasures, which, so far as they had not been paid in subsidies to Napoleon, were shut up in Mexico. Nothing but the shell was left of all that had made Spain great. This long depletion had not been effected without extreme anxiety on the part of the Spanish government. At any time after the Prince of Peace returned to power in 1801, he would gladly have broken with France, as he proved in 1806; but he stood in much the same position as Jefferson, between the selfishness of England and the immediate interests of Spain. King Charles, anxious beyond measure for his own repose and for the safety of his daughter the Queen of Etruria, shrank from every strong measure of resistance to Napoleon's will, yet was so helpless that only a traitor or a coward could have deserted him; and Godoy, with all his faults, was not so base as to secure his own interests by leaving the King to Napoleon's mercy. For a single moment the King yielded to Godoy's entreaties. When the fourth European coalition was formed against Napoleon, and Prussia declared war, the Prince of Peace was allowed to issue, Oct. 6, 1806, a proclamation calling the Spanish people to arms. October 14 the battle of Jena was fought, and the news reaching Madrid threw the King and court into consternation; Godoy's influence was broken by the shock; the proclamation was recalled, and the old King bowed his head to his fate. Had he held firm, and thrown in his fortunes with those of England, Russia, and Prussia, the battle of Eylau might have stopped Napoleon's career; and in any case the fate of Spain could not have been more terrible than it was.

The Prince of Peace begged in vain that King Charles would dismiss him and form a new ministry; the King could not endure a change. Napoleon laughed at the proclamation, but he knew Godoy to be his only serious enemy at Madrid. He took infinite pains, and exhausted the extraordinary resources of his cunning, in order to get possession of Spain without a blow. To do this, he forced Portugal into what he called a war. Without noticing Godoy's offence, immediately after the peace of Tilsit, as has been already told, the Emperor ordered the King of Portugal to execute the Berlin Decree. Unable to resist, Portugal consented to shut her ports to English commerce, but objected to confiscating British property. Without a moment's delay, Napoleon, October 12,[1] ordered General Junot, with an army of twenty thousand men, to enter Spain within twenty-four hours, and march direct to Lisbon; simultaneously he notified[2] the Spanish government that his troops would be at Burgos, November 1; and that this time "it was not intended to do as was done in the last war, — he must march straight to Lisbon."

[1] Napoleon to General Clarke, Oct. 12, 1807; Correspondance, xvi. 80.

[2] Napoleon to Champagny, Oct. 12, 1807; Correspondance, xvi. 79.

After the peace of Tilsit, no Power in Europe pretended to question Napoleon's will, and for Spain to do so would have been absurd. King Charles had to submit, and he sent an army to co-operate with Junot against Portugal. The Emperor, who might at a single word have driven King Charles as well as the King of Portugal from the throne, did not say the word. Godoy's proclamation had given France cause for war; but Napoleon took no notice of the proclamation. He did not ask for the punishment of Godoy; he not only left the old King in peace, but took extraordinary care to soothe his fears. On the same day when he ordered Junot to march, he wrote personally to reassure the King:[1] "I will concert with your Majesty as to what shall be done with Portugal; in any case the suzerainty shall belong to you, as you have seemed to wish." Yet four days later he ordered[2] another army of thirty thousand men to be collected at Bayonne, to support Junot, who had no enemy to fear. That his true campaign was against Spain, not against Portugal, never admitted of a doubt; his orders to Junot hardly concealed his object:[3] —

"Cause descriptions to be made for me of all the provinces through which you pass, — the roads, the na-

[1] Napoleon to Charles IV., Oct. 12, 1807; Correspondance, xvi. 83.

[2] Napoleon to General Clarke, Oct. 16, 1807; Correspondance, xvi. 91.

[3] Napoleon to Junot, Oct. 17, 1807; Correspondance, xvi. 98.

ture of the ground; send me sketches. Charge engineer officers with this work, which it is important to have; so that I can see the distance of the villages, the nature of the country, the resources it offers. . . . I learn this moment that Portugal has declared war on England and sent away the English ambassador: this does not satisfy me; continue your march; I have reason to believe that it is agreed upon with England in order to give time for the English troops to come from Copenhagen. You must be at Lisbon by December 1, as friend or as enemy. Maintain the utmost harmony with the Prince of Peace."

Junot entered Spain October 17, the same day that these orders were written, while Napoleon at Fontainebleau forced on the Spanish agent Izquierdo a treaty which might keep King Charles and Godoy quiet a little longer. This document, drafted by Napoleon himself, resembled the letter to Toussaint and the proclamation to the negroes of St. Domingo, with which Leclerc had been charged;[1] its motive was too obvious, and its appeal to selfishness too gross to deceive. It declared[2] that Portugal should be divided into three parts. The most northerly, with Oporto for a capital and a population of eight hundred thousand souls, should be given to the Queen of Etruria in place of Tuscany, which was to be swallowed up in the kingdom of Italy. The next provision was even more curious. The southern part

[1] See History of First Administration, i. 392.

[2] Correspondance de Napoleon I.; Projet de Convention, Oct. 23, 1807, xvi. 111.

of Portugal, with a population of four hundred thousand souls, should be given to the Prince of Peace as an independent sovereignty. The central part, with a population of two millions, and Lisbon for a capital, should be held by France subject to further agreement. By a final touch of dissimulation worthy of Shakespeare's tragic invention, Napoleon, in the last article of this treaty, promised to recognize Don Carlos IV. as Emperor of the two Americas.

The so-called treaty of Fontainebleau was signed Oct. 27, 1807. That it deceived Godoy or King Charles could hardly be imagined, but the internal and external difficulties of Spain had reached a point where nothing but ruin remained. In the whole of Spain hardly twenty thousand troops could be assembled; barely half-a-dozen frigates were fit for sea; the treasury was empty; industry was destroyed. Napoleon himself had no idea how complete was the process by which he had sucked the life-blood of this miserable land. Even in the court at Madrid and among the people signs of an immediate catastrophe were so evident that Napoleon could afford to wait until chaos should call for his control.

Meanwhile Junot marched steadily forward. He was at Burgos on the day fixed by Napoleon; he established permanent French depots at Valladolid and at Salamanca. Leaving Salamanca November 12, he advanced to Ciudad Rodrigo, and after establishing another depot there, he made a rapid dash at Lisbon. The march was difficult, but Junot was ready to destroy his army rather than fail to carry out his orders; and on the morning of November 30 he led a ragged remnant of fifteen hundred men into the city of Lisbon. He found it without a government. The Prince Regent of Portugal, powerless to resist Napoleon, had gone on board his ships with the whole royal family and court, and was already on his way to found a new empire at Rio Janeiro. Of all the royal houses of Europe, that of Portugal was the first to carry out a desperate resolution.

Napoleon's object was thus gained. Dec. 1, 1807, Junot was in peaceable possession of Lisbon, and French garrisons held every strategical point between Lisbon and Bayonne. In regard to Portugal Junot's orders were precise:[1] —

"So soon as you have the different fortified places in your hands, you will put French commandants in them, and will make yourself sure of these places. I need not tell you that you must not put any fortress in the power of the Spaniards, especially in the region which is to remain in my hands."

November 3, without the knowledge of Spain, the Emperor gave orders[2] that the army of reserve at Bayonne, under General Dupont, shall be ready to march by December 1; and November 11 he ordered[3]

[1] Napoleon to Junot, October 31, 1807; Correspondance, xvi. 128.

[2] Napoleon to General Clarke, Nov. 3, 1807; Correspondance, xvi. 136.

[3] Napoleon to General Clarke, Nov. 11, 1807; Correspondance, xvi. 149.

that the frontier fortresses on the Spanish border should be armed and supplied with provisions: —

"All this is to be done with the utmost possible secrecy, especially the armament of the places on the Spanish frontier on the side of the eastern Pyrenees. Give secret instructions, and let the corps march in such a manner that the first ostensible operations be not seen in that country before November 25."

At the same time a new army of some twenty thousand men was hurried across France to take the place, at Bayonne, of Dupont's army, which was to enter Spain. November 13, the Emperor ordered Dupont to move his first division across the frontier to Vittoria; and on the same day he despatched M. de Tournon, his chamberlain, with a letter to King Charles at Madrid, and with secret instructions[1] that revealed the reasons for these movements so carefully concealed from Spanish eyes: —

"You will also inform yourself, without seeming to do so, of the situation of the places of Pampeluna and of Fontarabia; and if you perceive armaments making anywhere, you will inform me by courier. You will be on the watch at Madrid to see well the spirit which animates that city."

Napoleon's orders were in all respects exactly carried out. Dec. 1, 1807, Junot was in possession of Portugal; Dupont was at Vittoria; twenty-five thousand French troops would, by December 20, hold

[1] Napoleon to M. de Tournon, Nov. 13, 1807; Correspondance, xvi. 159.

the great route from Vittoria to Burgos, and in two days could occupy Madrid.[1] The Spanish army was partly in Denmark, partly in Portugal. The Prince of Peace heard what was going on, and asked for explanations; but the moment for resistance had long passed. He had no choice but submission or flight, and Don Carlos was too weak to fly.

In Armstrong's despatch of November 15, already quoted, one more paragraph was worth noting. At the moment he wrote, Napoleon had just given his last orders; General Dupont had not yet received them, and neither Don Carlos IV. nor Lucien Bonaparte knew the change of plan that was intended. Only men like Talleyrand and Duroc could see that from the moment of the peace at Tilsit, Napoleon's movements had been rapidly and irresistibly converging upon Madrid, — until, by the middle of November, every order had been given, and the Spanish Peninsula lay, as the Emperor told Lucien, "in the hollow of his hand." Armstrong, writing a fortnight before the royal family of Portugal had turned their vessels' prows toward Brazil, asked a question which Napoleon himself would hardly have dared to answer:

"What will become of the royal houses of Portugal and Spain? I know not. By the way, I consider this question as of no small interest to the United States. If they were sent to America, or are even permitted to withdraw thither, we may conclude that the colonies which

[1] Napoleon to General Clarke, Dec. 6, 1807; Correspondance, xvi. 183.

excite the imperial longing, and which are in its opinion necessary to France, are not on our side of the Atlantic. If on the other hand they are retained in Europe, it will only be as hostages for the eventual delivery of their colonies; and then, at the distance of three centuries, may be acted over again the tragedy of the Incas, with some few alterations of scenery and names."

All these measures being completed by November 15, the day when Armstrong wrote his despatch, the Emperor left Fontainebleau and went to Italy. He passed through Milan and Verona to Venice; and on his return, stopped a few hours at Mantua,[1] on the night of December 13, to offer Lucien the throne of Spain.

Lucien's story[2] was that being summoned from Rome to an interview, he found his brother alone, at midnight of December 13, seated in a vast room in the palace at Mantua, before a great round table, almost entirely covered by a very large map of Spain, on which he was marking strategical points with black, red, and yellow pins. After a long interview, in which the Emperor made many concessions to his brother's resistance, Napoleon opened his last and most audacious offer:—

"'As for you, choose!' As he pronounced these words," continued Lucien, "his eyes sparkled with a flash of pride which seemed to me Satanic; he struck a great blow with his hand, spread out broadly in the

[1] Napoleon to Joseph, Dec. 17, 1807; Correspondance, xvi. 198.

[2] Lucien Bonaparte. Th. Jung. iii. 83, 113.

middle of the immense map of Europe which was extended on the table by the side of which we were standing. 'Yes, choose!' he said; 'you see I am not talking in the air. All this is mine, or will soon belong to me; I can dispose of it already. Do you want Naples? I will take it from Joseph, who, by the bye, does not care for it; he prefers Morfontaine. Italy, — the most beautiful jewel in my imperial crown? Eugene is but viceroy, and far from despising it he hopes only that I shall give it to him, or at least leave it to him if he survives me: he is likely to be disappointed in waiting, for I shall live ninety years; I must, for the perfect consolidation of my empire. Besides, Eugene will not suit me in Italy after his mother is repudiated. Spain? Do you not see it falling into the hollow of my hand, thanks to the blunders of your dear Bourbons, and to the follies of your friend the Prince of Peace? Would you not be well pleased to reign there where you have been only ambassador? Once for all, what do you want? Speak! Whatever you wish, or can wish, is yours, if your divorce precedes mine.'"

Lucien refused a kingdom on such terms, and Napoleon continued his journey, reaching Milan December 15. At that time his mind was intent on Spain and the Spanish colonies, with which the questions of English and American trade were closely connected. Spencer Perceval's Orders in Council had appeared in the "London Gazette" of November 14, and had followed the Emperor to Italy. Some weeks afterward war was declared between England and Russia. No neutral remained except Sweden, which was to be crushed by Russia, and the United States of

America, which Napoleon meant to take in hand. December 17, from the royal palace at Milan, in retaliation for the Orders in Council, and without waiting to consult President Jefferson, Napoleon issued a new proclamation, compared with which the Berlin Decree of the year before was a model of legality.

"Considering," began the preamble,[1] "that by these acts the English government has denationalized the ships of all the nations of Europe; that it is in the power of no government to compound its own independence and its rights, — all the sovereigns in Europe being jointly interested in the sovereignty and independence of their flag; that if by an inexcusable weakness, which would be an ineffaceable stain in the eyes of posterity, we should allow such a tyranny to pass into a principle and to become consecrated by usage, the English would take advantage of it to establish it as a right, as they have profited by the tolerance of governments to establish the infamous principle that the flag does not cover the goods, and to give to their right of blockade an arbitrary extension, contrary to the sovereignty of all States," —

Considering all these matters, so important to States like Denmark, Portugal, and Spain, whose flags had ceased to exist, and of whose honor and interests this mighty conqueror made himself champion, Napoleon decreed that every ship which should have been searched by an English vessel, or should have paid any duty to the British government, or should come

[1] Correspondance de Napoleon, xvi. 192; American State Papers, iii. 90.

from or be destined for any port in British possession in any part of the world, should be good prize; and that this rule should continue in force until England should have "returned to the principles of international law, which are also those of justice and honor."

CHAPTER VI.

Oct. 29, 1807, Monroe left London; and November 14, the day when the Orders in Council were first published in the official "Gazette," he sailed from Plymouth for home.

Nearly five years had passed since Monroe received the summons from Jefferson which drew him from his retirement in Virginia to stand forward as the diplomatic champion of the United States in contest with the diplomatists of Europe; and these five years had been full of unpleasant experience. Since signing the Louisiana treaty, in May, 1803, he had met only with defeat and disaster. Insulted by every successive Foreign Secretary in France, Spain, and England; driven from Madrid to Paris and from Paris to London; set impossible tasks, often contrary to his own judgment, — he had ended by yielding to the policy of the British government, and by meeting with disapproval and disavowal from his own. As he looked back on the receding shores of England, he could hardly fail to recall the circumstances of his return from France ten years before. In many respects Monroe's career was unparalleled, but he was singular above all in the experience of being disowned by two Presidents as strongly opposed to each other as Washington and Jefferson, and of being sacrificed by two secretaries as widely different as Timothy Pickering and James Madison.

In America only two men of much note were prepared to uphold his course, and of these the President was not one; yet Jefferson exerted himself to disguise and soften Monroe's discredit. He kept the treaty a secret when its publication would have destroyed Monroe's popularity and strengthened Madison. When at length, after eight months' delay, the British note appended to the treaty was revealed, Monroe's friend Macon, though anxious to make him President, privately admitted that "the extract of the treaty which has been published has injured Monroe more than the return of it by the President."[1] John Randolph alone held up Monroe and his treaty as models of statesmanship; and although Randolph was the only Republican who cared to go this length, Monroe found one other friend and apologist in a person who rivalled Randolph in his usual economy of praise. Timothy Pickering held that Merry and Erskine were no good Englishmen, but he was satisfied with Monroe.

"I sincerely wish an English minister here to be a very able man," he wrote[2] privately from Washington to a friend in Philadelphia, — "one who will feel and justly

[1] Macon to Nicholson, Dec. 2, 1807; Nicholson MSS.

[2] Pickering to Thomas Fitzsimons, Dec. 4, 1807; Pickering MSS.

estimate the dignity of his country, and bring down the supercilious looks of our strutting Administration. The feebleness of Merry and Erskine have encouraged them to assume a vain importance and haughtiness as remote from the genuine spirit and as injurious to the solid interests of our country as they are irritating to Great Britain. The ridiculous gasconade of our rulers has indeed disgraced our nation. The sentiment above expressed is excited by the consideration that Great Britain is our only shield against the overwhelming power of Bonaparte; and therefore I view the maintenance of her just rights as essential to the preservation of our own. I have regretted to see our newspapers continue to reproach Monroe. His abilities you know how to estimate, but I never considered him as wanting in probity. An *enragé* relative to the French, and implicitly relying on the advice of Jefferson, his deportment did not permit his remaining the minister of the United States at Paris [in 1797]; but I have certain information that at London no one could conduct with more propriety than he does; and, such is his sense of the proceedings of our rulers, he lately said he did not know how long the British government would bear with our petulance."

This letter, written while Monroe was at sea, betrayed a hope that the notorious quarrel between him and Jefferson would prove to be permanent; but Pickering could never learn to appreciate Jefferson's genius for peace. Doubtless only personal friendship and the fear of strengthening Federalist influence prevented President Jefferson from denouncing Monroe's conduct as forcibly as President Washington had denounced it ten years before; and Jefferson's grounds of complaint were more serious than Washington's. Monroe expected and even courted martyrdom, and never quite forgot the treatment he received. In private, George Hay, Monroe's son-in-law, who knew all the secrets of his career, spoke afterward of Jefferson as "one of the most insincere men in the world; . . . his enmity to Mr. Monroe was inveterate, though disguised, and he was at the bottom of all the opposition to Mr. Monroe in Virginia."[1] Peacemakers must submit to the charges which their virtues entail, but Jefferson's silence and conciliation deserved a better return than to be called insincere.

Monroe returned to Virginia, praised by George Canning and Timothy Pickering, to be John Randolph's candidate for the Presidency, while Jefferson could regard him in no other light than as a dupe of England, and Madison was obliged to think him a personal enemy. As a result of five years' honest, patient, and painstaking labor, this division from old friends was sad enough; but had Monroe been a nervous man, so organized as to feel the arrows of his outrageous fortune, his bitterest annoyance on bidding final farewell to Europe would have been, not the thought of his reception in America, not even the memory of Talleyrand's reproofs, or of the laurels won by Don Pedro Cevallos, or of Lord Harrowby's roughness, or Lord Mulgrave's indifference, or Lord Howick's friendly larcenies, or Canning's smooth impertinences, — as a diplomatist he would rather have

[1] Diary of J. Q. Adams, May 23, 1824, vi. 348.

felt most hurt that the British ministry had contrived a new measure of vital interest to America, and should have allowed him to depart without a word of confidence, explanation, or enlightenment as to the nature of the fresh aggression which was to close a long list of disasters with one which left to America only the title of an independent nation.

As early as October 3 the "Morning Post" announced at great length that his Majesty's government had adopted the principle of retaliation. November 10, while Monroe was still waiting at Portsmouth for a fair wind, the "Times" made known that a proclamation was in readiness for the King's signature, declaring France and all her vassal kingdoms in a state of siege: "The sum of all reasoning on the subject is included in this, that the Continent must and will have colonial productions in spite of the orders and decrees of its master, and we are to take care that she have no other colonial produce than our own." The fact that American commerce with the Continent was to be forbidden became a matter of public notoriety in London before November 13, and on Saturday, November 14, the day when Monroe's ship sailed from Portsmouth, the order appeared in the "Gazette;" yet Monroe himself would be obliged to appear before the President in official ignorance of a measure discussed and adopted under his eyes.

George Henry Rose, whom Canning selected as special envoy to settle the "Chesapeake" affair, and who sailed in the "Statira" frigate two days before

Monroe, knew officially as little as Monroe himself of the coming order; but this ignorance was due to Canning's settled plan of keeping the "Chesapeake" affair independent of every other dispute. Canning could have had no deep motive in withholding official knowledge of the order from Monroe, Pinkney, and Rose; he could not have foreseen when or how the winds would blow; yet, by mere accident, one day's delay added greatly to the coming embarrassments of the American government. The departure of vessels depended on a favorable wind, and for some weeks before November 14 westerly winds prevailed. About that day the weather changed, and all the ships bound to America sailed nearly together. The "Statira" and "Augustus," carrying Rose and Monroe, started from Portsmouth for Norfolk; the "Revenge" set sail from Cherbourg, with despatches from Armstrong; the "Brutus," with London newspapers of November 12, departed from Liverpool for New York; and the "Edward," with London newspapers and letters to November 10, left Liverpool for Boston. All were clear of land by November 14, when the "Gazette" published the Order in Council; but for weeks afterward no other vessels crossed the Atlantic.

After the "Revenge" sailed for Europe in July, on her errand of redress for the "Chesapeake" outrage, the Americans waited more and more patiently for her return. The excitement which blazed in midsummer from one end of the country to the other began to subside when men learned that Admiral Berkeley's orders had been issued without the authority or knowledge of his government, and would probably be disavowed. The news that came from Europe tended to chill the fever for war. The Peace of Tilsit, the Tory reaction in England, the bombardment of Copenhagen, the execution of the Berlin Decree in Holland, the threatened retaliation by Great Britain were events calculated to raise more than a doubt of the benefits which war could bring. In any case, the risks of commerce had become too great for legitimate trade; and every one felt that the further pursuit of neutral profits could end only in bringing America into the arms of one or the other of the Powers which were avowedly disputing pre-eminence in wrong.

The attack on the "Chesapeake," the trial of Aaron Burr, and the news from Copenhagen, Holland, and London made the summer and autumn of 1807 anxious and restless; but another event, under the eyes of the American people, made up a thousand fold, had they but known it, for all the losses or risks incurred through Burr, Bonaparte, or Canning. That the destinies of America must be decided in America was a maxim of true Democrats, but one which they showed little energy in reducing to practice. A few whose names could be mentioned in one or two lines,—men like Chancellor Livingston, Dr. Mitchill, Joel Barlow,—hailed the 17th of August, 1807, as the beginning of a new era in America,—a date which separated the colonial from the independent stage of growth; for on that day, at one o'clock in the afternoon, the steamboat "Clermont," with Robert Fulton in command, started on her first voyage. A crowd of bystanders, partly sceptical, partly hostile, stood about and watched the clumsy craft slowly forge its way at the rate of four miles an hour up the river; but Fulton's success left room for little doubt or dispute, except in minds impervious to proof. The problem of steam navigation, so far as it applied to rivers and harbors was settled, and for the first time America could consider herself mistress of her vast resources. Compared with such a step in her progress, the mediæval barbarisms of Napoleon and Spencer Perceval signified little more to her than the doings of Achilles and Agamemnon. Few moments in her history were more dramatic than the weeks of 1807 which saw the shattered "Chesapeake" creep back to her anchorage at Hampton Roads, and the "Clermont" push laboriously up the waters of the Hudson; but the intellectual effort of bringing these two events together, and of settling the political and economical problems of America at once, passed the genius of the people. Government took no notice of Fulton's achievement, and the public for some years continued, as a rule, to travel in sailing packets and on flat-boats. The reign of politics showed no sign of ending. Fulton's steamer went its way, waiting until men's time should become so valuable as to be worth saving.

The unfailing mark of a primitive society was to regard war as the most natural pursuit of man; and history with reason began as a record of war, because, in fact, all other human occupations were secondary to this. The chief sign that Americans had other qualities than the races from which they sprang, was shown by their dislike for war as a profession, and their obstinate attempts to invent other methods for obtaining their ends; but in the actual state of mankind, safety and civilization could still be secured only through the power of self-defence. Desperate physical courage was the common quality on which all great races had founded their greatness; and the people of the United States, in discarding military qualities, without devoting themselves to science, were trying an experiment which could succeed only in a world of their own.

In charging America with having lost her national character, Napoleon said no more than the truth. As a force in the affairs of Europe, the United States had become an appendage to England. The Americans consumed little but English manufactures, allowed British ships to blockade New York and Chesapeake Bay, permitted the British government to keep by force in its naval service numbers of persons who were claimed as American subjects, and to take from American merchant-vessels, at its free will, any man who seemed likely to be useful; they suffered their commerce with France and Spain to be plundered by Great Britain without resistance, or to be regulated in defiance of American rights. Nothing could exceed England's disregard of American dignity. When the "Bellona" and her consorts were ordered to depart from Chesapeake Bay, her captain not only disregarded the order, but threatened to take by force whatever he wanted on shore, and laughed at the idea of compulsion. On land still less respect was shown to American jurisdiction. When after the "Chesapeake" outrage the people talked of war, the first act of Sir James Craig, governor-general of Canada, was to send messages[1] to the Indian tribes in the Indiana Territory, calling for their assistance in case of hostilities; and the effect of this appeal was instantly felt at Vincennes and Greenville, where it gave to the intrigues of the Shawanese prophet an impulse that alarmed every settler on the frontier. Every subordinate officer of the British government thought himself at liberty to trample on American rights; and while the English navy controlled the coast, and the English army from Canada gave orders to the northwestern Indians, the British minister at Washington encouraged and concealed the conspiracy of Burr.

The evil had reached a point where some corrective must be found; but four years of submission had broken the national spirit. In 1805 the people were almost ready for war with England on the question of

[1] Sir James Craig to Lieutenant-Governor Gore, Dec. 6, 1807; Colonial Correspondence, Canada, 1807, 1808, vol. i., MSS. British Archives.

the indirect, or carrying, trade of the French and Spanish West Indies. After submitting on that point, in July, 1807, they were again ready to fight for the immunity of their frigates from impressment; but by the close of the year their courage had once more fallen, and they hoped to escape the necessity of fighting under any circumstances whatever, anxiously looking for some expedient, or compromise, which would reconcile a policy of resistance with a policy of peace. This expedient Jefferson and Madison had for fifteen years been ready to offer them.

So confident was Jefferson in his theory of peaceable coercion that he would hardly have thought his administrative career complete, had he quitted office without being allowed to prove the value of his plan. The fascination which it exercised over his mind was quite as much due to temperament as to logic; for if reason told him that Europe could be starved into concession, temperament added another motive still more alluring. If Europe persisted in her conduct America would still be safe, and all the happier for cutting off connection with countries where violence and profligacy ruled supreme. The idea of ceasing intercourse with obnoxious nations reflected his own personality in the mirror of statesmanship. In the course of the following year he wrote to a young grandson, Thomas Jefferson Randolph, a letter[1] of parental advice in regard to the conduct of life.

[1] Jefferson to T. J. Randolph, Nov. 24, 1808; Works, v. 388.

"Be a listener only," he said; "keep within yourself, and endeavor to establish with yourself the habit of silence, especially on politics. In the fevered state of our country no good can ever result from any attempt to set one of these fiery zealots to rights, either in fact or principle. They are determined as to the facts they will believe, and the opinions on which they will act. Get by them, therefore, as you would by an angry bull; it is not for a man of sense to dispute the road with such an animal."

The advice was good, and did honor to the gentleness of Jefferson's nature; but a course of conduct excellent in social life could not be made to suit the arena of politics. As President of the United States, Jefferson was bent upon carrying out the plan of keeping within himself; but the bull of which he spoke as unfit for a man of sense to dispute with, and which he saw filling the whole path before him, was not only angry, but mad with pain and blind with rage; his throat and flanks were torn and raw where the Corsican wolf had set his teeth; a pack of mastiffs and curs were baiting him and yelling at his heels, and his blood-shot eyes no longer knew friend from foe, as he rushed with a roar of stupid rage directly upon the President. To get by him was impossible. To fly was the only resource, if the President would not stand his ground and stop the animal by skill or force.

Few rulers ever succeeded in running from danger with dignity. Even the absolute Emperor of Russia had not wholly preserved the respect of his subjects after the sudden somersault performed at Tilsit; and the Prince Regent of Portugal had been forced to desert his people when he banished himself to Brazil. President Jefferson had not their excuse for flight; but resistance by force was already impossible. For more than six years he had conducted government on the theory of peaceable coercion, and his own friends required that the experiment should be tried. He was more than willing, he was anxious, to gratify them; and he believed himself to have solved the difficult problem of stopping his enemy, while running away from him without loss of dignity and without the appearance of flight.

General Turreau, after hoping for a time that the government would accept the necessity of war with England, became more and more bitter as he watched the decline of the war spirit; and September 4, barely two months after the assault on the "Chesapeake," and long before the disavowal of Berkeley was known, he wrote to Talleyrand a diatribe against the Americans: [1] —

"If the sentiments of fear and of servile deference for England with which the inhabitants of the American Union are penetrated, were not as well known as their indifference for everything which bears the name of French, what has passed since the attack on the frigate 'Chesapeake' would prove to the most vulgar observer

[1] Turreau to Talleyrand, Sept. 4, 1807; Archives des Aff. Étr. MSS.

not only that the Anglo-Americans have remained in reality dependent on Great Britain, but even that this state of subjection conforms with their affections as well as with their habits. He will also be convinced that France has, and will ever have, nothing to hope from the dispositions of a people that conceives no idea of glory, of grandeur, of justice; that shows itself the constant enemy of liberal principles; and that is disposed to suffer every kind of humiliation, provided it can satisfy both its sordid avarice and its projects of usurpation over the Floridas."

Scandalized at the rapid evaporation of American courage, Turreau could explain it only as due to the natural defects of "a motley people, that will never have true patriotism, because it has no object of common interest;" a nation which looked on the most shameless outrages of its own virtue as only "unfortunate events." Yet one point remained which, although to every American it seemed most natural, was incomprehensible to the Frenchman, whose anger with America was due not so much to the dependence of the United States on England, as to their independence of France.

"What will doubtless astonish those who know the Americans but imperfectly, and what has surprised me myself, — me, who have a very bad opinion of this people, and who believe it just, — is the aversion (*éloignement*) — and I soften the word — which it has preserved for the French at the very moment when everything should recall a glorious and useful memory. It is hardly to be believed, yet is the exact truth, that in perhaps five hundred banquets produced by the anniversary of July 4, and among ten thousand toasts, but one has been offered in favor of France; and even this was given at an obscure meeting, and was evidently dictated by Duane."

Even the Administration press, Turreau complained, had thought proper to repudiate the idea of a French alliance. From his complaints the truth could be easily understood. In spite of reason, and in defiance of every ordinary rule of politics, France possessed in America no friend, or influence. The conclusion to be drawn was inevitable. If the United States would not accept the only alliance which could answer their purpose, England had nothing to fear. "In this state of affairs and condition of minds, it appears to me difficult to believe that Congress will take measures vigorous enough to revenge the insult offered to the Union, and to prevent the renewal of outrages."

This conclusion was reached by Turreau September 4, while as early as September 1 the same opinion was expressed by Erskine, the British minister:[1]

"From all the consideration which I have been able to give to the present state of things in this country, I am confirmed most strongly in the opinion which I have ventured to express in my former despatches, that, although I fear it might be possible for this government to lead the people into a war with Great Britain on the point of searching her national armed ships, yet I do not believe

[1] Erskine to Canning, Sept. 1, 1807; MSS. British Archives.

that there are any other grounds which would be powerful enough to urge them to so dangerous a measure to the political existence perhaps, but certainly to the general prosperity of this country."

No two men in America were better informed or more directly interested than Turreau and Erskine, and they agreed in regarding America as passive in the hands of England.

During the month of September the news from Europe tended to show that while England would not sustain the attack on the "Chesapeake," she meant to cut off, for her own benefit, another share of American commerce. The report on the West Indian trade and the debates in Parliament foreshadowed the enforcement of the so-called Rule of 1756 or some harsher measure. That Congress must in some way resent this interference with neutral rights was evident, unless America were to become again a British province. Erskine knew the strength of British influence too well to fear war; but he warned his Government that no nation could be expected to endure without protest of some kind the indignities which the United States daily experienced:[1] —

"I am persuaded that more ill-will has been excited in this country toward Great Britain by a few trifling illegal captures immediately off this coast, and some instances of insulting behavior by some of his Majesty's naval commanders in the very harbors and waters of the United

[1] Erskine to Canning, Oct. 5, 1807; MSS. British Archives.

States, than by the most rigid enforcement of the maritime rights of Great Britain in other parts of the world. It may easily be conceived to be highly grating to the feelings of an independent nation to perceive that their whole coast is watched as closely as if it was blockaded, and every ship coming in or going out of their harbors examined rigorously in sight of the shore, by British squadrons stationed within their waters."

Erskine added that the causes of difference were so various as to make any good understanding improbable, and any commercial treaty impossible; that the Federalists thought even worse of Monroe's treaty than the Government did, which rejected it; and that a great sensation had been produced by the late Report on the West Indian trade: —

"This point, and his Majesty's Order in Council to prohibit all neutral trade from port to port of his Majesty's enemies, — which, as you would perceive by Mr. Madison's letters on the subject, which have been transmitted to you, has given great offence to this Government, — together with the other points of difference between the two countries, particularly that of the impressment of British seamen out of American ships, will be taken up by Congress upon their meeting at the close of the present month; and I am fully convinced that unless some amicable adjustment of these points of dispute should previously take place, or be in a train to be concluded, a system of commercial restrictions on the trade of Great Britain with this country will be immediately formed, and every step short of actual war taken to show their dissatisfaction."

Thus, on the eve of the session, the most careful critics agreed that Congress would avoid war, and would resist England, if at all, by commercial measures. The President and Madison, Turreau and Erskine, were united in expecting the same course of events. No one knew that Napoleon had enforced against American commerce the provisions of his Berlin Decree. France counted for nothing in the councils of America; but the conduct of England obliged Congress to offer some protest against aggression,—and the easiest form of protest was a refusal to buy what she had to sell. The moment for testing Jefferson's statesmanship had come; and at no time since he became President had his theories of peaceable coercion enjoyed so fair a prospect of success. Abroad, Napoleon had shut the whole Continent of Europe to English trade, which was henceforward limited to countries beyond the seas. If ever England could be coerced by peaceable means, this was the time; while at home, the prospect was equally favorable, for never in American history had the authority of the government been so absolute.

Jefferson's hope of annihilating domestic opposition was nearly gratified. In the three southernmost States he had never met with serious attack; beyond the Alleghanies, in Tennessee, Kentucky, and Ohio, his word was law; in Virginia, John Randolph grew weaker day by day, and even with Monroe's aid could not shake the President's popularity; Pennsylvania was torn by factions, but none of them troubled Jefferson; New York, purged of Burr, was divided between Clintons and Livingstons, who were united in matters of national policy. The greatest triumph of all was won in Massachusetts, where the election of April, 1807, after calling out 81,500 voters, resulted in the choice of the Democrat Sullivan over the head of Governor Strong by about 42,000 votes against 39,000, and in the return of a Democratic majority in the State legislature. Connecticut alone of the New England States held to her old conservative principles; but Connecticut was powerless without Massachusetts.

Still more decidedly the decline of organized opposition was shown in the character of the Tenth Congress, which was to meet October 26. Of the old Federalist senators, Plumer of New Hampshire had been succeeded by a Democrat; J. Q. Adams of Massachusetts had publicly pledged himself to support any measures of resistance to England; Tracy of Connecticut — a very able opponent — was dead. Only five senators could be rallied to partisan opposition on matters of foreign policy, — Timothy Pickering of Massachusetts; James Hillhouse and Chauncey Goodrich of Connecticut; James A. Bayard and Samuel White of Delaware. Pickering, who considered Plumer and Adams as deserters to the Administration, felt little confidence in Bayard; and the event proved him right. There were limits to Bayard's partisanship; but even had he been willing to abet Pickering, four or five senators could hope to effect little against a compact majority of twenty-nine.

In the House the whole strength of opposition could not control thirty votes, while Jefferson was supported by one hundred and ten members or more. The President was the stronger for Randolph's departure into decided opposition, where he could no longer divide and mislead the majority, but must act as a Federalist or alone. Of the twenty-four Federalist members, Josiah Quincy was probably the ablest speaker; but in the energy of his Federalism he was rivalled by two men, — Barent Gardenier of New York, and Philip Barton Key of Maryland, — who were likely to injure their cause more than they helped it.

In the country and in Congress, not only was Jefferson supreme, but his enemies were prostrate. Federalism in New England, for the first time, lay helpless under his feet; Burr and the "little band" in New York were crushed; the creoles in New Orleans, and the Western revolutionists, with Wilkinson at their head, were cowering before the outburst of patriotism which struck their projects dead. The hand of government rested heavily on them, and threatened nobler prey. Even Chief-Justice Marshall felt himself marked for punishment; while Monroe and Randolph were already under ban of the republic. These were triumphs which outweighed foreign disasters, and warranted Jefferson in self-confidence; but they were chiefly due to the undisputed success of his financial management. Jefferson and Madison, Dearborn and Robert Smith, might do what they would, so long as they left Gallatin free to control the results of their experiments; for Gallatin redeemed the mistakes of his party. Madison's foreign policy had brought only trouble to the government; Dearborn's army had shown itself to be more dangerous to the Union than to its enemies; Smith's gunboats were a laughing-stock; but Gallatin never failed to cover every weak spot in the Administration, and in October, 1807, the Treasury was profuse of prosperity. Congress might abolish the salt tax and Mediterranean Fund alike, and still the customs would yield fourteen millions a year; while the sales of public lands exceeded 284,000 acres and brought another half million into the Treasury. December 31, after providing for all payments of public debt, Gallatin had a balance of seven millions six hundred thousand dollars on hand. During the Presidency of Jefferson, twenty-five and a half millions had been paid to redeem the principal of the public debt, and only the restraints imposed by the law prevented more rapid redemption. Even in case of war, Gallatin offered to sustain it for a year without borrowing money or increasing taxes.

There was the secret of Jefferson's strength, of his vast popularity, and of the fate which, without direct act of his, never had failed to overwhelm his enemies. The American people pardoned everything except an empty Treasury. No foreign insults troubled them long, and no domestic incompetence roused their disgust; but they were sensitive to any taxation which they directly felt. Gallatin atoned for starving the government by making it rich; and if obliged to endure disgrace and robbery abroad, he gave the President popularity at home. Conscious of this reserved strength, the President cared the less for foreign aggressions. His was, according to theory, the strongest government on earth; and at worst he had but to withdraw from intercourse with foreign nations in order to become impregnable to assault. He had no misgivings as to the result. When he returned, about October 8, from Monticello to Washington, his only thought was to assert the strength he felt. Nothing had then been received from England in regard to the "Chesapeake" negotiation, except Canning's letter of August 3, promising to "make reparation for any alleged injury to the sovereignty of the United States, whenever it should be clearly shown that such injury has been actually sustained, and that such reparation is really due." The President justly thought that this letter, though it disavowed the pretension to search ships of war, held out no sufficient hope of reparation for the "Chesapeake" outrage; and in writing the first draft of his Message, he expressed strongly his irritation at the conduct of England. The draft was sent, as usual, to the members of his Cabinet, and called out a remonstrance from Gallatin:—

"Instead of being written in the style of the proclamation, which has been almost universally approved at home and abroad, the Message appears to me to be rather in the shape of a manifesto, issued against Great Britain on the eve of a war, than such as the existing undecided state of affairs seems to require. It may either be construed into a belief that justice will be denied, — a result not to be anticipated in an official communication, — or it may be distorted into an eagerness of seeing matters brought to issue by an appeal to arms." [1]

In truth, the draft rather showed that Jefferson was ready to see matters brought to an issue, provided that the issue should not be an appeal to arms.

A few days later, after Congress met, Gallatin wrote to his wife: —

"The President's speech was originally more warlike than was necessary; but I succeeded in getting it neutralized — this between us; but it was lucky, for Congress is certainly peaceably disposed." [2]

The situation lay in these few words. Not only Congress but also the Government and people were peaceably disposed; and between the attitude of Congress and that of the President was but the difference that the former knew not what to do, while the latter had a fixed policy to impose. "I observe among the members," wrote a non-partisan senator, "great embarrassment, alarm, anxiety, and

[1] Gallatin to Jefferson, Oct. 21, 1807; Gallatin's Writings, i. 853.

[2] Adams's Gallatin, p. 363.

confusion of mind, but no preparation for any measure of vigor, and an obvious strong disposition to yield all that Great Britain may require, to preserve peace under a thin external show of dignity and bravery."[1] In such a state of minds, and with such a reserve of popular authority, President Jefferson's power found no restraint.

[1] Diary of J. Q. Adams, Nov. 17, 1807 ; i. 476.

CHAPTER VII.

SUCH was the situation October 26, when Congress assembled in obedience to the President's call. An unusually large number of members attended on the opening day, when for the first time the House was installed in a chamber of its own. After seven years of residence at Washington, the government had so far completed the south wing of the Capitol as to open it for use. A covered way of rough boards still connected the Senate Chamber in the north wing with the Chamber of Representatives in the southern extension of the building, and no one could foresee the time when the central structure, with its intended dome, would be finished; but the new chamber gave proof that the task was not hopeless. With extraordinary agreement every one admitted that Jefferson's and Latrobe's combined genius had resulted in the construction of a room equal to any in the world for beauty and size. The oval hall, with its girdle of fluted sandstone columns draped with crimson curtains, its painted ceiling, with alternate squares of glass, produced an effect of magnificence which was long remembered. Unfortunately, this splendor had drawbacks. Many and bitter were Randolph's complaints of the echoes and acoustic defects which marred the usefulness of the chamber.

That Randolph should feel no love for it was natural. The first scene it witnessed was that of his overthrow. Macon, who for six years had filled the chair, retired without a contest, dragged down by Randolph's weight; and of the one hundred and seventeen members present, fifty-nine, a bare majority, elected Joseph Bradley Varnum of Massachusetts their Speaker; while the minority of fifty-eight scattered their votes among half-a-dozen candidates. Varnum, ignoring Randolph, appointed George Washington Campbell of Tennessee chairman of the Ways and Means Committee. Troublesome as the Virginia leader had been, he was still the only member competent to control the House, and his fall was greatly regretted by at least one member of the Cabinet. "Varnum has, much against my wishes, removed Randolph from the Ways and Means, and appointed Campbell of Tennessee," wrote Gallatin.[1] "It was improper as related to the public business, and will give me additional labor."

October 27 the President's Message was read.

> "The love of peace," it began, "so much cherished in the bosoms of our citizens, which has so long guided the proceedings of their public councils and induced forbearance under so many wrongs, may not insure our continuance in the quiet pursuits of industry."

[1] Adams's Gallatin, p. 363.

An account of Monroe's negotiation and treaty followed this threatening preamble; and the warmest friends of Monroe and Pinkney could hardly find fault with the President's gentle comments on their conduct.

"After long and fruitless endeavors to effect the purposes of their mission, and to obtain arrangements within the limits of their instructions, they concluded to sign such as could be obtained, and to send them for consideration; candidly declaring to their other negotiators, at the same time, that they were acting against their instructions, and that their Government, therefore, could not be pledged for ratification."

The provisions of the proposed treaty proved to be, in certain points, "too highly disadvantageous," and the minister had been instructed to renew negotiation. The attack on the "Chesapeake" followed, aggravated by the defiant conduct of the British commanders at Norfolk. Lord Howick's Order in Council had swept away by seizures and condemnations the American trade in the Mediterranean. Spain, too, had issued a decree in conformity with Napoleon's decree of Berlin. Of France alone no complaint was made, and the President could even say that commerce and friendly intercourse had been maintained with her on their usual footing. He had not yet heard of the seizures made two months before, by Napoleon's order, in the ports of Holland.

In the face of these alarming events, it had been thought better to concentrate all defensive resources on New York, Charleston, and New Orleans; to purchase such military stores as were wanted in excess of the supply on hand; to call all the gunboats into service, and to warn the States to be ready with their quotas of militia. "Whether a regular army is to be raised, and to what extent, must depend on the information so shortly expected."

If this language had the meaning which in other times and countries would have been taken for granted, it implied a resort to measures of force against foreign aggressions; yet neither the President nor his party intended the use of force, except for self-defence in case of actual invasion. The Message was, in reality, silent in regard to peace and war. The time had not yet come for avowing a policy; but even had the crisis been actually at hand, Jefferson would not have assumed the responsibility of pointing out a policy to Congress. The influence he exerted could rarely be seen in his official and public language; it took shape in private, in the incessant talk that went on, without witnesses, at the White House.

More pointed than the allusion to England was the menace to Chief-Justice Marshall. The threat against the court, which the President made in the summer, reappeared in the Message as a distinct invitation to Congress.

"I shall think it my duty to lay before you the proceedings and the evidence publicly exhibited on the arraignment of the principal offenders before the Circuit

Court of Virginia. You will be enabled to judge whether the defect was in the testimony or in the law, or in the administration of the law; and wherever it shall be found, the Legislature alone can apply or originate the remedy. The framers of our Constitution certainly supposed they had guarded as well their government against destruction by treason, as their citizens against oppression under pretence of it; and if these ends are not attained, it is important to inquire by what means more effectual they may be secured."

This strong hint was quickly followed up. Burr's trial at Richmond had hardly closed when the President sent this Message to Congress; and within another month, November 23, another Message was sent, conveying a copy of the evidence and judicial opinions given at the trial, on which Congressional action might be taken.

So far as concerned foreign relations, no one could say with certainty whether the Annual Message leaned toward war or toward peace; but Gallatin's Report, which followed November 5, could be understood only as an argument to show that if war was to be made at all, it should be made at once. The Treasury had a balance of seven or eight millions in specie; the national credit was intact; taxes were not yet reduced; the Bank was still in active existence; various incidental resources were within reach; the first year of war would require neither increase of debt nor of taxation, and for subsequent years loans, founded on increased customs duties, would suffice. Calmly and easily Gallatin yielded to the impulse of the time, and dropping the objects for which — as he said — he had been brought into office, took up again the heavy load of taxation and debt which his life had been devoted to lightening. No one could have supposed, from his language in 1807, that within only ten years he and his party had regarded debt as fatal to freedom and virtue.

"An addition to the debt is doubtless an evil," he informed Congress; "but experience having now shown with what rapid progress the revenue of the Union increases in time of peace, with what facility the debt formerly contracted has in a few years been reduced, a hope may confidently be entertained that all the evils of the war will be temporary and easily repaired, and that the return of peace will, without any effort, afford ample resources for reimbursing whatever may have been borrowed during the war."

If Gallatin was so willing to abandon his dogma, the Federalists might at least be forgiven for asking why he had taken it up. For what practical object had he left the country helpless and defenceless for six years in order to pay off in driblets the capital of a petty debt which, within much less than a century, could be paid in full from the surplus of a single year? The success of his policy depended on the correctness of Jefferson's doctrine, that foreign nations could be coerced by peaceable means into respect for neutral rights; but Gallatin seemed to have already abandoned the theory of peaceable coercion before it had been tried.

The same conflict of ideas was felt in Congress, which had nothing to do but to wait for news from Europe that did not arrive. The month of November was passed in purposeless debate. That the time had come when some policy must be adopted for defending the coasts and frontiers was conceded, but no policy could be contrived which satisfied at once the economical and the military wants of the country. In this chaos of opinions, Jefferson alone held fixed theories; and as usual his opinions prevailed. He preferred gunboats to other forms of armament, and he had his way.

The Cabinet had not adopted the gunboat policy without protest. When in the preceding month of February the President sent to Congress his Message recommending that two hundred gunboats should be built, at a cost, as Gallatin thought, of a million dollars, the secretary remonstrated. In his opinion not one third that number were needed in peace, while in case of war any required number could be built within thirty days. "Exclusively of the first expense of building and the interest of the capital thus laid out, I apprehend that, notwithstanding the care which may be taken, they will infallibly decay in a given number of years, and will be a perpetual bill of costs for repairs and maintenance."[1] The President overruled these objections, affirming that the necessary gunboats could not be built even in six months; that after the beginning of a war they

[1] Gallatin's Writings, i. 330.

could not be built in the seaports, "because they would be destroyed by the enemy on the stocks;" and the first act of the enemy "would be to sweep all our seaports of their vessels at least;" finally, the expense of building and preserving them would be trifling.[1] Gallatin did not persist in the argument. Jefferson was determined to have gunboats, and gunboats were built.

The "Chesapeake" disaster riveted the gunboat policy on the government. Nearly every one, except the Federalists, agreed in Randolph's unwillingness to vote money for the support of a "degraded and disgraced navy."[2] Robert Smith made no apparent attempt to counteract this prejudice; he sacrificed the frigates for gunboats. October 22, 1807, at a full Cabinet meeting, according to Jefferson's memoranda, the following order was taken in regard to the frigates, in view of war with England:[3] —

"The 'Constitution' is to remain at Boston, having her men discharged; the 'Wasp' is to come to New York; the 'Chesapeake' to remain at Norfolk; and the sending the 'United States' frigate to New York is reserved for further consideration, inquiring in the mean time how early she could be ready to go. It is considered that in case of war these frigates would serve as receptacles for enlisting seamen, to fill the gunboats occasionally."

[1] Jefferson to Gallatin, Feb. 9, 1807; Works, v. **42.**

[2] Annals of Congress, 1807–1808, p. 823.

[3] Cabinet Memoranda, Oct. 22, 1807; Jefferson MSS.

A government which could imagine no other use for its frigates than as receiving ships for gunboats in time of war naturally cared to build none. When Congress took up the subject of naval defence, gunboats alone were suggested by the department. November 8 Robert Smith wrote to Dr. Mitchill, chairman of the Senate Committee on defences, a letter asking for eight hundred and fifty thousand dollars to build one hundred and eighty-eight more gunboats in order to raise the whole number to two hundred and fifty-seven.[1] A bill was at once introduced, passed the Senate without a division, and went to the House, where the Federalists sharply assailed it. Randolph ridiculed the idea of expelling by such means even so small a squadron as that which at Lynnhaven Bay had all summer defied the power of the United States. Josiah Quincy declared that except for rivers and shallow waters these gunboats were a danger rather than a defence; and that at all times and places they were uncomfortable, unpopular in the service, and dangerous to handle and to fight. Imprisonment for weeks, months, or years in a ship of the line was no small hardship, but service in a coop not wide enough to lie straight in, with the certainty of oversetting or running ashore or being sunk, in case of bad weather or hostile attack, was a duty intolerable to good seamen and fatal to the navy.

[1] Robert Smith to S. L. Mitchill, Nov. 8, 1807; Annals of Congress, 1807–1808, p. 32.

All this and much more was true. Fulton's steamer, the "Clermont," with a single gun would have been more effective for harbor defence than all the gunboats in the service, and if supplemented by Fulton's torpedoes would have protected New York from any line-of-battle ship; but President Jefferson, lover of science and of paradox as he was, suggested no such experiment. By the enormous majority of 111 to 19, the House, December 11, passed the bill for additional gunboats. A million dollars were voted for fortifications. In all, an appropriation of one million eight hundred and fifty thousand dollars for defences was the work accomplished by Congress between October 26 and December 18, 1807. In face of a probable war with England, such action was equivalent to inaction; and in this sense the public accepted it.

While Congress wrangled about systems of defence almost equally inefficient,— gunboats and frigates, militia and volunteers, muskets, movable batteries, and fixed fortifications,— the country listened with drawn breath for news from England. Time dragged on, but still the "Revenge" did not return. About the end of November, despatches[1] dated October 10 arrived from Monroe, announcing that Canning refused to couple the "Chesapeake" affair with the impressment of merchant seamen; that he was about to send a special envoy to Washington with the exclusive object of settling the "Chesapeake" affair; that

[1] Monroe to Madison, Oct. 10, 1807; State Papers, iii. 191.

Monroe had taken his final audience of King George, and that William Pinkney was henceforward sole minister of the United States in London. Of the treaty not a hope seemed to exist. Monroe's return was ominous of failure.

Erskine, uneasy at hearing these reports, hastened to the White House, and without delay reported Jefferson's conversation to his Government:[1]—

"I found from my interview with the President that he was much disappointed at the result of the discussions which had taken place, and, as he expressed himself, greatly alarmed by some of the passages in your letters that a satisfactory redress of the injuries complained of was not likely to be afforded to the United States. He informed me that the reasons which had induced him to instruct the American ministers to endeavor to obtain some arrangement upon the point of impressment of British seamen out of American ships, at the same time that a reparation for the attack on the 'Chesapeake' by his Majesty's ship 'Leopard' was demanded, were that he conceived that if a satisfactory security against the injuries arising to the United States from such impressments could have been obtained, a redress for the attack upon their national ship would have been much easier settled; but that if the point of honor was to be taken into consideration by itself, he foresaw greater difficulties in the way of an amicable adjustment of it. . . . The President further observed, however, that although he feared the separating the two subjects would increase the difficulty of the negotiation, and that he considered

[1] Erskine to Canning, Dec. 2, 1807; MSS. British Archives.

the determination of his Majesty's government to postpone the consideration of the point of impressment — which he said was the most serious ground of difference — as an unfavorable symptom of their ultimate intentions upon that subject, yet that he certainly would not refuse upon the ground of form only that the affair of the 'Chesapeake' should be first concluded; but expressed a hope that the minister who should be sent to this country to settle that subject of complaint should also be invested by his Majesty with powers to negotiate upon the point of impressment."

The sanguine temperament which challenged a duel accorded ill with the afterthought which shrank from it. Voluntarily, coolly, with mature reflection, Jefferson had invited Canning's blow; and when Canning struck, Jefferson recoiled. Monroe might well claim that such conditions as were imposed on him should never have been made, or should never have been withdrawn; that at moments of violent irritation no nation could afford to tease another with demands not meant to be enforced.

To increase the President's embarrassment, the Secretary of War Dearborn made a natural mistake. The original instructions to Monroe, decided in Cabinet meeting July 2,[1] did not connect the "Chesapeake" outrage with impressments of merchant seamen. Neither July 4 nor July 5, when full Cabinet meetings were held, did the subject come up.[2] The final instructions, dated July 6, changed the original

[1] See p. 31.

[2] Cabinet Memoranda; Jefferson MSS.

demand by extending the required redress over all cases of impressment; but meanwhile General Dearborn had left Washington for New York, and was not told of the change.[1] So it happened that when in October the Federalist newspapers began to attack Jefferson, on the authority of the English press, for coupling the subject of general impressment with the attack on the "Chesapeake," Dearborn, who chanced to be in Massachusetts, denied the charge; and on his authority the Republican newspapers asserted that the alleged instructions had not been given. This denial created no little confusion among Republicans, who could not understand why the instructions had been changed, or on what ground the Administration meant to defend them.

In truth, the change had been an afterthought, founded on the idea that as abandonment of impressments was a *sine qua non* in the commercial negotiation, and a point on which the Government meant inflexibly to insist, it should properly be made a *sine qua non* in this or any other agreement.[2] This decision had been made in July, with knowledge that England would rather fight than yield a point so vital to her supposed interests. In December, on hearing that Canning refused to yield, the President told Erskine that the *sine qua non*, so formally adopted, would be abandoned.

That conduct in appearance so vacillating should

[1] Dearborn to Jefferson, Oct. 18, 1807; Jefferson MSS.

[2] R. Smith to Jefferson, July 17, 1807; Jefferson MSS.

perplex Jefferson's friends and irritate his enemies was natural; but in reality nothing vacillating was in the President's mind. These negotiations were but outpost skirmishes, and covered his steady retreat to the fortress which he believed to be impregnable. He meant to coerce Canning, but his method of coercion needed neither armies nor negotiators. While telling Erskine that the *sine qua non* should not prevent a settlement of the "Chesapeake" affair, he set in motion the first of the series of measures which were intended to teach England to respect American rights.

December 14, against strong remonstrances from the merchants, the Non-importation Act of April 18, 1806, went into effect. The exact amount of British trade affected by that measure was not known. All articles of leather, silk, hemp, glass, silver, paper, woollen hosiery, ready-made clothing, millinery, malt liquors, pictures, prints, playing-cards, and so forth, if of English manufacture, were henceforward prohibited; and any person who had them in his possession incurred forfeiture and fine. The measure was in its nature coercive. The debates in Congress showed that no other object than that of coercion was in the mind of the American government; the history of the Republican party and the consistent language of Jefferson, Madison, and the Virginian school proclaimed that the policy of prohibition was their substitute for war. England was to be punished, by an annual fine of several million dollars, for interference with American trade to the continent of Europe.

Two days after this law went into effect Madison received from the British government a document which threw the Non-importation Act into the background, and made necessary some measure more energetic. The King's proclamation of October 17, requiring all British naval officers to exercise the right of impressment to its full extent over neutral merchant-vessels, was printed in the "National Intelligencer" of December 17; and if Sir William Scott's decision in the case of the "Essex" required the Non-importation Act as its counterpoise, the Impressment Proclamation could be fairly balanced only by a total cessation of relations.

In rapid succession the ships which had sailed a month before from Europe arrived in American harbors, after unusually quick voyages. Monroe, in the "Augustus," reached Norfolk December 13; the "Edward" arrived at Boston December 12; the "Brutus" got in at New York December 14, preceded December 12 by the "Revenge." All these ships brought news to the same effect. Armstrong's despatches by the "Revenge" announced Napoleon's enforcement of the Berlin Decree. London newspapers of November 12 agreed in predicting some immediate and sweeping attack by the British government upon American commerce; and from Pinkney and Monroe came the official papers which put an end to all hope of a commercial treaty with England.

Private letters bore out the worst public rumors. Among other persons who were best informed as to the intentions of the British government was Senator Pickering of Massachusetts, whose nephew Samuel Williams had been removed by Jefferson from the London consulate, and remained in that city as an American merchant, in connection with his brother Timothy Williams of Boston. December 12 Timothy Williams in Boston wrote to his uncle Senator Pickering at Washington,[1] —

"My brother writes me on the 9th of November 'that he was informed the Government would in a few days declare Cuba, Martinique, and Guadeloupe in a state of blockade, and restrict still more the trade of neutrals with the Continent.' The British no doubt had or would issue an Order above referred to, to counteract our friend Bonaparte's decree of Nov. 21, 1806. I cannot however think the intercourse with the Continent will be entirely cut off. The influence of the West Indian planters will procure the blockading of the enemy's islands, no doubt. What has not this country lost by the miserable policy of the Administration! Your prudence will know to whom you can or cannot communicate any of the above paragraphs."

"With much solicitude respecting the present state of things," Timothy Williams concluded this letter of warning; and his anxiety was shared by every one who read the newspapers which proclaimed the danger of war. At Washington the alarming news arrived December 17, at the heels of the Impressment

[1] T. Williams to T. Pickering, Dec. 12, 1807; Pickering MSS.

Proclamation. The President instantly called his Cabinet together. Under less serious circumstances in 1794, Congress had imposed an embargo for thirty days, forbidding clearances to all foreign-bound vessels while the question of war or peace was deciding. By common consent an embargo was the proper measure to be taken in the face of an expected attack on commerce. On reading the news from France and England, every one assumed that an embargo would be imposed until the exact nature of the French and British aggressions should be learned; but safe precedent required that the law should restrict its own operation within some reasonable limit of time. An embargo for thirty or sixty days, or even for three months, might be required before reaching some decision as to peace or war.

On a loose sheet of letter-paper, which happened to bear the address of General Mason, the President wrote a hasty draft of an embargo message to Congress.[1] After referring to Armstrong's despatch announcing the Emperor's decision to enforce the Berlin Decree, Jefferson's draft noticed the threatened orders of England: —

"The British regulations had before reduced us to a direct voyage to a single port of their enemies, and it is now believed they will interdict all commerce whatever with them. A proclamation, too, of that Government (not officially, indeed, communicated to us, yet so given

[1] Jefferson to Gen. J. Mason; Works, v. 217. Cf. Jefferson to Madison, July 14, 1824; Works, vii. 373.

out to the public as to become a rule of action with them) seems to have shut the door on all negotiation with us, except as to the single aggression on the 'Chesapeake.' The sum of these mutual enterprises on our national rights is that France and her allies, reserving for future consideration the prohibiting our carrying anything to the British territories, have virtually done it by restraining our bringing a return cargo from them; and Great Britain, after prohibiting a great proportion of our commerce with France and her allies, is now believed to have prohibited the whole. The whole world is thus laid under interdict by these two nations, and our vessels, their cargoes, and crews are to be taken by the one or the other for whatever place they may be destined out of our own limits. If, therefore, on leaving our harbors we are certainly to lose them, is it not better, as to vessels, cargoes, and seamen, to keep them at home? This is submitted to the wisdom of Congress, who alone are competent to provide a remedy."

Unfortunately, no official document could be produced in proof of the expected British interdict, and mere newspaper paragraphs could not be used for the purpose. To avoid this difficulty Madison wrote, in pencil, another draft which omitted all direct mention of the expected British order. He proposed to send Congress the official letter in which the Grand Judge Regnier announced that the Berlin Decree would be enforced, and with this letter a copy of the British Impressment Proclamation as printed in the "National Intelligencer." On these two documents he founded his draft of a Message: —

"The communications now made showing the great and increasing danger with which our merchandise, our vessels, and our seamen are threatened on the high seas and elsewhere by the belligerent Powers of Europe, and it being of the greatest importance to keep in safety these essential resources, I deem it my duty to recommend the subject to the consideration of Congress, who will doubtless perceive all the advantages which may be expected from an immediate inhibition of the departure of our vessels from the ports of the United States."[1]

The Cabinet, every member being present, unanimously concurred in the recommendation to Congress;[2] but at least one member would have preferred that the embargo should be limited in time. The Cabinet meeting was held in the afternoon or evening of December 17, and early the next morning Gallatin wrote to the President suggesting a slight change in the proposed measure, and adding a serious warning which Jefferson would have done well to regard: —

"I also think," said Gallatin,[3] "that an embargo for a limited time will at this moment be preferable in itself and less objectionable in Congress. In every point of view — privations, sufferings, revenue, effect on the enemy, politics at home, etc. — I prefer war to a permanent embargo. Governmental prohibitions do always more

[1] Draft of Embargo Message, Jefferson MSS. Cf. Jefferson to Madison, July 14, 1824; Works, vii. 373.

[2] Jefferson to John G. Jackson, Oct. 13, 1808; Jefferson MSS.

[3] Gallatin to Jefferson, Dec. 18, 1807; Gallatin's Writings, i. 368.

mischief than had been calculated; and it is not without much hesitation that a statesman should hazard to regulate the concerns of individuals, as if he could do it better than themselves. The measure being of a doubtful policy, and hastily adopted on the first view of our foreign intelligence, I think that we had better recommend it with modifications, and at first for such a limited time as will afford us all time for reconsideration, and if we think proper, for an alteration in our course without appearing to retract. As to the hope that it may have an effect on the negotiation with Mr. Rose, or induce England to treat us better, I think it entirely groundless."

To this remarkable letter the President immediately replied by summoning the Cabinet together at ten o'clock in the morning.[1] No record of the consultation was preserved; but when the Senate met at noon the Message was read by the Vice-president as it had been shaped by Madison. The suggestion of Gallatin as to a limit of time had not been adopted.

The Senate instantly referred the Message to a committee of five, with General Smith and J. Q. Adams at its head: —

"We immediately went into the committee-room," recorded Senator Adams in his Diary,[2] "and after some discussion, in which I suggested very strong doubts as to the propriety of the measure upon the papers sent with the President's Message, I finally acquiesced in it as a compliance with the special call for it in the Message.

[1] Jefferson to Gallatin, Dec. 18, 1807; Gallatin's Writings, i. 369.

[2] Diary of J. Q. Adams, Dec. 18, 1807, i. 491.

I inquired whether there were other reasons for it besides the diplomatic papers sent with the Message, as *they* appeared to me utterly inadequate to warrant such a measure. Smith, the chairman, said that the President wanted it to aid him in the negotiation with England upon which Mr. Rose is coming out, and that perhaps it might enable us to get rid of the Non-importation Act. I yielded. But I believe there are yet other reasons, which Smith did not tell. There was no other opposition in committee."

Senator Adams was right in believing that other reasons existed; but although the "National Intelligencer" of the same morning had published the warnings of British newspapers, — doubtless in order to affect the action of Congress, — no one of the Republican senators seemed to rely on the expected British order as the cause of the embargo. In foreign affairs Jefferson maintained the reserve of a European monarch. He alone knew what had been done or was doing, and on him rested the whole responsibility of action. The deference paid by the Senate to the Executive in matters of foreign policy seemed patriotic, but it proved fatal to one senator at least, whose colleague had grievances to revenge. When the committee, after a short deliberation, reported an Embargo Bill, and some of the senators appealed for delay, Adams, who was chafing under the delays which had already lowered the self-respect of Government and people, broke into a strenuous appeal for energy. "The President has recommended the measure on his high responsibility. I would not consider, I would not deliberate; I would act!" The words were spoken in secret session, but Senator Pickering noted them for future use.[1] Among the antipathies and humors of New-England politics none was more characteristic than this personal antagonism, beginning a new conspiracy which was to shake the Union to its foundations.

The Senate agreed with the committee that if an embargo was to be laid it should be laid promptly; and the bill, probably drawn by the President, passed through its three stages on the same day, by a vote of twenty-two to six. At the second reading it was strongly opposed by Hillhouse, Pickering, and Sumter of South Carolina; while William H. Crawford, the new senator from Georgia, asked only time for consideration.[2] Within four or five hours after hearing the Message read, the Senate sent its Embargo Act to the House.

Meanwhile the House also had received the President's Message, and had, like the Senate, gone at once into secret session. No sooner was the Message read than John Randolph and Jacob Crowninshield sprang at the same moment to their feet. The Speaker recognized Randolph, who instantly offered a Resolution, "that an embargo be laid on all shipping, the property of citizens of the United States, now in port,

[1] Pickering's Letter to Governor Sullivan, April 22, 1808. Cf. New-England Federalism, p. 174, *n.*

[2] Diary of J. Q. Adams, i. 491, 492.

or which shall hereafter arrive." After some time passed in discussion, on receiving the Senate bill the House laid Randolph's Resolution aside, and in secret session began a long and warm debate, which continued all day, and was not concluded on Saturday, December 19, when the House adjourned over Sunday.

The loss of this debate was unfortunate; for no private citizen ever knew the reasons which Congress considered sufficient to warrant a strain of the Constitution so violent as a permanent embargo implied. The debate was certainly dramatic: it was not only the first great political crisis witnessed in the new scenery of the Representatives' Chamber, but it also brought John Randolph forward in an attitude which astonished even those who had witnessed the Virginian's growing eccentricity. On Friday Randolph "scrambled" with Crowninshield for the floor, eager to force on the House a policy of embargo which he had again and again recommended as the only proper measure of national defence. On Saturday he rose again, but only to denounce his own measure as one that crouched to the insolent mandates of Napoleon, and led to immediate war with England.[1] The cry of French influence, raised by him and by the Federalist members, began on that day, and echoed in louder and louder tones for years.

On Monday, December 21, the debate closed, and the House consumed the day in voting. Amendment

[1] Adams's Randolph, p. 227.

after amendment was rejected. Most significant of all these votes was the list of yeas and nays on the question of limiting the embargo to the term of two months. Forty-six members voted in the affirmative; eighty-two in the negative. The New England and Pennsylvania Democrats obeyed the wishes of Jefferson, and riveted a permanent embargo on the people, without public discussion of the principle or explanation of the effect which was expected from a measure more trying than war itself to patriotism. The bill then passed by a vote of eighty-two to forty-four.

So small a part was played in this debate by the expected Order in Council that members afterward disputed whether the subject was mentioned at all. Probably the Administration preferred silence in public, either for fear of prejudicing the expected negotiation with Rose, or of weakening the effect of arguments which without the order were sufficiently strong; but in private no such reticence was shown. The British minister on Monday, before the bill had become law, notified Canning not only that an embargo was about to be laid, but of the cause which produced the measure:[1] —

"It has been confidentially communicated to me that an embargo on all the shipping in the United States has been proposed in Congress, and although it is strongly resisted, it is expected that it will be carried, on the ground of expecting that a proclamation by his Majesty

[1] Erskine to Canning, Dec. 21, 1807; MSS. British Archives.

will be issued declaring France and her dependencies in a state of blockade. I hasten to send you this letter for fear of the effect of an embargo."

The person from whom Erskine received this confidential communication was probably the Secretary of State; for two days afterward, when the British minister wrote to say that the embargo had been laid, he added:[1] —

"I propose to send off his Majesty's packet-boat with this intelligence immediately, and avail myself of this opportunity by a private ship to inform you that the embargo is not intended, as this Government declares, as a measure of hostility against Great Britain, but only as a precaution against the risk of the capture of their ships in consequence of the decree of Bonaparte of Nov. 21, 1806, which they have just learned is to be rigorously enforced; and also from an apprehension of a retaliatory order by Great Britain."

Thus the embargo was imposed; and of all President Jefferson's feats of political management, this was probably the most dexterous. On his mere recommendation, without warning, discussion, or publicity, and in silence as to his true reasons and motives, he succeeded in fixing upon the country, beyond recall, the experiment of peaceable coercion. His triumph was almost a marvel; but no one could fail to see its risks. A free people required to know in advance the motives which actuated government, and the intended consequences of important laws. Large

[1] Erskine to Canning, Dec. 23, 1807; MSS. British Archives.

masses of intelligent men were slow to forgive what they might call deception. If Jefferson's permanent embargo should fail to coerce Europe, what would the people of America think of the process by which it had been fastened upon them? What would be said and believed of the President who had challenged so vast a responsibility?

CHAPTER VIII.

DECEMBER 22 Jefferson signed the Embargo Act; four days afterward George Rose arrived at Norfolk. The avowed object of his mission was to offer satisfaction for the attack upon the "Chesapeake;" the true object could be seen only in the instructions with which he was furnished by Canning.[1]

These instructions, never yet published, began by directing that in case any attempt should be made to apply the President's proclamation of July 2 to Rose's frigate, the "Statira," he should make a formal protest, and if the answer of the American government should be unsatisfactory, or unreasonably delayed, he should forthwith return to England. Should no such difficulty occur, he was on arriving at Washington to request an audience of the President and Secretary of State, and to announce himself furnished with full powers to enter into negotiation on the "Chesapeake" affair, but forbidden to entertain any proposition on any other point.

"With respect to that object, you will express your conviction that the instructions under which you act

[1] Instructions to G. H. Rose, Oct. 24, 1807; MSS. British Archives.

would enable you to terminate your negotiation amicably and satisfactorily. But you will state that you are distinctly instructed, previously to entering into any negotiation, to require the recall of the proclamation of the President of the United States, and the discontinuance of the measures which have been adopted under it."

After explaining that the disavowal and recall of Admiral Berkeley had taken away the excuse for interdicting free communication with British ships, and that thenceforward the interdict became an aggression, Canning directed that if the request be refused, Rose should declare his mission at an end; but supposing the demand to be satisfied, he was to disavow at once the forcible attack on the "Chesapeake."

"You will state further that Admiral Berkeley has been recalled from his command for having acted in an affair of such importance without authority. You will add that his Majesty is prepared to discharge those men who were taken by this unauthorized act out of the American frigate; reserving to himself the right of reclaiming such of them as shall prove to have been deserters from his Majesty's service, or natural-born subjects of his Majesty; and further, that in order to repair as far as possible the consequences of an act which his Majesty disavows, his Majesty is ready to secure to the widows and orphans (if such there be) of such of the men who were unfortunately killed on board the 'Chesapeake' as shall be proved not to have been British subjects, a provision adequate to their respective situation and condition in life."

This disavowal, and the removal of Berkeley from command, were to be the limit of concession. The circumstances of provocation under which Berkeley had acted, greatly extenuated his procedure; "and his Majesty therefore commands me to instruct you peremptorily to reject any further mark of his Majesty's displeasure toward Admiral Berkeley."

The remainder of Canning's instructions admits of no abridgment: —

"You will next proceed to state that after this voluntary offer of reparation on his Majesty's part, his Majesty expects that the Government of the United States will be equally ready to remove those causes of just complaint which have led to this unfortunate transaction.

"His Majesty requires this, not only as a due return for the reparation which he has thus voluntarily tendered, but as indispensable to any well-founded expectation of the restoration and continuance of that harmony and good understanding between the two governments which it is equally the interest of both to cultivate and improve.

"However much his Majesty may regret the summary mode of redress which has been resorted to in the present instance, it cannot be supposed that his Majesty is prepared to acquiesce in an injury so grievous to his Majesty as the encouragement of desertion from his naval service.

"The extent to which this practice has been carried is too notorious to require illustration; but the instance of the 'Chesapeake' itself is sufficient to justify the demand of adequate satisfaction.

"The protestation of Commodore Barron is contradicted in the face of the world by the conviction and confession of one of those unhappy men who had been seduced from his allegiance to his Majesty, and to whom Commodore Barron had promised his protection.

"His Majesty, however, does not require any proceeding of severity against Commodore Barron; but he requires a formal disavowal of that officer's conduct in encouraging deserters from his Majesty's service, in retaining them on board his ship, and in denying the fact of their being there; and he requires that this disavowal shall be such as plainly to show that the American government did not countenance such proceedings, and to deter any officer in their service from similar misconduct in future.

"He requires a disavowal of other flagrant proceedings, — detailed in papers which have been communicated to you, — unauthorized, his Majesty has no doubt, but with respect to which it ought to be known to the world that the American government did not authorize and does not approve them.

"You will state that such disavowals, solemnly expressed, would afford to his Majesty a satisfactory pledge on the part of the American government that the recurrence of similar causes will not on any occasion impose on his Majesty the necessity of authorizing those means of force to which Admiral Berkeley has resorted without authority, but which the continued repetition of such provocations as unfortunately led to the attack upon the 'Chesapeake' might render necessary, as a just reprisal on the part of his Majesty.

"And you will observe, therefore, that if the American government is animated by an equally sincere desire with that which his Majesty entertains to preserve the relations of peace between the two countries from being violated by the repetition of such transactions, they can have no difficulty in consenting to make these disavowals.

"This consent is to be the express and indispensable condition of your agreeing to reduce into an authentic and official form the particulars of the reparation which you are instructed to offer."

Rose came, not to conciliate, but to terrify. His apology was a menace. So little was the President prepared for such severity, that from the moment of his consent to treat the "Chesapeake" affair by itself he rather regarded the mission and reparation as a formality. So completely had Monroe been beguiled by Canning's courteous manners, that no suspicion of the truth crossed his mind or crept into his despatches. No prominent American, except Giles, ventured to hint that this mission of peace and friendship was intended only to repeat the assertion of supremacy which had led to the original offence.

George Henry Rose was chiefly remembered as the father of Lord Strathnairn; but his merits were quite different from those of his son. Without the roughness which sometimes marked English character, Rose's manners betrayed a dignified and slightly patronizing courteousness, — a certain civil condescension, — impressive to Americans of that day, who rarely felt at ease in the presence of an Englishman, or were quite certain that an American gentleman knew the habits of European society. Benevolent superiority and quiet assumption, so studied as to be natural and simple, were the social weapons with which George Rose was to impose an unparalleled indignity on a government which, in professing contempt for forms, invited discourtesies. No man could have been chosen with qualities better suited for enforcing Canning's will on the yielding moods of Jefferson.

Rose's first act after arriving in Hampton Roads was to notify the President that he could not land until assured that the proclamation of July 2 would not be enforced against his ship. Canning had been already officially informed that the proclamation expressly excepted vessels on a service like that of the "Statira," as he might have seen for himself by a moment's inquiry; but his instructions were written to suit the temper of Tory constituents. Rose was obliged to wait from December 26 until January 9 before leaving his ship, while messengers carried explanations and notes between Norfolk and Washington.

Monroe, who sailed from England a day later than Rose, reached Washington December 22. Rose arrived only January 14. January 16 he was received by the President, and made no complaint of the mode of reception. In the four years that had passed since Merry's arrival, Jefferson had learned to be less strict in Republican etiquette; but although Rose suffered no indignity at the White House, he found much to disapprove in the government. January 17, in a despatch to Canning, he mentioned that Congress contained one tailor, one weaver, six or seven tavern-keepers, four notorious swindlers, one butcher, one grazier, one curer of hams, and several schoolmasters and Baptist preachers.[1]

The most aristocratic American of the twentieth century will probably agree with the most extreme socialist in admitting that Congress, in 1808, might with advantage have doubled its proportion of tailors, butchers, and swindlers, if by doing so it could have lessened the number of its conspirators. To the latter class belonged Senator Pickering, whose power for mischief and whose appetite for intrigue combined to make him a valuable ally for Rose. Within forty-eight hours after Rose's arrival, the senator from Massachusetts had fallen under the fascination of the British envoy's manners and conversation. January 18 he wrote to his nephew Timothy Williams,[2]—

"I now take up my pen merely to mention an unexpected interview with Mr. Rose. I met him last Saturday [January 16] at Georgetown, at the table of Mr. Peter, whose lovely wife is a granddaughter of Mrs. Washington. Mr. Rose's face is indicative of a placid temper, and his conversation confirms it. He possesses good sense and a disposition perfectly conciliatory. Such also is the disposition of the minister, Canning, by whom he was selected for this mission. Canning was his school-fellow and intimate friend. It seemed to me a sort of friendly compulsion that sent him hither. It was

[1] Rose to Canning, Jan. 17, 1808; MSS. British Archives.

[2] Pickering to T. Williams, Jan. 18, 1808; Pickering MSS.

a sacrifice for a domestic man who left a wife and seven children behind him, and from whom he had never before been separated. Thus much I gathered from his conversation with me, which was marked with ease and candor; indeed with singular openness, as if I had been an old acquaintance. He expressed his surprise that the real state of the negotiation with Mr. Monroe had not become officially known to the people by an open communication to Congress. No minister of Great Britain, he observed, would have used such concealment as existed here. He manifested a solicitude even to anxiety for a pacific adjustment of all our differences. What our Government will demand as a reparation for the attack on the 'Chesapeake' I do not know, nor what Mr. Rose is authorized to concede; but I run no hazard in saying that nothing in reality will be denied, and that if after all a war with England should ensue, the fault will be our own."

In giving this account of Rose's singular openness and candor, Senator Pickering did not repeat his own remarks in the conversation; but they could be inferred from the rest of his letter.

"I wrote last week to Mr. Cabot that I had the best authority for saying that our Government had abandoned the ground taken in London, — to treat of the 'Chesapeake' affair only in connection with the old subjects of dispute. They have now determined to negotiate on this separately, and even say that it is an affair by itself and ought to be so treated. Perhaps they may demand that Admiral Berkeley be brought to a British court-martial, — that at any rate he be removed from command; and that the three rascals of deserters who remain unhung should be restored.

"*Confidence* now seems to be in Mr. Jefferson's hands as effectual in producing a compliance with his recommendations as soldiers in the hands of Bonaparte in procuring submission to his commands. With the like implicit, blind confidence which enacted the Embargo, the legislatures of Virginia and Maryland have approved it. To this day if you ask any member of Congress the cause and the object of the Embargo, he can give no answer which common-sense does not spurn at. I have reason to believe that Mr. Jefferson expected to get some credit for it by having it ready just in time to meet the retaliating order of England for Napoleon's decree of Nov. 21, 1806. With much solicitude he, two or three weeks ago, expressed his wonder that it did not arrive, apparently desiring it as a material justification with the people for the Embargo. He will doubtless be utterly disappointed."

That Jefferson in recommending the Embargo had the Orders in Council in his mind was therefore known to Pickering,[1] and was the general talk of Federalists in Washington during the month which followed the Embargo Act; but the orders themselves reached America only the day after this letter was written, and were published in the "National Intelligencer" of January 22. In full view of the official command that American trade with Europe should pass through British ports and pay duty to the Brit-

[1] Cf. Letters addressed to the People of the United States, by Col. Timothy Pickering. London (reprinted), 1811. Letter xiii. p. 96. Review of Cunningham Correspondence, by Timothy Pickering (Salem, 1824), pp. 56–58.

ish Treasury, doubt as to the wisdom of an Embargo seemed at an end. No further dispute appeared possible except on the question whether or when the Embargo should be raised in order to declare war. Already, January 11, Senator Adams offered a Resolution for appointing a committee to consider and report when the Embargo could be taken off and vessels permitted to arm; but the Senate silently rejected the Resolution, January 21, by a vote of seventeen to ten.[1] Neither decision nor debate on so serious a point could be profitably undertaken before the result of Rose's diplomacy should be revealed.

Saturday, January 16, before meeting Senator Pickering at dinner, Rose had delicately explained to Madison that the President's "Chesapeake" proclamation was likely to prove a stumbling-block. In conversations which consumed another week he urged its withdrawal, while Madison replied that the exclusion of British ships was not a punishment but a precaution, that the "Leopard's" attack was but one of its causes, and that it was a measure taken in the interests of peace. Argument against Canning's positive instructions answered no purpose. Rose could not give way, and when he had been one week in Washington, January 21, the negotiation was already at a stand-still. There it would under any other Administration have been permitted to remain. Rose had come to offer an apology and to restore the captured seamen. He had only to do this and go home.

[1] Diary of J. Q. Adams, i. 504.

Rose, after an interview with the Secretary of State about January 21, waited until January 27 before writing to Canning. Then he resumed his story:[1] —

"Within a few hours after my last conference with Mr. Madison, an indirect and confidential communication was made to me from one of the members of the Government to the following purport: that the real difficulty as to the recall of the proclamation was that of finding grounds upon which the President could found his declared motives for such a measure without exposing himself to the charge of inconsistency and disregard of the national honor, and without compromising his own personal weight in the State; that it was earnestly wished that I could make, as it were, a bridge over which he might pass; and that I would develop just so much of the tenor of my instructions as to the conditions of reparation as might justify him in the course which I required should be taken; that should however this be impossible, and should the negotiation fail, the United States would not commence war with Great Britain, but would continue their Embargo, and adopting a sort of Chinese policy would shut themselves up from the rest of the world; that if we attacked them they would sally out just far enough to repel us, and would invade Canada. . . . Communications of a similar nature were repeated to me on subsequent days; and it did not seem advisable to address Mr. Madison in writing until the utmost point to which they would go was ascertained. At length I had a conversation with the gentleman in question. He avowed to me that what had passed was with the knowl-

[1] Rose to Canning, Jan. 27, 1808; MSS. British Archives.

edge of the President, whose difficulty arose from the sacrifice of public opinion which he apprehended must follow from the abandonment of the proclamation. He said I must be aware how dear to Mr. Jefferson his popularity must be, and especially at the close of his political career, and that this consideration must be held particularly in view by him; and he pressed me earnestly to take such steps as would conciliate the President's wish to give his Majesty satisfaction on the point in question and yet to maintain the possession of what was pre-eminently valuable to him. He expressed his own personal anxiety for the accommodation of the present difference, — an anxiety heightened by his knowledge that the United States had forever lost all hope of obtaining the Floridas, the negotiation for them having totally failed, and by his intimate persuasion that France is the dormant owner of them. He said, moreover, that since America could not obtain those provinces, he sincerely wished to see them in the hands of Great Britain, whose possession of them could never be anxious to the United States."

The supplications of this Cabinet minister were reinforced by entreaties from leading Federalists, who begged Rose not to follow a course which would aid the President in rousing popular feeling against England; but the British envoy could yield only so far as not to break the negotiation abruptly. January 26 he wrote to the Secretary a note, in courteous language announcing himself authorized to express the conviction — which he certainly could not have felt — that if the proclamation were withdrawn, he should be able "to terminate the negotiation amicably and satisfactorily." Madison sent no answer to the note, but kept the negotiation alive by private interviews. January 29 Rose suggested the idea of his friendly return to England with a representation of the difficulty. Madison reported this suggestion to the President, who on the following Monday, February 1, decided against the idea, preferring to yield the point of dignity so far as to offer a recall of the proclamation, conditional upon an informal disclosure by Rose of the terms in which the atonement would be made.[1]

Throughout this tortuous affair Rose stood impassive. He made no advance, offered no suggestion of aid, showed no anxiety. Republicans and Federalists crowded about him with entreaties and advice. Rose listened in silence. Amateur diplomacy never showed its evils more plainly than in the negotiation with Rose; and when Madison allowed the President to take the affair into his own hands, employing another Cabinet officer to do what no Secretary of State could permit himself to undertake, the nuisance became a scandal. In the despatch of January 27 Rose concealed the name of the deputy Secretary of State; but in a despatch of February 6 he revealed it: —

"I should here add that a member of the Cabinet (the Secretary of the Navy), who informed me that all his communications with me were with the President's knowl-

[1] Negotiations with Mr. Rose; Madison's Works, ii. 411.

edge, assures me that a rupture with France is inevitable and at hand."

That Robert Smith acted in the matter as negotiator for the President was afterward made known by Jefferson himself.[1]

Jefferson clung with touching pathos to the love and respect of his fellow-citizens, who repaid his devotion with equal attachment; but many an American President who yearned no less passionately for the people's regard would have died an outcast rather than have trafficked in their dignity and his own self-respect in order to seek or save a personal popularity. Perhaps Jefferson never knew precisely what was said of him by his Secretary of the Navy, — a passing remark by such a man as Robert Smith, repeated through such a medium as George Rose, need count for little; but the truth must be admitted that in 1808 — for the first and probably for the last time in history — a President of the United States begged for mercy from a British minister.

In obedience to the President's decision, Madison yielded to the British demand on condition that the Executive should not be exposed to the appearance of having yielded.[2] He arranged with Rose the "bridge" which Robert Smith had previously prepared for the President to cross. In a "secret and

[1] Jefferson to W. Wirt, May 2, 1811; Works, v. 593.

[2] Negotiations with Mr. Rose, Feb. 4, 1808; Madison's Works, ii. 12.

confidential" despatch dated Feb. 6, 1808, Rose explained to Canning, with evident uneasiness, the nature of the new proposal:[1] —

"The proposition made to me by Mr. Madison at the close of our conference of yesterday was that he should put into my hands a proclamation recalling the original proclamation, sealed and signed by the President, bearing date on the day of adjustment of differences, and conceived in such terms as I should agree to; that on this being done we should proceed to sign the instruments adjusting the reparation. I answered that positive as my instructions were to the effect I had invariably stated to him, such was the knowledge I had of the disposition of his Majesty's government to act with the utmost conciliation toward this country that I would attempt the experiment, but premising distinctly that it must be made unofficially through the whole of it, and with the assurance of our mutual good faith to that effect; and that as it must be completely and essentially informal, — for the purpose of getting over difficulties which appeared insuperable in any other way, — it must be distinctly understood that if the attempt failed, the regular and official communication must be resumed on my explanatory note of January 26, and on that alone."

In the defence which Rose offered for thus disregarding his instructions, the cause of his embarrassment was plain. Duty required him to act as though England had hitherto endured with magnanimity the

[1] Rose to Canning, Feb. 6, 1808; MSS. British Archives. Cf. Madison's Writings, ii. 413.

wrongs inflicted by America, but might find herself obliged soon to resent them This attitude could have been maintained against ordinary forms of diplomacy, but Rose found himself stifled in the embraces of men whose hatred was necessary to warrant his instructions. He would gladly have assumed that Madison's concessions and Robert Smith's cajoleries were treacherous; but his Federalist friends, whose interests were actively English, assured him that if America could avoid a war with England, she would inevitably drift into a war with France. The temptation to show equal courtesy to that which was shown to him, the instinctive shrinking from a harsh act, the impossibility of obeying instructions without putting himself in the wrong, and finally perhaps an incapacity to understand the full humiliation implied in his unrevealed demands, — led him to give way, and to let Madison partially into the secret of Canning's instructions.

On the evening of February 5 Rose and Erskine went to the house of the Secretary, and a draft of the proposed proclamation was there offered to them and accepted. The next day, at the Department, Rose delicately began to reveal the further disavowals he was instructed to demand. Even then he seemed ashamed to betray the whole, but delayed and discussed, knowing that he had done too much or too little for the objects of his mission. Not until after repeated interviews did he at last, February 14, mention "with an apology for omitting it before, when he intended to do it," that a disavowal of Commodore Barron would be required.[1]

So cautious was Madison on his side that he offered to make a part of the required disavowals, provided these should be mutual. Rose declined this offer, but proposed nothing more, and seemed rather to invite a friendly failure of agreement. He ended the conversation of February 14 by addressing to Madison the usual words of rupture: "I will not dissemble that I leave you with the most painful impressions."[2] February 16 Madison closed these informal interviews with the dry remark that the United States could not be expected to "make as it were an expiatory sacrifice to obtain redress, or beg for reparation."[3]

The delay had strengthened Rose by weakening the President. The embargo was beginning to work. That the people should long submit to it was impossible, reported Rose; even North Carolina was turning against it. Monroe's influence made itself felt.

"I learn this day," wrote the British envoy February 17, "that Mr. Monroe has been indefatigable in representing through Virginia the contrasted systems of Great Britain and France in their true lights, the certain destruction which must result to America from the prevalence of the latter, and the necessity of uniting for existence with the former. He has undoubtedly acquired

[1] Madison's Writings, ii. 416.

[2] Rose to Canning, Feb. 16, 1808; MSS. British Archives.

[3] Rose to Canning, Feb. 17, 1808; MSS. British Archives.

a very strong party in that State, — it is now said a decided majority in its legislature, and one entirely brought over to the views above enounced."

February 22, only a few days after the rupture of negotiation, the Milan Decree arrived, and was published in the "National Intelligencer." This violent act of Napoleon did much to divert popular indignation from England. Under the influence of this good fortune, Rose so little feared war as a consequence of his failure that he speculated rather as to the policy of accepting the United States as an ally:

"It would certainly be highly desirable," he wrote,[1] "that a rupture between France and America should take place; but the latter under its present Constitution and Administration could take but a very feeble part in the warfare, and I know not if it is to be wished that it should be roused to greater exertions, which must lead to a more efficient form of government, a knowledge of its strength, and the development of extensive views of ambition."

Nothing remained but to revert to Rose's note of January 26, and to close the affair by a formal correspondence. No further attempt was made to conciliate the British envoy, or to obtain concessions from him; but February 24 he was told by Madison of two steps to be taken by the Government which bore on his negotiation. The President would recommend to Congress an increase of the army to ten thousand men, and a levy of twenty-four thousand

[1] Rose to Canning, Feb. 27, 1808; MSS. British Archives.

volunteers. Madison added that these were to be considered as "measures of preparation, but not as leading to war, or as directed against any particular nation." The Secretary added that an order had been issued to discharge all British subjects from national ships, — "an act of complaisance in its effects which he observed Great Britain could lay no claim to; which was done gratuitously, but from views of policy and fitness entertained by this Government."

March 5 Madison at last sent his reply to Rose's note of January 26. After repeating the reasons which forbade a withdrawal of the President's proclamation, the Secretary closed by informing Rose that the President "has authorized me, in the event of your disclosing the terms of reparation which you believe will be satisfactory, and on its appearing that they are so, . . . to proceed to concert with you a revocation of that act."[1] Rose waited till March 17, as though hoping for some further overture, but finally replied, "It is with the most painful sensations of regret that I find myself . . . under the necessity of declining to enter into the terms of negotiation which by direction of the President you therein offer."[2]

Rose's professions of regret were doubtless sincere. Apart from the wish felt by every young diplomatist to avoid the appearance of failure, Rose could not but

[1] Madison to Rose, March 5, 1808; State Papers, iii. 214.

[2] Rose to Madison, March 17, 1808; State Papers, iii. 217.

see that his Government must wish to be relieved of the three American seamen imprisoned at Halifax, whose detention, admitted to be an act of violence, must become a festering sore in the relations of the two countries. That the American government meant to profit by it was evident. By leaving the "Chesapeake" affair unsettled, Rose played into the hands of a national party. For the first time since 1794 language began to be used to a British minister in the United States which he could not hear without loss of dignity or sense of discredit. The word "war" was semi-officially pronounced.

When on Monday, March 21, Rose made his parting visits, he found the President silent; the Secretary of State studiously avoided all political topics, while if Rose's report was accurate, Gallatin and Robert Smith talked with intentional freedom.

"Mr. Gallatin, the Secretary of the Treasury, has little influence in the Government, though by far the ablest and best informed member of it; and he probably does not interfere materially beyond the limits of his own department; but his utility in that department, in which no adequate successor to him is contemplated, is such that, as they feel they cannot do without him, they are anxious to retain him at the head of it, and consequently are obliged to keep him informed of their proceedings. . . . Mr. Gallatin said at once and spontaneously that *nothing* of real difficulty remained between the two countries but his Majesty's Orders in Council. This he repeated twice, dwelling upon the word 'nothing' with particular emphasis. He added that if the belligerent Powers persisted in enforcing their restrictions on the neutral commerce, the embargo must be continued until the end of the year, and that then America must take part in the war; that England had officially declared that she would revoke the restrictions she had imposed if her enemy would do the same; but that though France had professed as much, she had neither done it to the minister of the United States at Paris nor directly to this Government; neither had she made any communication to it of her restrictive edicts, or relative to them; and that this Government felt sensibly the difference of the conduct held toward it by those of Great Britain and France in those respects."[1]

Gallatin's assertion that if the Orders in Council were enforced America within a year must declare war, went far beyond any threat ever made before by President Jefferson or his party. The Secretary of the Navy held a somewhat different tone: —

"Mr. Smith told me that all would remain quiet if no new vexations were committed on their coast, and that the only measure which the Government would carry into effect would be the levy of the body of regulars to consist nominally of six thousand, but really of four thousand men."

Senator Giles and other Republican leaders avowed readiness for war with England. Before Rose's departure, the new policy had become defined. Its first object was to unite America in resisting England and France; the second, to maintain the embargo till the country should be ready for war.

[1] Rose to Canning, March 22, 1808; MSS. British Archives.

With these ends in view, the Administration threw aside the "Chesapeake" affair as a matter which concerned England rather than America. Madison notified Erskine that the subject had lost its consequence, and that if England wished a settlement she must seek it.

"It will throw some light upon the views of this Government," wrote Rose in his last despatch,[1] "if I state that in a recent conversation with Mr. Erskine, Mr. Madison observed that since England has thus publicly disclaimed the right of search of national ships for deserters, and Admiral Berkeley has been recalled from command of the Halifax squadron, although a more formal mode of terminating the business would have been more acceptable to this Government, it would consider itself as satisfied on the restoration of the seamen taken away by an act of force disavowed by his Majesty; but that it would not again ask for reparation upon this matter."

From that moment all eyes turned toward the embargo. The President had chosen his ground. Unless his experiment succeeded, he might yet be forced into the alternative of a second submission or war.

[1] Rose to Canning, March 22, 1808; MSS. British Archives. Cf. Madison to Pinckney, April 4, 1808; State Papers, iii. 221.

CHAPTER IX.

All winter Congress waited for the result of Rose's negotiation. The huge majority, without leadership, split by divergent interests, a mere mob guided from the White House, showed little energy except for debate, and no genius except for obedience.

The first political effect of the embargo was shown in the increased virulence of debate. The Act of December 22, passed on the spur of the moment, was powerless to prevent evasions in the seaports, and left untouched the trade with Canada and Florida. A supplementary Act was necessary; but to warrant a law for stopping all commerce by sea and land, the Government could no longer profess a temporary purpose of protecting ships, merchandise, and seamen, but must admit the more or less permanent nature of the embargo, and the policy of using it as a means of peaceable coercion. The first Supplementary Act passed Congress as early as January 8, but applied only to coasting and fishing vessels, which were put under heavy bonds and threatened with excessive penalties in case of entering a foreign port or trading in foreign merchandise. Finding that this measure was not effective, and that neither England nor France showed a sign of relaxing the so-called system of retaliation, Government was obliged to complete its restrictions. February 11 the House instructed its Committee of Commerce to inquire what further legislation was necessary "to prevent the exportation of goods, wares, and merchandise of foreign or domestic growth or manufacture to any foreign port or place." The committee instantly reported a bill; and as Rose's negotiation broke down, February 19 the House went into committee to debate a second supplementary Embargo Act, which was to stop by land and sea all commerce with the world.

The next day, February 20, Barent Gardenier of New York, who surpassed Josiah Quincy in hatred of the Administration, attacked the new bill in a speech which showed much rough power and more temper. He said with force that between the original embargo and this Supplementary Act no connection existed. The one was an embargo, the other was non-intercourse; and he charged that the original embargo was a fraud, intended to trick the country into a permanent system of non-intercourse: —

"The more the original measure develops itself, the more I am satisfied that my first view of it was correct; that it was a sly, cunning measure; that its real object was not merely to prevent our vessels from going out, but to effect a non-intercourse. Are the nation prepared for this? If you wish to try whether they are, tell them at once what is your object. Tell them what you mean. Tell them you mean to take part with the Grand Pacificator. Or else stop your present course. Do not go on forging chains to fasten us to the car of the Imperial Conqueror."

Interrupted by a dozen Republican members who leaped to their feet in anger, Gardenier for a time returned to his argument and dropped the assertion of subservience to Napoleon: —

"I ask the intelligent and candid men of this House whether to prevent the farmers of Vermont from selling their pigs in Canada is calculated to increase or diminish our essential resources; whether the object which the President professed to have in view is counteracted by a traffic of this kind. . . . I could wish gentlemen would, instead of bolting at me in the fulness of their rage, endeavor to satisfy my poor understanding by cool reasoning that they are right; that they would show me how this measure will prepare us for war; how the weakening by distressing every part of the country is to increase its strength and its vigor."

Had Gardenier stopped there, his argument would have admitted no answer; but he had the defect of a Federalist temper, and could not control his tongue.

"Sir, I cannot understand it. I am astonished, — indeed I am astonished and dismayed. I see effects, but I can trace them to no cause. Yes, sir, I do fear that there is an unseen hand which is guiding us to the most dreadful destinies, — unseen because it cannot endure the light. Darkness and mystery overshadow this House and this whole nation. We know nothing; we are permitted to know nothing; we sit here as mere automata; we legislate without knowing — nay, sir, without wishing to know — why or wherefore. We are told what we are to do, and the Council of Five Hundred do it. We move, but why or wherefore no man knows. We are put in motion, but how I for one cannot tell."

Gardenier was believed to be the author of a letter written during the secret session, December 19, and published in the "New York Evening Post," which began the cry of French influence.[1] His speech of February 20, insulting to the House, disorderly and seditious, resting on innuendo but carrying the weight of a positive assertion, outraged every member of the majority. Even John Randolph had never gone so far as to charge his opponents with being the willing and conscious tools of a foreign despot. The House was greatly exasperated, and at the next session, Monday, February 22, three members — Richard M. Johnson of Kentucky, George W. Campbell of Tennessee, and John Montgomery of Maryland — rose successively and declared that Gardenier's expressions were a slander, which if not supported by proof made their author an object of contempt. Gardenier challenged Campbell, and March 2 a duel took place at Bladensburg. Gardenier was severely wounded, but escaped with life, while the bitterness of party feeling became more violent than before.

Yet no member ventured fairly to avow and defend the policy of non-intercourse as a policy of coercion. Campbell, the leader of the majority, admitted that the embargo was intended to distress England and

[1] Annals of Congress, 1807–1808, p. 1251, *n.*

France, but treated it mainly as a measure of defence. No full and fair discussion of the subject was attempted; and the bill passed both Houses and was approved by the President March 12, without calling from the Government a hint in regard to the scope of its policy or the length of time during which the system of seclusion was to last. Even Jefferson kept silence upon what was uppermost in his mind, and defended the embargo on every ground except that which with him, if with no one else, was strongest. In private he said that the measure was intended to last until the return of peace in Europe, or as long as the orders and decrees of England and France should be maintained: —

"Till they return to some sense of moral duty we keep within ourselves. This gives time. Time may produce peace in Europe; peace in Europe removes all causes of difference till another European war; and by that time our debt may be paid, our revenues clear, and our strength increased."[1]

With such reasoning the opponents of the embargo were far from pleased. Nevertheless, Jefferson carried his point, and could for the moment afford to disregard criticism. His experiment of peaceable coercion was sure of a trial. His control over Congress seemed absolute. Only twenty-two members voted against the Supplementary Embargo Act, and in the Senate no opposition was recorded.

With such influence Jefferson might promise him-

[1] Jefferson to John Taylor, Jan. 6, 1808; Works, v. 226.

self success in any undertaking; and if he had at heart one object more momentous than the embargo, it was the punishment of Chief-Justice Marshall for his treatment of Burr. As early as Nov. 5, 1807, Senator Tiffin of Ohio began his career in the Senate by moving, as an amendment to the Constitution, that all judges of the United States should hold office for a term of years, and should be removed by the President on address by two-thirds of both Houses. Governor Tiffin's motion was not an isolated or personal act. The State legislatures were invoked. Vermont adopted the amendment. The House of Delegates in Virginia, both branches of the Pennsylvania legislature, the popular branch in Tennessee, and various other State governments, in whole or in part, adopted the principle and urged it upon Congress. In the House, George W. Campbell moved a similar amendment January 30, and from time to time other senators and members made attempts to bring the subject forward. In the Senate, Giles aided the attack by bringing in a bill for the punishment of treason. February 11 he spoke in support of his proposed measure, advancing doctrines which terrified Democrats as well as Federalists. Joseph Story was one of his audience, and wrote an account of this alarming speech: —

"Giles exhibits in his appearance no marks of greatness; he has a dark complexion and retreating eyes, black hair, and robust form. His dress is remarkably plain and in the style of Virginia carelessness. Having broken his leg a year or two since, he uses a crutch, and perhaps this adds somewhat to the indifference or doubt with which you contemplate him. But when he speaks, your opinion immediately changes. . . . I heard him a day or two since in support of a bill to define treason, reported by himself. Never did I hear such all-unhinging and terrible doctrines. He laid the axe at the root of judicial power, and every stroke might be distinctly felt. His argument was very specious and forensic, sustained with many plausible principles and adorned with various political axioms, designed *ad captandum*. One of its objects was to prove the right of the Legislature to *define* treason. My dear friend, look at the Constitution of the United States and see if any such construction can possibly be allowed! . . . He attacked Chief-Justice Marshall with insidious warmth. Among other things he said, 'I have learned that judicial opinions on this subject are like changeable silks, which vary their colors as they are held up in political sunshine.'"[1]

Had Giles's proposed definition of treason become law, it would in another half-century have had singular interest for Virginians of his school. According to this bill any persons, without exception, "owing allegiance to the United States of America," who should assemble with intent forcibly to change the government of the United States, or to dismember them or any one of them, or to resist the general execution of any public law, should suffer death as a traitor; and even though not personally present at the assemblage or at the use of force, yet should any person aid or

[1] Story's Life and Letters of Joseph Story, i. 158–159.

assist in doing any of the acts proscribed, such person should also suffer death as a traitor.[1] Fortunately for Southern theories the bill, although it passed the Senate by means of Southern votes, was lost in the House, where John Randolph had introduced a bill of his own more moderate in character.[2]

Although the attack on the Supreme Court was more persistent and was carried further than ever before, it met with passive resistance which foreshadowed failure, and probably for this reason was allowed to exhaust its strength in the committee-rooms of Congress. The chief-justice escaped without a wound. Under the shadow of the embargo he could watch in security the slow exhaustion of his antagonist. Jefferson had lost the last chance of reforming the Supreme Court. In another six months Congress would follow the will of some new Executive chief; and if in the full tide of Jefferson's power Marshall had repeatedly thwarted or defied him with impunity, the chance was small that another President would meet a happier fate.

The failure of his attack on the Supreme Court was not the only evidence that Jefferson's authority when put to the test was more apparent than real. If in the President's eyes Marshall deserved punishment, another offender merited it still more. Senator Smith of Ohio was deeply implicated in Burr's conspiracy.

[1] Bill for the Punishment of Treason and other crimes; Annals of Congress, 1807–1808, p. 108.

[2] Annals of Congress, 1807–1808, p. 1717.

The dignity of the President and of Congress demanded inquiry, and an investigation was made. The evidence left no reasonable doubt that Smith had been privy to Burr's scheme; but the motion to expel him from the Senate failed by a vote of nineteen to ten, two thirds being required for this purpose. In the House, John Randolph brought charges against General Wilkinson which could neither be admitted nor met. The Administration was obliged to cover and ignore the military scandals brought to light by Burr's trial.

Even in regard to more serious matters the Government could hardly feel secure. In February, Sloan of New Jersey offered a motion that the seat of government should be removed from Washington to Philadelphia. The House, February 2, by a vote of sixty-eight to forty-seven, agreed to consider the resolution, and a debate followed which proved how far from stable the actual arrangement was supposed to be. Republicans and Federalists alike assailed the place in which they were condemned to live. Fifteen million dollars, it was said, had been spent upon it with no other result than to prove that a city could never be made to exist there. One day they were choked with dust; the next they were wallowing in mire. The climate was one of violent changes and piercing winds. Members sickened and died in greater numbers than ever before, but in case of illness they could find no physician except by sending to the navy yard some miles away. At the last session the House had been driven from its old hall by the wind breaking its windows. The new hall, however magnificent was unfit for its purpose; to hear was impossible; its ventilation was so bad as to have caused the illness of Jacob Crowninshield, one of its leading members, then lying at the point of death. The prices of everything in Washington were excessive. Butter was fifty cents a pound; a common turkey cost a dollar and a half; in Philadelphia members would save one hundred and fifty dollars a day in hack-hire alone. Even these objections were trifling compared with the inconvenience of governing from a wilderness where no machinery existed to make administration easy. As an example of the absurdities of such a system, members pointed to the navy yard, only to be reached by following the windings of the shallow Potomac, while the Navy Department was obliged at extravagant cost to bring every article of use from the seaboard, besides recruiting seamen at the commercial ports for every ship fitted out at Washington.

Sloan desisted from his motion only after the House had shown itself strongly inclined toward his opinion. On another point the divergence of ideas became more marked, and Jefferson found himself obliged to strain his influence.

In the Republican party any vote for a standing army had been hitherto considered a crime. The Federalists in 1801 had left a force of five thousand men; Jefferson reduced it to three thousand. The

Republican party believed in a militia, but neglected it. Throughout the Southern States the militia was undisciplined and unarmed; but in Massachusetts, as President Jefferson was beginning to notice, the Federalists took much care of their State soldiery. The United States fort at Newport was garrisoned only by goats, and the strategic line of Lake Champlain and the Hudson River, which divided New England from the rest of the Union, lay open to an enemy. In view of war with England such negligence became wanton. Jefferson saw that an army must be raised; but many of his truest followers held that militia alone could be trusted, and that the risk of conquest from abroad was better than the risk of military despotism at home.

For a people naturally brave, Americans often showed themselves surprisingly unwilling to depend upon their own strength. To defy danger, to rush into competition with every foreign rival, to take risks without number, and to depend wholly on themselves were admitted characteristics of Americans as individuals; but the same man who, when left to his own resources, delighted in proving his skill and courage, when brought within the shadow of government never failed to clamor for protection. As a political body the American people shrank from tests of its own capacity. "American systems" of politics, whether domestic or foreign, were systems for evading competition. The American system in which the old Republican party believed was remarkable for avowing want of self-confidence as the foundation of domestic as well as of foreign policy. The Republican party stood alone in refusing, on principle, to protect national rights from foreign outrage; but it defied imitation when the sacrifice of national rights was justified by the argument that if American liberties were not abandoned to foreign nations they would be destroyed by the people themselves. War, which every other nation in history had looked upon as the first duty of a State, was in America a subject for dread, not so much because of possible defeat as of probable success. No truer Republican could be found in Virginia than John W. Eppes, one of Jefferson's sons-in-law; and when the House debated in February a Senate bill for adding two regiments to the regular army, Eppes declared the true Republican doctrine:[1] —

"If we have war, this increase of the army will be useless; if peace, I am opposed to it. I am in favor of putting arms into the hands of our citizens and then let them defend themselves. . . . If we depend on regular troops alone, the liberty of the country must finally be destroyed by that army which is raised to defend it. Is there an instance in which a nation has lost its liberty by its own citizens in time of peace? It is by standing armies and very often by men raised on an emergency and professing virtuous feelings, but who eventually turned their arms against their country. . . . I never yet have voted for a regular army or soldier in time

[1] Annals of Congress, Feb. 17, 1808; Thirteenth Congress, pp. 1627, 1631.

of peace. Whenever an opportunity has offered I have voted them down; and so help me God! I will as long as I live."

One week after Eppes spoke these words, President Jefferson sent to Congress a Message asking for an immediate addition of six thousand men to the regular army.[1] No such blow had ever been given to the established practices of Republican administration. Ten years before, every leader of the party had denounced the raising of twelve regiments at a time of actual hostilities with France, although the law limited their service to the term of the expected war. The eight regiments demanded by Jefferson were to be raised for five years in a time of peace. The Southern Republicans saw themselves required to walk, publicly and avowedly, in the footsteps of their monarchical predecessors; while John Randolph stood by and jeered at them.

The House waited until Rose had fairly sailed and the session drew near its end, with embargo fastened upon the country, and no alternative visible but war; then slowly and unwillingly began its recantations. April 4 John Clopton of Virginia[2] admitted that in 1798 he had voted against the army. His excuse for changing his vote was that in 1798 he thought there was no ground for fearing war, while in 1808 he saw little ground for hoping peace. Yet he voted

[1] Message of Feb. 25, 1808; Annals of Congress, 1807–1808, p. 1691.

[2] Annals of Congress, 1807–1808, p. 1901.

for the new regiments only because they were so few; and even in the event of actual war "he could scarcely imagine that he could be induced to admit the expediency of increasing the regular forces to a number much greater than they would be" under the present bill. Clopton was answered by Randolph, who warmly opposed the new army for the same reasons which had led him to oppose the old one. Randolph was followed by George M. Troup of Georgia, — a young man not then so prominent as he was destined to become, who declared that no one had more confidence than he felt in militia; but "it is well known that the present defective system of militia in our quarter of the country at least is good for nothing;" and a small standing army was not dangerous but necessary, because it would preserve peace by preparing for war.[1] Smilie of Pennsylvania added another reason. He argued that John Randolph had favored raising troops in the year 1805 to protect the Southern frontier "from Spanish inroad and insult." Smilie had then opposed the motion and the House had rejected it, but to Smilie the argument that Randolph had once favored an increase of the army, seemed decisive.

A much respected member from South Carolina — David R. Williams, one of Randolph's friends — then took the floor.[2] He could not bring himself to vote for the bill, because no half-way measure would an-

[1] Annals of Congress, 1807–1808, p. 1916.
[2] Annals of Congress, 1807–1808, p. 1922.

swer. War would require not six but sixty thousand men; defensive armies were worse than none, either in war or peace. Williams's argument was so evidently weak that it failed to convince even Macon, who had voted against the twelve regiments in 1798, but meant to change his ground and believed himself able to prove his consistency. In contradiction to the bill itself he maintained that the new army was not a peace establishment; that if it were so he would not vote for it. He condemned the maxim that to preserve peace nations must be prepared for war, and asserted that no analogy existed between 1798 and 1808, for that in 1808 America was attacked by foreign powers, while in 1798 she attacked them.[1]

Discordant as these voices were, the debate was the next day enlivened by a discord more entertaining. Richard Stanford of North Carolina, one of the oldest members of the House, a close ally of Randolph, Macon, and Williams, made a speech which troubled the whole body of Southern Republicans.[2] Stanford voted for the twelve regiments in 1798, but like the majority of Republicans he did so in deference to a party caucus, in order to ward off the danger of a larger force. He said it was the only Federalist vote he ever gave, and he promised his friends never again to be caught in the same mistake. With candor intended to irritate, he arrayed the occasions on

[1] Annals of Congress, 1807–1808, p. 1937.
[2] Annals of Congress, 1807–1808, p. 1939.

which his party had refused to increase the military establishment: first, in a state of actual hostilities in 1798; again, when Spain defied and insulted the government in 1805; still again, on the brink of a Spanish war during Burr's conspiracy in 1806. He quoted Jefferson's first Inaugural Address, which counted among the essential principles of the government "a well-disciplined militia, our best reliance in peace and for the first moments of war till regulars may relieve them;" and the Annual Message of 1806, which said, "Were armies to be raised whenever a speck of war is visible in our horizon, we never should have been without them; our resources would have been exhausted on dangers which have never happened, instead of being reserved for what is really to take place." He quoted also pungent resolutions of 1798, speeches of Eppes and Wilson Cary Nicholas, of Varnum and Gallatin; he showed the amount of patronage once abolished but restored by this bill; and when at last he sat down, the Southern members were ruffled until even Macon lost his temper.

Soon John Randolph rose again, and if Stanford's speech was exasperating in its candor, Randolph's was stinging in its sarcasm.[1] He treated the new defensive system with ridicule. The Navy Department, he said, had dwindled to a Gunboat Department. Congress built gunboats to protect shipping and coasts, and built forts to protect gunboats. The

[1] Annals of Congress, 1807–1808, p. 1959.

army was equally feeble; and both were at odds with the embargo: —

"When the great American tortoise draws in his head you do not see him trotting along; he lies motionless on the ground; it is when the fire is put on his back that he makes the best of his way, and not till then. The system of embargo is one system, withdrawing from every contest, quitting the arena, flying the pit. The system of raising troops and fleets of whatever sort is another and opposite to that dormant state. . . . They are at war with each other, and cannot go on together."

Even if not inconsistent with the embargo, the army was still useless: —

"My worthy friend from Georgia has said that the tigress, prowling for food for her young, may steal upon you in the night. I would as soon attempt to fence a tiger out of my plantation with a four-railed fence as to fence out the British navy with this force."

Randolph ventured even to ridicule the State of Virginia which was said to demand an army: —

"My friend and worthy colleague tells us that the State of Virginia, so much opposed to armies, has now got to the war pitch so far as to want one regiment for the defence of half a million of souls and seventy thousand square miles. . . . Yes, sir; the legislature of Virginia, my parent State, of whom I cannot speak with disrespect, nor will I suffer any man worth my resentment to speak of her with disrespect in my hearing, has been carried away by the military mania, and they want one regiment!"

Yet Randolph approved the embargo as little as he liked the army and navy.

"I am not one of those who approve the embargo," he said in another speech.[1] "It gives up to Great Britain all the seamen and all the commerce, — their feet are not now upon your decks, for your vessels are all riding safely moored along your slips and wharves; and this measure absolutely gives Agriculture a blow which she cannot recover till the embargo is removed. What has become of your fisheries? Some gentleman has introduced a proposition for buying their fish to relieve the fishermen. Indeed, I would much sooner assent to buying their fish than to raising these troops, except indeed we are raising the troops to eat the fish."

Randolph broke into shrill laughter at his own joke, delighted with the idea of six thousand armed men paid to eat the fish that were rotting on the wharves at Gloucester and Marblehead.

Keenly as Randolph enjoyed the pleasure of ridiculing his colleagues and friends, he could expect to gain no votes. George W. Campbell and the other Administration speakers admitted that the embargo might yield to war and that an army had become necessary. Even Eppes had the courage to defy ridicule, and in full recollection of having vowed to God February 17 that as long as he lived he would vote down a regular army, he rose April 7 to support the bill for raising eight regiments: —

"I consider it as part of the system designed to meet the present crisis in our affairs. . . . The period

[1] Annals of Congress, 1807–1808, p. 2037.

must arrive when the embargo will be a greater evil than war. When that period shall arrive it will be taken off."[1]

On the same day the bill passed by a vote of ninety-five to sixteen, and the Republican party found itself poorer by the loss of one more traditional principle. Events were hurrying the Government toward dangers which the party had believed to be preventable under the system invented by Virginia and Pennsylvania. In 1804 Jefferson wrote to Madison: "It is impossible that France and England should combine to any purpose."[2] The impossible had happened, and every practice founded on the theory of mutual jealousy between European Powers became once more a subject of dispute. On the day of Rose's departure Jefferson, abandoning the secrecy in which until that moment he had wrapped his diplomacy, sent to Congress a mass of diplomatic correspondence with England and France, running back to the year 1804. A few days later, March 30, he sent a secret message accompanied by documents which gave to Congress, with little exception, everything of importance that had passed between the governments. Only one subject was kept back: — the tenebrous negotiation for Florida remained secret.

From these documents Congress could see that the time for talking of theories of peace and friendship or of ordinary commercial interests had passed. Vio-

[1] Annals of Congress, 1807–1808, p. 2049.

[2] Jefferson to Madison, Aug. 15, 1804; Works, iv. 557.

lence and rapine marked every page of the latest correspondence. February 23 Erskine had at last notified the Government officially of the existence and purpose of the Orders in Council. His note repeated the words of Canning's instructions.[1] After asserting that America had submitted to the French Decrees, and had thereby warranted England in forbidding if she pleased all American commerce with France, Erskine pointed out that the Orders in Council, by not prohibiting but limiting this commerce, gave proof of his Majesty's amicable disposition. The Americans might still transport French and Spanish colonial produce to England, and re-export it to the continent of Europe under certain regulations: —

"The object of these regulations will be the establishment of such a protecting duty as shall prevent the enemy from obtaining the produce of his own colonies at a cheaper rate than that of the colonies of Great Britain. In this duty it is evident that America is no otherwise concerned than as being to make an advance to that amount, for which it is in her power amply to indemnify herself at the expense of the foreign consumer."

Further, the orders licensed the importation through England into France of all strictly American produce, except cotton, without paying duty in transit: —

"The reason why his Majesty could not feel himself at liberty, consistent with what was necessary for the execution of his purpose in any tolerable degree, to

[1] Erskine to Madison, Feb. 23, 1808; State Papers, iii. 209.

allow this relaxation to apply to cotton is to be found in the great extent to which France has pushed the manufacture of that article, and the consequent embarrassment upon her trade which a heavy import upon cotton as it passes through Great Britain to France must necessarily produce."

Erskine's note claimed credit for England because the orders were not abruptly enforced, but allowed time for neutrals to understand and conform to them. The concluding sentences were intended to soothe the suffering merchants: —

"The right of his Majesty to resort to retaliation cannot be questioned. The suffering occasioned to neutral parties is incidental, and not of his Majesty's seeking. In the exercise of this undoubted right, his Majesty has studiously endeavored to avoid aggravating unnecessarily the inconveniences suffered by the neutral; and I am commanded by his Majesty especially to represent to the Government of the United States the earnest desire of his Majesty to see the commerce of the world restored once more to that freedom which is necessary for its prosperity; and his readiness to abandon the system which has been forced upon him whenever the enemy shall retract the principles which have rendered it necessary."

From this note — a model of smooth-spoken outrage — Congress could understand that until the King of England should make other regulations American commerce was to be treated as subject to the will and interest of Great Britain. At the same moment Congress was obliged to read a letter from Champagny to Armstrong, dated Jan. 15, 1808, in defence of the Berlin and Milan Decrees.[1] Written in words dictated by Napoleon, this letter asserted rude truths which irritated Americans the more because they could not be denied: —

"The United States, more than any other Power, have to complain of the aggressions of England. It has not been enough for her to offend against the independence of their flag, — nay, against that of their territory and of their inhabitants, — by attacking them even in their ports, by forcibly carrying away their crews; her decrees of the 11th November have made a fresh attack on their commerce and on their navigation as they have done on those of all other Powers.

"In the situation in which England has placed the Continent, especially since her decrees of the 11th November, his Majesty has no doubt of a declaration of war against her by the United States. Whatever transient sacrifices war may occasion, they will not believe it consistent either with their interest or dignity to acknowledge the monstrous principle and the anarchy which that government wishes to establish on the seas. If it be useful and honorable for all nations to cause the true maritime law of nations to be re-established, and to avenge the insults committed by England against every flag, it is indispensable for the United States, who from the extent of their commerce have oftener to complain of those violations. War exists then in fact between England and the United States; and his Majesty con-

[1] Champagny to Armstrong, Jan. 15, 1808; State Papers, iii. 248.

siders it as declared from the day on which England published her decrees."

Two such letters could hardly have been written to the chief of an independent people and submitted to a free legislature in Europe without producing a convulsion. Patient as Congress was, the temper excited by Champagny's letter obliged the President, April 2, to withdraw the injunction of secrecy after the House had twice rejected a motion to do so without his permission; but the motive of the Federalists in publishing Champagny's letter was not so much to resent it as to divert popular anger from England to France. No outburst of national self-respect followed the appearance of the two letters. During the next week the House debated and passed the bill for raising the army to ten thousand men, but on all sides the friends and opponents of the measure equally deprecated war. The report of a special committee in the Senate, April 16, expressed on that point the general feeling of Congress:[1] —

"With respect to a resort to war as a remedy for the evils experienced, the committee will offer no other reflection than that it is in itself so great an evil that the United States have wisely considered peace and honest neutrality as the best foundation of their general policy. It is not for the committee to say under what degree of aggravated injuries and sufferings a departure from this policy may become a duty, and the most pacific nation find itself compelled to exchange for the calamities of

[1] Annals of Congress, 1807–1808, p. 364.

war the greater distresses of longer forbearance. In the present state of things the committee cannot recommend any departure from that policy which withholds our commercial and agricultural property from the licensed depredations of the great maritime belligerent Powers. They hope that an adherence to this policy will eventually secure to us the blessings of peace without any sacrifice of our national rights; and they have no doubt that it will be supported by all the manly virtue which the good people of the United States have ever discovered on great and patriotic occasions."

The Senate passed a bill authorizing the President during the recess to suspend the embargo in whole or in part if in his judgment the conduct of the belligerent Powers should render suspension safe. After a hot debate, chiefly on the constitutionality of the measure, it passed the House, and April 22 became law. April 25 the session ended.

As the result of six months' labor, Congress could show besides the usual routine legislation a number of Acts which made an epoch in the history of the Republican party. First came the Embargo, its two Supplements, and the Act empowering the President to suspend it at will. Next came the series of appropriation Acts which authorized the President to spend in all four million dollars in excess of the ordinary expenditures, — for gunboats, eight hundred and fifty thousand dollars; for land fortifications, one million; for five new regiments of infantry, one of riflemen, one of light artillery, and one of light dragoons, two million dollars; and two hundred thousand dollars for arming the militia. Such progress toward energy was more rapid than could have been expected from a party like that which Jefferson had educated and which he still controlled.

CHAPTER X.

"THIS six months' session has worn me down to a state of almost total incapacity for business," wrote President Jefferson to his attorney-general.[1] "Congress will certainly rise to-morrow night, and I shall leave this for Monticello on the 5th of May, to be here again on the 8th of June." More earnestly than ever he longed for repose and good-will. "For myself," he said,[2] "I have nothing further to ask of the world than to preserve in retirement so much of their esteem as I may have fairly earned, and to be permitted to pass in tranquillity, in the bosom of my family and friends, the days which yet remain to me." He could not reasonably ask from the world more than he had already received from it; but a whole year remained, during which he must still meet whatever demand the world should make upon him. He had brought the country to a situation where war was impossible for want of weapons, and peace was only a name for passive war. He was bound to carry the government through the dangers he had braved; and

[1] Jefferson to Rodney, April 24, 1808; Works, v. 275.

[2] Jefferson to Monroe, March 10, 1808; Works, v. 253.

for the first time in seven years American democracy, struck with sudden fear of failure, looked to him in doubt, and trembled for its hopes.

Fortunately for Jefferson's ease, no serious opposition was made in the Republican party to his choice of a successor. Giles and Nicholas, who managed Madison's canvass in Virginia, caused a caucus to be held, January 21, at Richmond, where one hundred and twenty-three members of the State legislature joined in nominating electors for Madison. Randolph's friends held another caucus, at which fifty-seven members of the same legislature joined in nominating electors for Monroe. To support the Virginia movement for Madison, a simultaneous caucus was held at Washington, where, January 20, Senator Bradley of Vermont issued a printed circular inviting the Republican members of both Houses to consult, January 23, respecting the next Presidential election. Bradley's authority was disputed by Monroe's partisans, and only Madison's friends, or indifferent persons, obeyed the call. Eighty-nine senators and members attended; and on balloting, eighty-three votes were given for Madison as President, seventy-nine for George Clinton as Vice-President; but the names of the persons present were never published, and the caucus itself seemed afraid of its own action. About sixty Republican members or senators held aloof. John Randolph and sixteen of his friends published a protest against the caucus and its candidate: —

"We ask for energy, and we are told of his moderation. We ask for talents, and the reply is his unassuming merit. We ask what were his services in the cause of public liberty, and we are directed to the pages of the 'Federalist,' written in conjunction with Alexander Hamilton and John Jay, in which the most extravagant of their doctrines are maintained and propagated. We ask for consistency as a Republican, standing forth to stem the torrent of oppression which once threatened to overwhelm the liberties of the country. We ask for that high and honorable sense of duty which would at all times turn with loathing and abhorrence from any compromise with fraud and speculation. We ask in vain."[1]

Jefferson had commanded the warm and undisputed regard of his followers; Madison held no such preeminence. "Every able diplomatist is not fit to be President," said Macon. George Clinton, who had yielded unwillingly to Jefferson, held Madison in contempt. While Monroe set up a Virginia candidacy which the Republicans of Randolph's school supported, George Clinton set up a candidacy of his own, in New York, supported by Cheetham's "Watch-Tower," and by a portion of the country press. Before long, the public was treated to a curious spectacle. The regular party candidate for the Vice-presidency became the open rival of the regular candidate for the Presidency. Clinton's newspapers attacked Madison without mercy, while Madison's

[1] Address to the People of the United States, National Intelligencer, March 7, 1808.

friends were electing Clinton as Madison's Vice-president.

In this state of things successful opposition to Madison depended upon the union of his enemies in support of a common candidate. Not only must either Monroe or Clinton retire, but one must be able to transfer his votes to the other; and the whole Federalist party must be induced to accept the choice thus made. The Federalists were not unwilling; but while they waited for the politicians of Virginia and New York to arrange the plan of campaign, they busied themselves with recovering control of New England, where they had been partially driven from power. The embargo offered them almost a certainty of success.

From the first moment of the embargo, even during the secret debate of Dec. 19, 1807, its opponents raised the cry of French influence; and so positively and persistently was Jefferson charged with subservience to Napoleon, that while a single Federalist lived, this doctrine continued to be an article of his creed. In truth, Jefferson had never stood on worse terms with France than when he imposed the embargo. He acted in good faith when he enclosed Armstrong's letter and Regnier's decision in his Embargo Message. Turreau was annoyed at his conduct, thinking it intended to divert public anger from England to France in order to make easier the negotiation with Rose. Instead of dictating Jefferson's course, as the Federalists believed, Turreau was vexed and alarmed by it. He complained of Armstrong, Madison, and Jefferson himself. The Embargo Message, he said, exposed the Administration in flank to the Federalists, and gave the English envoy free play. "For me it was a useless proof — one proof the more — of the usual awkwardness of the Washington Cabinet, and of its falsity (*faussetê*) in regard to France."[1] His contempt involved equally people, Legislature, and Executive: —

"Faithful organs of the perverse intentions of the American people, its representatives came together before their usual time, in accordance with the President's views, and in their private conversation and in their public deliberations seemed entirely to forget the offences of England, or rather to have been never affected by them. This temper, common to the men of all parties, proved very evidently what was the state of popular opinion in regard to Great Britain, against whom no hostile project will ever enter into an American's thoughts. The Annual Message was not calculated to inspire energy into the honorable Congress. All these political documents from the President's pen are cold and colorless."[2]

The result of Rose's negotiation confirmed Turreau's disgust: —

"It can be no longer doubtful that the United States, whatever insults they may have to endure, will never make war on Great Britain unless she attacks them.

[1] Turreau to Champagny, May 20, 1808; Archives des Aff. Étr. MSS.

[2] Turreau to Champagny, May 20, 1808; Archives des Aff. Étr. MSS.

Every day I have been, and still am, met with the objection that the decrees of the French government have changed the disposition of the members of the Executive, and especially of members of Congress. Both have seized this incident as a pretext to color their cowardice (*lâcheté*), and extend it over their system of inaction; since it is evident that however severe the measures of the French government may have been, they weigh light in the balance when set in opposition to all the excesses, all the outrages, that England has permitted herself to inflict on the United States."[1]

During the winter and spring nothing occurred to soothe Turreau's feelings. On the contrary, his irritation was increased by the President's communication to Congress of Champagny's letter of January 15, and by the "inconceivable weakness" which made this letter public:—

"Although I could hardly have calculated on this new shock, which has considerably weakened our political credit in the United States, I well knew that we had lost greatly in the opinion of the Cabinet at Washington and of its chief. After Mr. Rose's departure,—that is to say, about three weeks before the end of the session,—I quitted the city for reasons of health, which were only too well founded. I had seen Mr. Jefferson only a week before I went to take leave of him. Perhaps I should tell your Excellency that I commonly see the President once a week, and always in the evening,—a time when I am sure of finding him at home, and nearly always alone. I

[1] Turreau to Champagny, May 20, 1808; Archives des Aff. Étr. MSS.

never open upon the chapter of politics, because it seems more proper for me to wait for him to begin this subject, and I never wait long. At the interview before the last I found him extremely cool in regard to the interests of Europe and the measures of the Powers coalesced against England. At the last interview he asked me if I had recent news from Europe. I told him — what was true — that I had nothing official since two months. 'You treat us badly,' he replied. 'The governments of Europe do not understand this government here. Even England, whose institutions have most analogy with ours, does not know the character of the American people and the spirit of its Administration,' etc. I answered that Great Britain having violated the law of nations in regard to every people in succession, the nature and the difference of their institutions mattered little to a Power which had abjured all principles. He interrupted me to say: 'When severe measures become necessary we shall know how to take them, but we do not want to be dragged into them (*y être entrainés*).' Although this was directly to the address of the minister of France, I thought best to avoid a retort, and contented myself with observing that generally France gave the example of respect for governments which sustained their dignity, and that the object of the coalition of all the European States against England was to constrain that Power to imitate her. The rest of the conversation was too vague and too insignificant to be worth remembering. Nevertheless, Mr. Jefferson repeated to me what he tells me at nearly every interview, — that he has much love for France."

Turreau drew the inference "that the federal government intends to-day more than ever to hold an equal balance between France and England." Erskine saw matters in the same light. Neither the Frenchman nor the Englishman, although most directly interested in the bias of President Jefferson, reported any word or act of his which showed a wish to serve Napoleon's ends.

The interests of the Federalists required them to assert the subservience of Jefferson to France. They did so in the most positive language, without proof, and without attempting to obtain proof. Had this been all, they would have done no worse than their opponents had done before them; but they also used the pretext of Jefferson's devotion to France in order to cover and justify their own devotion to England.

After the failure of Rose, in the month of February, to obtain further concessions from Madison, the British envoy cultivated more closely the friendship of Senator Pickering, and even followed his advice. As early as March 4 he wrote to his Government on the subject,[1] —

"It is apprehended, should this Government be desirous that hostilities should take place with England, it will not venture to commence them, but will endeavor to provoke her to strike the first blow. In such a case it would no doubt adopt highly irritating measures. On this head I beg leave, but with great diffidence, to submit the views which I have formed here, and which I find coincide completely with those of the best and most en-

[1] Rose to Canning, March 4, 1808; MSS. British Archives.

lightened men of this country, and who consider her interests as completely identified with those of Great Britain. I conceive it to be of extreme importance in the present state of the public mind in this nation, and especially as operated upon by the embargo, such as I have endeavored to represent it in preceding despatches, to avoid if possible actual warfare, — should it be practicable consistently with the national honor, to do no more than retort upon America any measures of insolence and injury falling short of it which she may adopt. Such a line of conduct would, I am persuaded, render completely null the endeavors exerted to impress upon the public mind here the persuasion of the inveterate rancor with which Great Britain seeks the destruction of America, and would turn their whole animosity, — goaded on, as they would be, by the insults and injuries offered by France, and the self-inflicted annihilation of their own commerce, — against their own Government, and produce an entire change in the politics of the country. A war with Great Britain would, I have no doubt, prove ultimately fatal to this Government; but it is to be feared that the people would necessarily rally round it at the first moment and at the instant of danger; and an exasperation would be produced which it might be found impossible to eradicate for a series of years. Their soundest statesmen express to me the utmost anxiety that their fellow-citizens should be allowed to bear the whole burden of their own follies, and suffer by evils originating with themselves; and they are convinced that the effects of punishment inflicted by their own hands must ere long bring them into co-operation with Great Britain, whilst if inflicted by hers, it must turn them perhaps irrevocably against her."

"The best and most enlightened men of the country," — who "considered her interests as completely identified with those of Great Britain," and who thus concerted with Canning a policy intended to bring themselves into power as agents of Spencer Perceval and Lord Castlereagh, — were Senator Pickering and his friends. To effect this coalition with the British ministry Pickering exerted himself to the utmost. Not only by word of mouth, but also by letter, he plied the British envoy with argument and evidence. Although Rose, March 4, wrote to Canning in the very words of the Massachusetts senator, March 13 the senator wrote to Rose repeating his opinion:[1] —

"You know my solicitude to have peace preserved between the two nations, and I have therefore taken the liberty to express to you my opinion of the true point of policy to be observed by your Government toward the United States, in case your mission prove unsuccessful; that is, to let us alone; to bear patiently the wrongs we do ourselves. In one word, amidst the irritations engendered by hatred and folly, to maintain a dignified composure, and to abstain from war, — relying on this, that whatever disposition exists to provoke, there is none to commence a war on the part of the United States."

To support his views Pickering enclosed a letter from Rufus King. "I also know," he continued, "that in the present unexampled state of the world

[1] Pickering to Rose, March 13, 1808; New England Federalism, p. 366.

our own best citizens consider the interests of the United States to be interwoven with those of Great Britain, and that our safety depends on hers. . . . Of the opinions and reasonings of such men I wish you to be possessed." He held out a confident hope that the embargo would end in an overthrow of the Administration, and that a change in the head of the government would alter its policy "in a manner propitious to the continuance of peace." A few days afterward he placed in Rose's hands two letters from George Cabot. Finally, on the eve of Rose's departure, March 22, he gave the British envoy a letter to Samuel Williams of London. "Let him, if you please, be the medium of whatever epistolary intercourse may take place between you and me." [1]

To these advances Rose replied in his usual tone of courteous superiority: —

"I avail myself thankfully of your permission to keep that gentleman's [Rufus King's] letter, which I am sure will carry high authority where I can use it confidentially, and whither it is most important that what I conceive to be right impressions should be conveyed. It is not to you that I need protest that rancorous impressions of jealousy or ill-will have never existed there; but it is to be feared that at some time or another the extremest point of human forbearance may be reached. Yet at the present moment there is, I think, a peculiarity of circumstances most strange indeed, which enables the offended party to leave his antagonist to his own sui-

[1] Pickering to G. H. Rose, March 22, 1808; New England Federalism, p. 368.

cidal devices, unless, in his contortions under them, he may strike some blow which the other might not be able to dissemble."[1]

No senator of the United States could submit, without some overpowering motive, to such patronage. That Pickering should have invited it was the more startling because he knew better than any other man in America the criminality of his act. Ten years before, at a time when Pickering was himself Secretary of State, the Pennsylvania Quaker, Dr. Logan, attempted, with honest motives, to act as an amateur negotiator between the United States government and that of France. In order to prevent such mischievous follies for the future, Congress, under the inspiration of Pickering, passed a law known as "Logan's Act," which still stood on the statute book:[2] —

"Every citizen of the United States, whether actually resident or abiding within the same, or in any foreign country, who, without the permission or authority of the government, directly or indirectly commences or carries on any verbal or written correspondence or intercourse with any foreign government, or any officer or agent thereof, with an intent to influence the measures or conduct of any foreign government, or of any officer or agent thereof, in relation to any disputes or controversies with the United States, or to defeat the measures of

[1] G. H. Rose to Pickering, March 18, 1808; New England Federalism, p. 367.

[2] Rev. Stat. sec. 5335. Cf. Act of Jan. 30, 1799; Annals of Congress, 1797-1799, p. 3795.

the government of the United States; and every person . . . who counsels, advises, or assists in any such correspondence, with such intent, shall be punished by a fine of not more than five thousand dollars, and by imprisonment during not less than six months, nor more than three years."

When Pickering defied fine and imprisonment under his own law, in order to make a concert of political action with George Canning to keep the British government steady in aggression, he believed that his end justified his means; and he avowed his end to be the bringing of his friends into power For this purpose he offered himself to Canning as the instrument for organizing what was in fact a British party in New England, asking in return only the persistence of Great Britain in a line of policy already adopted, which was sure to work against the Republican rule. Pickering knew that his conduct was illegal; but he had in his hands an excuse which justified him, as he chose to think, in disregarding the law. He persuaded himself that Jefferson was secretly bound by an engagement with Napoleon to effect the ruin of England.

Then came Pickering's master-stroke. The April election — which would decide the political control of Massachusetts for the coming year, and the choice of a senator in the place of J. Q. Adams — was close at hand. February 16, the day when Rose's negotiation broke down, Pickering sent to Governor Sullivan of Massachusetts a letter intended for official communication to the State legislature.[1] "I may claim some share of attention and credit," he began, — "that share which is due to a man who defies the world to point, in the whole course of a long and public life, at one instance of deception, at a single departure from Truth." He entered into speculations upon the causes which had led Congress to impose the embargo. Omitting mention of the Orders in Council, he showed that the official reasons presented in the President's Embargo Message were not sufficient to justify the measure, and that some secret motive must lie hidden from public view: —

"Has the French Emperor declared that he will have no neutrals? Has he required that our ports, like those of his vassal States in Europe, be shut against British commerce? Is the embargo a substitute, a milder form of compliance, with that harsh demand, which if exhibited in its naked and insulting aspect the American spirit might yet resent? Are we still to be kept profoundly ignorant of the declarations and avowed designs of the French Emperor, although these may strike at our liberty and independence? And in the mean time are we, by a thousand irritations, by cherishing prejudices, and by exciting fresh resentments, to be drawn gradually into a war with Great Britain? Why amid the extreme anxiety of the public mind is it still kept on the rack of fearful expectation by the President's portentous silence respecting his French despatches? In this concealment there is danger. In this concealment must be wrapt up

[1] Letter from the Hon. Timothy Pickering to His Excellency James Sullivan (Boston, 1808).

the real cause of the embargo. On any other supposition it is inexplicable."

Never was Jefferson's sleight-of-hand more dexterously turned against him than in this unscrupulous appeal to his own official language. In all Pickering's voluminous writings this letter stood out alone stamped by a touch of genius.

"By false policy," he continued, "or by inordinate fears, our country may be betrayed and subjugated to France as surely as by corruption. I trust, sir, that no one who knows me will charge it to vanity when I say that I have some knowledge of public men and of public affairs; and on that knowledge, and with solemnity, I declare to you that I have no confidence in the wisdom or correctness of our public measures; that our country is in imminent danger; that it is essential to the public safety that the blind confidence in our rulers should cease; that the State legislatures should know the facts and the reasons on which important general laws are founded; and especially that those States whose farms are on the ocean and whose harvests are gathered in every sea, should immediately and seriously consider how to preserve them."

To those Federalists leaders who had been acquainted with the plans of 1804, the meaning of this allusion to the commercial States could not be doubtful. Least of all could Pickering's colleague in the Senate, who had so strenuously resisted the disunion scheme, fail to understand the drift of Pickering's leadership. John Quincy Adams, at whose growing influence this letter struck, had been from his earliest recollection, through his father's experience or his own, closely connected with political interests. During forty years he had been the sport of public turbulence, and for forty years he was yet to undergo every vicissitude of political failure and success; but in the range of his chequered life he was subjected to no other trial so severe as that which Pickering forced him to meet. In the path of duty he might doubtless face social and political ostracism, even in a town such as Boston then was, and defy it. Men as good as he had done as much, in many times and places; but to do this in support of a President whom he disliked and distrusted, for the sake of a policy in which he had no faith, was enough to shatter a character of iron. Fortunately for him, his temper was not one to seek relief in half-way measures. He had made a mistake in voting for an embargo without limit of time; but since no measure of resistance to Europe more vigorous than the embargo could gain support from either party, he accepted and defended it. He attended the Republican caucus January 23, and voted for George Clinton as President; and when Pickering flung down his challenge in the letter of February 16, Adams instantly took it up.

Governor Sullivan naturally declined to convey Senator Pickering's letter to the Legislature; but a copy had been sent to George Cabot, who caused it, March 9, to be published. The effect was violent. Passion took the place of reason, and swept the Federalists into Pickering's path. Governor Sullivan published a vigorous reply, but lost his temper in doing so, and became abusive where he should have been cool.[1] When Pickering's letter was received at Washington, Adams wrote an answer,[2] which reached Boston barely in time to be read before the election. He went over the history of the embargo; pointed out its relation to the Orders in Council; recapitulated the long list of English outrages; turned fiercely upon the British infatuation of Pickering's friends, and called upon them to make their choice between embargo and war: —

"If any statesman can point out another alternative I am ready to hear him, and for any practicable expedient to lend him every possible assistance. But let not that expedient be submission to trade under British licenses and British taxation. We are told that even under these restrictions we may yet trade to the British dominions, to Africa and China, and with the colonies of France, Spain, and Holland. I ask not how much of this trade would be left when our intercourse with the whole continent of Europe being cut off would leave us no means of purchase and no market for sale. I ask not what trade we could enjoy with the colonies of nations with which we should be at war. I ask not how long Britain would leave open to us avenues of trade which even in these very Orders of Council she boasts of leaving open as a special indulgence. If we yield the principle, we abandon all pretence to national sovereignty."

1 Interesting Correspondence (Boston, 1808).

2 Letter to the Hon. Harrison Gray Otis, by John Quincy Adams (Boston, 1808).

Thus the issue between a British and American party was sharply drawn. Governor Sullivan charged Pickering with an attempt to excite sedition and rebellion, and to bring about a dissolution of government. Adams made no mention of his colleague's name. In Massachusetts the modern canvass was unknown; newspapers and pamphlets took the place of speeches; the pulpit and tavern bar were the only hustings; and the public opinions of men in high official or social standing weighed heavily. The letters of Pickering, Sullivan, and Adams penetrated every part of the State, and on the issues raised by them the voters made their choice.

The result showed that Pickering's calculation on the embargo was sound. He failed to overthrow Governor Sullivan, who won his re-election by a majority of some twelve hundred in a total vote of about eighty-one thousand; but the Federalists gained in the new Legislature a decided majority, which immediately elected James Lloyd to succeed J. Q. Adams in the Senate, and adopted resolutions condemning the embargo. Adams instantly resigned his seat. The Legislature chose Lloyd to complete the unfinished term.

Thus the great State of Massachusetts fell back into Federalism. All, and more than all, that Jefferson's painful labors had gained, his embargo in a few weeks wasted. Had the evil stopped there no harm need have been feared; but the reaction went far beyond that point. The Federalists of 1801 were the national party of America; the Federalists of 1808 were a British faction in secret league with George Canning.

The British government watched closely these events. Rose's offensive and defensive alliance with Timothy Pickering and with the Washington representatives of the Essex Junto was not the only tie between Westminster and Boston. Of all British officials, the one most directly interested in American politics was Sir James Craig, then Governor of Lower Canada, who resided at Quebec, and had the strongest reason to guard against attack from the United States. In February, 1808, when the question of peace or war seemed hanging on the fate of Rose's mission, Sir James Craig was told by his secretary, H. W. Ryland, that an Englishman about to visit New England from Montreal would write back letters as he went, which might give valuable hints in regard to the probable conduct of the American government and people. The man's name was John Henry; and in reporting his letters to Lord Castlereagh as they arrived, Sir James Craig spoke highly of the writer: —

"Mr. Henry is a gentleman of considerable ability, and, I believe, well able to form a correct judgment on what he sees passing. He resided for some time in the United States, and is well acquainted with some of the leading people of Boston, to which place he was called very suddenly from Montreal, where he at present lives, by the intelligence he received that his agent there was among the sufferers by the recent measures of the American government. He has not the most distant idea that I should make this use of his correspondence, which therefore can certainly have no other view than that of an unreserved communication with his friend who is my secretary."[1]

Sir James Craig had something to learn in regard to volunteer diplomatists of Henry's type; but being in no way responsible for the man, he read the letters which came addressed to Ryland, but which were evidently meant for the Governor of Canada, and proved to be worth his reading. The first was written March 2, from Swanton in Vermont, ten miles from the Canada border: —

"You will have learned that Congress has passed a law prohibiting the transport of any American produce to Canada, and the collector at this frontier post expects by this day's mail instructions to carry it into rigorous execution. The sensibility excited by this measure among the inhabitants in the northern part of Vermont is inconceivable. The roads are covered with sleighs, and the whole country seems employed in conveying their produce beyond the line of separation. The clamor against the Government — and this measure particularly — is such that you may expect to hear of an engagement between the officers of government and the sovereign people on the first effort to stop the introduction of that vast quantity of lumber and produce which is prepared for the Montreal market."

[1] Sir J. H. Craig to Lord Castlereagh, April 10, 1808; MSS. British Archives.

From Windsor in Vermont, March 6, Henry wrote again, announcing that the best-informed people believed war to be inevitable between the United States and England. From Windsor Henry went on to Boston, where he found himself at home. Acquainted with the best people, and admitted freely into society,[1] he heard all that was said. March 10, when he had been not more than a day or two in Boston, he wrote to Ryland, enclosing a Boston newspaper of the same morning, in which Senator Pickering's letter to Governor Sullivan appeared and the approaching departure of Rose was announced. Already he professed to be well-advised of what was passing in private Federalist councils.

"The men of talents, property, and influence in Boston are resolved to adopt without delay every expedient to avert the impending calamity, and to express their determination not to be at war with Great Britain in such a manner as to indicate resistance to the government in the last resort. . . . Very active, though secret, measures are taken to rouse the people from the lethargy which if long continued must end in their subjection to the modern Attila."

March 18 Henry wrote again, announcing that the fear of war had vanished, and that Jefferson meant to depend upon his embargo and a system of irritation: —

"It is, however, to be expected that the evil will produce its own cure, and that in a few months more of

[1] Quincy's Life of Josiah Quincy, p. 250.

suffering and privation of all the benefits of commerce the people of the New England States will be ready to withdraw from the confederacy, establish a separate government, and adopt a policy congenial with their interests and happiness. For a measure of this sort the men of talents and property are now ready, and only wait until the continued distress of the multitude shall make them acquainted with the source of their misery, and point out an efficient remedy."

These letters, immediately on their receipt at Quebec, were enclosed by Sir James Craig to Lord Castlereagh in a letter marked "Private," dated April 10, and sent by the Halifax mail, as the quickest mode of conveyance.[1] Meanwhile Henry completed his business in Boston and returned to Montreal, where he arrived April 11, and three days afterward wrote again to Ryland at Quebec: —

"I attended a private meeting of several of the principal characters in Boston, where the questions of *immediate* and *ultimate* necessity were discussed. In the first, all agreed that memorials from all the towns (beginning with Boston) should be immediately transmitted to the Administration, and a firm determination expressed that they will not co-operate in a war against England. I distributed several copies of a memorial to that effect in some of the towns in Vermont on my return. The measure of ultimate necessity which I suggested I found in Boston some unwillingness to consider. It was 'that in case of a declaration of war the State of Massachu-

[1] Sir James Craig to Lord Castlereagh, April 10, 1808; MSS. British Archives, Lower Canada, vol. cvii.

setts should treat separately for itself, and obtain from Great Britain a guaranty of its integrity.' Although it was not deemed necessary to decide on a measure of this sort at this moment, it was considered as a very probable step in the last resort. In fine, every man whose opinion I could ascertain was opposed to a war, and attached to the cause of England."

That Henry reported with reasonable truth the general character of Federalist conversation was proved by the nearly simultaneous letters of Pickering to Rose; but his activity did not stop there. In a final letter of April 25 he gave a more precise account of the measures to be taken: —

"In my last I omitted to mention to you that among the details of the plan for averting from the Northern States the miseries of French alliance and friendship, individuals are selected in the several towns on the seaboard and throughout the country to correspond and act in concert with the superintending committee at Boston. The benefits of any organized plan over the distinct and desultory exertions of individuals are, I think, very apparent. Whether this confederacy of the men of talents and property be regarded as a diversion of the power of the nation, as an efficient means of resistance to the general government in the event of a war, or the nucleus of an English party that will soon be formidable enough to negotiate for the friendship of Great Britain, it is in all respects very important; and I have well-founded reason to hope that a few months more of suffering and the suspension of everything collateral to commerce will reconcile the multitude to any men and any system which will promise them relief."

May 5 the second part of Henry's correspondence was forwarded by Sir James Craig to Lord Castlereagh, who could compare its statements with those of Pickering, and with the reports of Rose. The alliance between the New England Federalists and the British Tories was made. Nothing remained but to concentrate against Jefferson the forces at their command.

CHAPTER XI.

THE embargo had lasted less than four months, when April 19 the President at Washington was obliged to issue a proclamation announcing that on Lake Champlain and in the adjacent country persons were combined for the purpose of forming insurrections against the laws, and that the military power of the government must aid in quelling such insurrections.[1] Immense rafts of lumber were collecting near the boundary line; and report said that one such raft, near half a mile long, carried a ball-proof fort, and was manned by five or six hundred armed men prepared to defy the custom-house officers. This raft was said to contain the surplus produce of Vermont for a year past, — wheat, potash, pork, and beef, — and to be worth upward of three hundred thousand dollars.[2] The governor of Vermont ordered out a detachment of militia to stop this traffic, and the governor of New York ordered another detachment to co-operate with that of Vermont. May 8 rumors of a battle were afloat, and of forty men killed or

[1] Proclamation of April 19, 1808; Annals of Congress, 1808–1809, p. 580.

[2] New York Evening Post, May, 1808

wounded.[1] The stories were untrue, but the rafts escaped, the customs officials not venturing to stop them.

Reports of this open defiance and insurrection on the Canada frontier reached Washington at the same time with other reports which revealed endless annoyances elsewhere. If the embargo was to coerce England or France, it must stop supplies to the West Indian colonies, and prevent the escape of cotton or corn for the artisans of Europe. The embargo aimed at driving England to desperation, but not at famishing America; yet the President found himself at a loss to do the one without doing the other. Nearly all commerce between the States was by coasting-vessels. If the coasting-trade should be left undisturbed, every schooner that sailed from an American port was sure to allege that by stress of weather or by the accidents of navigation it had been obliged to stop at some port of Nova Scotia or the West Indies, and there to leave its cargo. Only the absolute prohibition of the coasting-trade could prevent these evasions; but to prohibit the coasting-trade was to sever the Union. The political tie might remain, but no other connection could survive. Without the coasting-trade New England would be deprived of bread, and her industries would perish; Charleston and New Orleans would stagnate in unapproachable solitude.

Jefferson proclaimed the existence of an insur-

[1] National Intelligencer, May 23, 1808.

rection on the Canadian frontier shortly before the adjournment of Congress. Immediately after the adjournment he took in hand the more serious difficulties of the coasting-trade. The experiment of peaceable coercion was at last to have full trial, and Jefferson turned to the task with energy that seemed to his friends excessive, but expressed the vital interest he felt in the success of a theory on which his credit as a statesman depended. The crisis was peculiarly his own; and he assumed the responsibility for every detail of its management.

May 6 the President wrote to Gallatin a letter containing general directions to detain in port every coasting-vessel which could be regarded as suspicious. His orders were sweeping. The power of the embargo as a coercive weapon was to be learned.

"In the outset of the business of detentions," said the President,[1] "I think it impossible to form precise rules. After a number of cases shall have arisen, they may probably be thrown into groups and subjected to rules. The great leading object of the Legislature was, and ours in execution of it ought to be, to give complete effect to the embargo laws. They have bidden agriculture, commerce, navigation to bow before that object, — to be nothing when in competition with that. Finding all their endeavors at general rules to be evaded, they finally gave us the power of detention as the panacea; and I am clear we ought to use it freely, that we may by a fair experiment know the power of this great weapon, the embargo."

[1] Jefferson to Gallatin, May 6, 1808; Works, v. 287.

A few days later Jefferson repeated the warning in stronger language: "I place immense value in the experiment being fully made, how far an embargo may be an effectual weapon in future as well as on this occasion."[1]

"Where you are doubtful," continued the instructions to Gallatin, "consider me as voting for detention;" and every coasting-vessel was an object of doubt. On the same day with the letter of May 6 to the Secretary of the Treasury, the President wrote a circular to the governors of New Hampshire, Massachusetts, South Carolina, Georgia, and Orleans,—portions of the Union which consumed more wheat than they produced,—requesting them to issue certificates for such quantities of flour as were likely to be needed beyond their local supply. The certificates, directed to the collector of some port usually exporting flour, were to be issued to "any merchant in whom you have confidence."[2] All other shipments of produce were objects of suspicion. "I really think," wrote the President to Gallatin, "it would be well to recommend to every collector to consider every shipment of provisions, lumber, flaxseed, tar, cotton, tobacco, etc.,—enumerating the articles,—as sufficiently suspicious for detention and reference here." He framed new instructions to the governors

[1] Jefferson to the Secretary of the Treasury, May 15, 1808; Works, v. 289.

[2] Jefferson to the Governors of Orleans, etc., May 6, 1808; Works, v. 285.

on this idea: "We find it necessary to consider every vessel as suspicious which has on board any articles of domestic produce in demand at foreign markets, and most especially provisions."[1]

Gallatin, having early declared his want of faith in the embargo as a coercive measure, was the more bound to prove that his private opinion did not prevent him from giving full trial to the experiment which Executive and Legislature had ordered him to make. He set himself resolutely to the unpleasant task. Instead of following the President's plan of indiscriminate suspicion and detention, he preferred to limit the suspicious cargo in value, so that no vessel could carry provisions to the amount of more than one-eighth of the bond; but before he could put his system in force, new annoyances arose. Governor Sullivan of Massachusetts, under the President's circular, issued certificates before July 15 to the amount of fifty thousand barrels of flour and one hundred thousand bushels of corn, besides rice and rye. Gallatin complained to the President,[2] who instantly wrote to the governor of Massachusetts an order to stop importing provisions:—

"As these supplies, although called for within the space of two months, will undoubtedly furnish the consumption of your State for a much longer time, I have

[1] Jefferson to Gallatin, May 16, 1808; Gallatin's Writings, i. 389.

[2] Gallatin to Jefferson, July 15, 1808; Gallatin's Writings, i. 394.

thought advisable to ask the favor of your Excellency, after the receipt of this letter, to discontinue issuing any other certificates, that we may not unnecessarily administer facilities to the evasion of the embargo laws."[1]

That Massachusetts already on the brink of rebellion should tolerate such dictation could hardly be expected; and it was fortunate for Jefferson that the Federalists had failed to elect a governor of their own stripe. Even Sullivan, Democrat as he was, could not obey the President's request, and excused his disobedience in a letter which was intended to convince Jefferson that the people of Massachusetts were the best judges of the amount of food they needed.

"The seaport towns," Sullivan wrote,[2] "are supported almost entirely by bread from the Southern and Middle States. The interior of this State live on a mixture of Indian corn and rye in common regimen, but their fine bread and pastry depend on the importations from the southward, carted into the interior. The country towns consume more imported flour than is equivalent for all the grain they carry to market in the seaport towns. Their hogs and poultry consume much Indian corn. The rice imported here from the southward, since the Embargo Act, has been very inconsiderable. The Indian corn is in greater quantities, but that would not find a market in the British or French dominions if there was no embargo. This is an article of great demand here,

[1] Jefferson to Sullivan, July 16, 1808; Works, v. 317.

[2] Sullivan to Jefferson, July 23, 1808; Jefferson MSS.

not as bread, but as sustenance for carriage-horses, draft-horses, etc., and the quantity consumed is really astonishing."

Sullivan admitted that the habits of the Massachusetts people, contracted under the royal government and still continued, led to the evasion of commercial laws; but he told the President what would be the result of an arbitrary interference with their supplies of food:—

"You may depend upon it that three weeks after these certificates shall be refused, an artificial and actual scarcity will involve this State in mobs, riots, and convulsions, pretendedly on account of the embargo. Your enemies will have an additional triumph, and your friends suffer new mortifications."[1]

Governor Sullivan was a man of ability and courage. Popular and successful, he had broken the long sway of Federalism in Massachusetts, and within a few months had carried his re-election against the utmost exertions of the Essex Junto; but he had seen John Quincy Adams fall a sacrifice to the embargo, and he had no wish to be himself the next victim of Jefferson's theories. His situation was most difficult, and he warned the President that the embargo was making it worse:—

"The embargo has been popular with what is denominated the Republican part of the State; but as it does not appear from anything that has taken place in the European Powers that it has had the expected effect

[1] Sullivan to Jefferson, July 21, 1808; Jefferson MSS.

there, it has begun to lose its support from the public opinion. . . . There are judicious men in this State who are friends to the present Administration, and who have been in favor of the embargo as a measure of expedience which ought to have been adopted by the government, but who now express great doubts as to the power of enforcing it much longer under present circumstances. They do not perceive any of the effects from it that the nation expected; they do not perceive foreign Powers influenced by it, as they anticipated. They are convinced, as they say, that the people of this State must soon be reduced to suffering and poverty. . . . These men consider the embargo as operating very forcibly to the subversion of the Republican interest here. Should the measure be much longer continued, and then fail of producing any important public good, I imagine it will be a decisive blow against the Republican interest now supported in this Commonwealth."[1]

Jefferson resented Sullivan's conduct. A few days afterward he wrote to General Dearborn, the Secretary of War, who was then in Maine, warning him to be ready to support the measure which Sullivan had declined to adopt.

"Yours of July 27 is received," Jefferson said.[2] "It confirms the accounts we receive from others that the infractions of the embargo in Maine and Massachusetts are open. I have removed Pope, of New Bedford, for worse than negligence. The collector of Sullivan is on the totter. The Tories of Boston openly threaten insurrection if their importation of flour is stopped. The next

[1] Sullivan to Jefferson, July 23, 1808; Jefferson MSS.

[2] Jefferson to Lincoln, Aug. 9, 1808; Works, v. 334.

post will stop it. I fear your Governor [Sullivan] is not up to the tone of these parricides, and I hope on the first symptom of an open opposition of the law by force you will fly to the scene, and aid in suppressing any commotion."

Blood was soon shed, but Jefferson did not shrink. The new army was stationed along the Canada frontier. The gunboats and frigates patrolled the coast. On every side dangers and difficulties accumulated. "I did not expect a crop of so sudden and rank growth of fraud and open opposition by force could have grown up in the United States."[1] At Newburyport an armed mob on the wharf prevented the custom-house officers from detaining a vessel about to sail. The collectors and other officers were ill-disposed, or were harassed by suits at law for illegal detentions. Rebellion and disunion stared Jefferson in the face, but only caused him to challenge an outbreak and to invite violence.

"That the Federalists may attempt insurrection is possible," he wrote to Gallatin,[2] "and also that the governor would sink before it; but the Republican part of the State, and that portion of the Federalists who approve the embargo in their judgments, and at any rate would not court mob law, would crush it in embryo. I have some time ago written to General Dearborn to be on the alert on such an occasion, and to take direction of the public authority on the spot. Such an incident will rally the whole body of Republicans of every

[1] Jefferson to Gallatin, Aug. 11, 1808; Works, v. 336.

[2] Jefferson to Gallatin, Aug. 19, 1808; Works, v. 346.

shade to a single point, — that of supporting the public authority."

The Federalists knew when to rebel. Jefferson could teach them little on that subject. They meant first to overthrow Jefferson himself, and were in a fair way to gratify their wish; for the people of New England — Republican and Federalist alike — were rapidly rallying to common hatred of the President. As winter approached, the struggle between Jefferson and Massachusetts became on both sides vindictive. He put whole communities under his ban. He stopped the voyage of every vessel "in which any person is concerned, either in interest or in navigating her, who has ever been concerned in interest or in the navigation of a vessel which has at any time before entered a foreign port contrary to the views of the embargo laws, and under any pretended distress or duress whatever."[1] When a permit was asked for the schooner "Caroline," of Buckstown on the Penobscot, Jefferson replied, —

"This is the first time that the character of the place has been brought under consideration as an objection. Yet a general disobedience to the laws in any place must have weight toward refusing to give them any facilities to evade. In such a case we may fairly require positive proof that the individual of a town tainted with a general spirit of disobedience has never said or done anything himself to countenance that spirit."[2]

[1] Jefferson to Gallatin, Dec. 7, 1808; Works, v. 396.
[2] Jefferson to Gallatin, Nov. 13, 1808; Works, v. 386.

Jefferson went still further in his reply to a petition from the island of Nantucket for food. "Our opinion here is that that place has been so deeply concerned in smuggling, that if it wants it is because it has illegally sent away what it ought to have retained for its own consumption."[1]

Of all the old Republican arguments for a policy of peace, the commonest was that a standing army would be dangerous, not to foreign enemies, but to popular liberties; yet the first use of the new army and gunboats was against fellow-citizens. New England was chiefly controlled by the navy; but in New York the army was needed and was employed. Open insurrection existed there. Besides forcible resistance offered to the law, no one was ignorant that the collectors shut their eyes to smuggling, and that juries, in defiance of court and President, refused to indict rioters. Governor Tompkins announced that Oswego was in active insurrection, and called on the President to issue a proclamation to that effect.[2] Jefferson replied by offering to take into the United States service the militia required to suppress the riots, and begged Governor Tompkins to lead his troops in person. "I think it so important in example to crush these audacious proceedings and to make the offenders feel the consequences of individuals daring to oppose a law by

[1] Jefferson to Levi Lincoln, Nov. 13, 1808; Works, v. 387.

[2] Gallatin to Jefferson, July 29, 1808; Gallatin's Writings, i, 396.

force, that no effort should be spared to compass this object."[1]

When permission was asked to establish a packet on Lake Champlain, "I do not think this is a time," replied Jefferson, "for opening new channels of intercourse with Canada and multiplying the means of smuggling."[2] The people who lived on the shores of Lake Champlain might object to such interference in their affairs, but could not deny the force of Jefferson's reasoning. Another application of a different kind was rejected on grounds that seemed to give to the President general supervision over the diet of the people: —

> "The declaration of the bakers of New York that their citizens will be dissatisfied, under the present circumstances of their country, to eat bread of the flour of their own State, is equally a libel on the produce and citizens of the State. . . . If this prevails, the next application will be for vessels to go to New York for the pippins of that State, because they are higher flavored than the same species of apples growing in other States."[3]

The same sumptuary rule applied to Louisiana. "You know I have been averse to letting Atlantic flour go to New Orleans merely that they may have the *whitest* bread possible."[4]

[1] Jefferson to Governor Tompkins, Aug. 15, 1808; Works, v. 343.

[2] Jefferson to the Secretary of the Treasury, Sept. 9, 1808; Works, v. 363.

[3] Jefferson to Gallatin, July 12, 1808; Works, v. 307.

[4] Jefferson to Gallatin, Sept. 9, 1808; Works, v. 363.

The President seemed alone to feel this passionate earnestness on behalf of the embargo. His Cabinet looked on with alarm and disgust. Madison took no share in the task of enforcement. Robert Smith sent frigates and gunboats hither and thither, but made no concealment of his feelings. "Most fervently," he wrote to Gallatin, "ought we to pray to be relieved from the various embarrassments of this said embargo. Upon it there will in some of the States, in the course of the next two months, assuredly be engendered monsters. Would that we could be placed on proper ground for calling in this mischief-making busy-body."[1] Smith talked freely, while Gallatin, whose opinion was probably the same, said little, and labored to carry out the law, but seemed at times disposed to press on the President's attention the deformities of his favorite monster.

"I am perfectly satisfied," wrote Gallatin to the President July 29,[2] "that if the embargo must be persisted in any longer, two principles must necessarily be adopted in order to make it sufficient: First, that not a single vessel shall be permitted to move without the special permission of the Executive; Second, that the collectors be invested with the general power of seizing property anywhere, and taking the rudders, or otherwise effectually preventing the departure of any vessel in harbor, though ostensibly intended to remain there, — and that

[1] Smith to Gallatin, Aug. 1, 1808; Adams's Gallatin, p. 373.

[2] Gallatin to Jefferson, July 19, 1808; Gallatin's Writings, i. 396.

without being liable to personal suits. I am sensible that such arbitrary powers are equally dangerous and odious; but a restrictive measure of the nature of the embargo, applied to a nation under such circumstances as the United States, cannot be enforced without the assistance of means as strong as the measure itself. To that legal authority to prevent, seize, and detain, must be added a sufficient physical force to carry it into effect; and although I believe that in our seaports little difficulty would be encountered, we must have a little army along the Lakes and British lines generally. . . . That in the present situation of the world every effort should be attempted to preserve the peace of this nation, cannot be doubted; but if the criminal party-rage of Federalists and Tories shall have so far succeeded as to defeat our endeavors to obtain that object by the only measure that could possibly have effected it, we must submit and prepare for war."

"I mean generally to express an opinion," continued the secretary, "founded on the experience of this summer, that Congress must either invest the Executive with the most arbitrary powers and sufficient force to carry the embargo into effect, or give it up altogether." That Jefferson should permit a member of his Cabinet to suggest the assumption of "the most arbitrary powers;" that he should tolerate the idea of using means "equally dangerous and odious," — seemed incredible; but his reply showed no sign of offence. He instantly responded, —

"I am satisfied with you that if Orders and Decrees are not repealed, and a continuance of the embargo is preferred to war (which sentiment is universal here), Congress must legalize all means which may be necessary to obtain its end."[1]

If repeated and menacing warnings from the people, the State authorities, and officers of the national government failed to produce an impression on the President's mind, he was little likely to regard what came from the Judiciary; yet the sharpest of his irritations was caused by a judge whom he had himself, in 1804, placed on the Supreme Bench to counteract Marshall's influence. Some merchants of Charleston, with consent of the collector and district-attorney, applied for a mandamus to oblige the collector of that town to clear certain ships for Baltimore. The collector admitted that he believed the voyage to be intended in good faith, and that under the Embargo Law he had no right of detention; but he laid Secretary Gallatin's instructions before the court. The case was submitted without argument, and Justice William Johnson, of the South Carolina circuit, — a native of South Carolina, and a warm friend of the President, — decided that the Act of Congress did not warrant detention, and that without the sanction of law the collector was not justified by instructions from the Executive in increasing the restraints upon commerce. The mandamus issued.

These proceedings troubled but did not check the President. "I saw them with great concern," he

[1] Jefferson to Gallatin, Aug. 11, 1808; Works, v. 336.

wrote to the governor of South Carolina,[1] "because of the quarter from whence they came, and where they could not be ascribed to any political waywardness." Rodney, the attorney-general, undertook to overrule Justice Johnson's law, and wrote, under the President's instructions, an official opinion that the court had no power to issue a mandamus in such a case. This opinion was published in the newspapers at the end of July, "an act unprecedented in the history of executive conduct," which in a manner forced Justice Johnson into a newspaper controversy. The Judge's defence of his course was temperate and apparently convincing to himself, although five years afterward he delivered an opinion[2] of the whole Supreme Court in a similar case, "unquestionably inconsistent" with his embargo decision, which he then placed on technical ground. He never regained Jefferson's confidence; and so effective was the ban that in the following month of December the Georgia grand-jury, in his own circuit, made him the object of a presentment for "improper interference with the Executive."

If the conduct of Justice Johnson only stimulated the President's exercise of power, the constitutional arguments of Federalist lawyers and judges were unlikely to have any better effect; yet to a Virginia Republican of 1798 no question could have deeper

[1] Jefferson to Governor Pinckney, July 18, 1808; Works, v. 322.

[2] McIntyre *v*. Wood, March, 1813; 7 Cranch, p. 504.

interest than that of the constitutionality of the embargo. The subject had already been discussed in Congress, and had called out a difference of opinion. There, Randolph argued against the constitutionality in a speech never reported, which turned on the distinction between regulating commerce and destroying it; between a restriction limited in time and scope, and an interdict absolute and permanent. The opponents of the embargo system, both Federalists and Republicans, took the same ground. The Constitution, they said, empowered Congress "to *regulate* commerce with foreign nations, and among the several States, and with the Indian tribes;" but no one ever supposed it to grant Congress the power "to *prohibit* commerce with foreign nations, and among the several States, and with the Indian tribes." Had such words been employed, the Constitution could not have gained the vote of a single State.

History has nothing to do with law except to record the development of legal principles. The question whether the embargo was or was not Constitutional depended for an answer on the decision of Congress, President, and Judiciary, and the assent of the States. Whatever unanimous decision these political bodies might make, no matter how extravagant, was law until it should be reversed. No theory could control the meaning of the Constitution; but the relation between facts and theories was a political matter, and between the embargo and the old Virginia theory of the Constitution no relation could be imagined. Whatever else was doubtful, no one could doubt that under the doctrine of State-rights and the rules of strict construction the embargo was unconstitutional. Only by the widest theories of liberal construction could its constitutionality be sustained.

The arguments in its favor were arguments which had been once regarded as fatal to public liberty. The first was made by Richard M. Johnson of Kentucky: "If we have power to lay an embargo for one day, have we not the power to renew it at the end of that day? If for sixty days, have we not the power to renew it again? Would it not amount to the same thing? If we pass a law to expire within a limited term, we may renew it at the end of that term; and there is no difference between a power to do this, and a power to pass laws without specified limit."[1] This principle, if sound, might be applied to the right of habeas corpus or of free speech, to the protection of American manufactures or to the issue of paper money as a legal tender; and whenever such application should be made, the Union must submit to take its chance of the consequences sure to follow the removal of specified limits to power. Another argument was used by David R. Williams, a representative South Carolinian. "The embargo is not an annihilation but a suspension of commerce," he urged,[2] "to regain the advantages of which it has

[1] Annals of Congress, 1807–1808, p. 2091.
[2] Annals of Congress, 1807–1808, p. 2130.

been robbed." If Congress had the right to regulate commerce for such a purpose in 1808, South Carolina seemed to have no excuse for questioning, twenty years later, the constitutionality of a protective system. Still another argument was used by George W. Campbell of Tennessee.

"A limited embargo," he said,[1] "can only mean an embargo that is to terminate at some given time; and the length of time, if a hundred years, will not change the character of the embargo, — it is still limited. If it be constitutional to lay it for one day, it must be equally so to lay it for ten days or a hundred days or as many years, — it would still be a limited embargo; and no one will, I presume, deny that an embargo laid for such a length of time, and one laid without limitation, would in reality and to all practical purposes be the same."

This reasoning was supported by an immense majority in both Houses of Congress; was accepted as sound by the Executive, and roused no protest from the legislature of any Southern State. So far as concerned all these high political authorities, the principle was thus settled that the Constitution, under the power to regulate commerce, conferred upon Congress the power to suspend foreign commerce forever; to suspend or otherwise regulate domestic and inter-state commerce; to subject all industry to governmental control, if such interference in the opinion of Congress was necessary or

[1] Annals of Congress, p. 2147.

proper for carrying out its purpose; and finally, to vest in the President discretionary power to execute or to suspend the system, in whole or in part.

The Judiciary had still to be consulted. In the September Term, 1808, an embargo case was argued at Salem before John Davis, judge of the District Court for Massachusetts; and Samuel Dexter, the ablest lawyer in New England, urged the constitutional objections to the embargo with all the force that ability and conviction could give. No sounder Federalist than Judge Davis sat on the bench; but although the newspapers of his party were declaiming against the constitutionality of the law, and although Chief-Justice Parsons, of the Massachusetts Supreme Court, the most eminent legal authority in the State, lent his private influence on the same side, Judge Davis calmly laid down the old Federalist rule of broad construction. His opinion, elaborately argued and illustrated, was printed in every newspaper.

"Stress has been laid in argument," he said, "on the word 'regulate,' as implying in itself a limitation. Power to 'regulate,' it is said, cannot be understood to give a power to annihilate. To this it may be replied that the Acts under consideration, though of very ample extent, do not operate as a prohibition of all foreign commerce. It will be admitted that partial prohibitions are authorized by the expression; and how shall the degree or extent of the prohibition be adjusted but by the discretion of the national government, to whom the subject appears to be committed."

In the Federalist spirit the Judge invoked the "necessary and proper" clause, which had been the cloak for every assumption of doubtful powers; and then passed to the doctrine of "inherent sovereignty," the radical line of division between the party of President Washington and that of President Jefferson: —

"Further, the power to regulate commerce is not to be confined to the adoption of measures exclusively beneficial to commerce itself, or tending to its advancement; but in our national system, as in all modern sovereignties, it is also to be considered as an instrument for other purposes of general policy and interest. The mode of its management is a consideration of great delicacy and importance; but the national right or power to adapt regulations of commerce to other purposes than the mere advancement of commerce appears to me unquestionable."

After drawing these conclusions from the power to regulate commerce, the Judge went a step further, and summoned to his aid the spirits which haunted the dreams of every true Republican, — the power of war, and necessity of State: —

"Congress has power to declare war. It of course has power to prepare for war; and the time, the manner, and the measure, in the application of constitutional means, seem to be left to its wisdom and discretion. Foreign intercourse becomes in such times a subject of peculiar interest, and its regulation forms an obvious and essential branch of federal administration. . . . It seems to have been admitted in the argument that State necessity might justify a limited embargo, or suspension of all foreign commerce; but if Congress have the power, for purposes of safety, of preparation, or counteraction, to suspend commercial intercourse with foreign nations, where do we find them limited as to the duration more than as to the manner and extent of the measure?"

Against this remarkable decision Dexter did not venture to appeal. Strong as his own convictions were, he knew the character of Chief-Justice Marshall's law too well to hope for success at Washington. One of Marshall's earliest constitutional decisions had deduced from the power of Congress to pay debts the right for government to assume a preference over all other creditors in satisfying its claims on the assets of a bankrupt.[1] Constructive power could hardly go further; and the habit of mind which led to such a conclusion would hardly shrink from sustaining Judge Davis's law.

Yet the embargo, in spite of Executive, Legislative, Judicial, and State authorities, rankled in the side of the Constitution. Even Joseph Story, though in after life a convert to Marshall's doctrines, could never wholly reconcile himself to the legislation of 1808.

"I have ever," he wrote, "considered the embargo a measure which went to the utmost limit of constructive power under the Constitution. It stands upon the ex-

[1] United States *v.* Fisher and others, February Term, 1805; Cranch's Reports, ii. 358–405.

treme verge of the Constitution, being in its very form and terms an unlimited prohibition or suspension of foreign commerce."[1]

That President Jefferson should exercise "dangerous and odious" powers, carrying the extremest principles of his Federalist predecessors to their extremest results; that he should in doing so invite bloodshed, strain his military resources, quarrel with the State authorities of his own party and with judges whom he had himself made; that he should depend for constitutional law on Federalist judges whose doctrines he had hitherto believed fatal to liberty,—these were the first fruits of the embargo. After such an experience, if he or his party again raised the cry of State-rights, or of strict construction, the public might, with some foundation of reason, set such complaints aside as factious and frivolous, and even, in any other mouth than that of John Randolph, as treasonable.

[1] Story's Life of Story, i. 185.

CHAPTER XII.

THE embargo was an experiment in politics well worth making. In the scheme of President Jefferson's statesmanship, non-intercourse was the substitute for war, — the weapon of defence and coercion which saved the cost and danger of supporting army or navy, and spared America the brutalities of the Old World. Failure of the embargo meant in his mind not only a recurrence to the practice of war, but to every political and social evil that war had always brought in its train. In such a case the crimes and corruptions of Europe, which had been the object of his political fears, must, as he believed, sooner or later teem in the fat soil of America. To avert a disaster so vast, was a proper motive for statesmanship, and justified disregard for smaller interests. Jefferson understood better than his friends the importance of his experiment; and when in pursuing his object he trampled upon personal rights and public principles, he did so, as he avowed in the Louisiana purchase, because he believed that a higher public interest required the sacrifice: —

"My principle is, that the conveniences of our citizens shall yield reasonably, and their taste greatly, to the importance of giving the present experiment so fair a trial that on future occasions our legislators may know with certainty how far they may count on it as an engine for national purposes."[1]

Hence came his repeated entreaties for severity, even to the point of violence and bloodshed:—

"I do consider the severe enforcement of the embargo to be of an importance not to be measured by money, for our future government as well as present objects."[2]

Everywhere, on all occasions, he proclaimed that embargo was the alternative to war. The question next to be decided was brought by this means into the prominence it deserved. Of the two systems of statesmanship, which was the most costly,—which the most efficient?

The dread of war, radical in the Republican theory, sprang not so much from the supposed waste of life or resources as from the retroactive effects which war must exert upon the form of government; but the experience of a few months showed that the embargo as a system was rapidly leading to the same effects. Indeed, the embargo and the Louisiana purchase taken together were more destructive to the theory and practice of a Virginia republic than any foreign war was likely to be. Personal liberties and rights of property were more directly curtailed in the United States by embargo than in Great Britain by centuries of almost continuous foreign war. No one denied

[1] Jefferson to Gallatin, July 12, 1808; Works, v. 307.

[2] Jefferson to Robert Smith, July 16, 1808; Works v. 316.

that a permanent embargo strained the Constitution to the uttermost tension; and even the Secretary of the Treasury and the President admitted that it required the exercise of most arbitrary, odious, and dangerous powers. From this point of view the system was quickly seen to have few advantages. If American liberties must perish, they might as well be destroyed by war as be stifled by non-intercourse.

While the constitutional cost of the two systems was not altogether unlike, the economical cost was a point not easily settled. No one could say what might be the financial expense of embargo as compared with war. Yet Jefferson himself in the end admitted that the embargo had no claim to respect as an economical measure. The Boston Federalists estimated that the net American loss of income, exclusive of that on freights, could not be less than ten per cent for interest and profit on the whole export of the country,— or ten million eight hundred thousand dollars on a total export value of one hundred and eight millions.[1] This estimate was extravagant, even if the embargo had been wholly responsible for cutting off American trade; it represented in fact the loss resulting to America from Napoleon's decrees, the British orders, and the embargo taken together. Yet at least the embargo was more destructive than war would have been to the interests of foreign commerce. Even in the worst of foreign wars American commerce could

[1] Speech of Josiah Quincy, Nov. 28, 1808; Annals of Congress, 1808, 1809, p. 543.

not be wholly stopped, — some outlet for American produce must always remain open, some inward bound ships would always escape the watch of a blockading squadron. Even in 1814, after two years of war, and when the coast was stringently blockaded, the American Treasury collected six million dollars from imports; but in 1808, after the embargo was in full effect, the customs yielded only a few thousand dollars on cargoes that happened to be imported for some special purpose. The difference was loss, to the disadvantage of embargo. To this must be added loss of freight, decay of ships and produce, besides enforced idleness to a corresponding extent; and finally the cost of a war if the embargo system should fail.

In other respects the system was still costly. The citizen was not killed, but he was partially paralyzed. Government did not waste money or life, but prevented both money and labor from having their former value. If long continued, embargo must bankrupt the government almost as certainly as war; if not long continued, the immediate shock to industry was more destructive than war would have been. The expense of war proved, five years afterward, to be about thirty million dollars a year, and of this sum much the larger portion was pure loss; but in 1808, owing to the condition of Europe, the expense need not have exceeded twenty millions, and the means at hand were greater. The effect of the embargo was certainly no greater than the effect of war in stimulating domestic industry. In either case the stimulus was temporary and ineffective; but the embargo cut off the resources of credit and capital, while war gave both an artificial expansion. The result was that while embargo saved perhaps twenty millions of dollars a year and some thousands of lives which war would have consumed, it was still an expensive system, and in some respects more destructive than war itself to national wealth.

The economical was less serious than the moral problem. The strongest objection to war was not its waste of money or even of life; for money and life in political economy were worth no more than they could be made to produce. A worse evil was the lasting harm caused by war to the morals of mankind, which no system of economy could calculate. The reign of brute force and brutal methods corrupted and debauched society, making it blind to its own vices and ambitious only for mischief. Yet even on that ground the embargo had few advantages. The peaceable coercion which Jefferson tried to substitute for war was less brutal, but hardly less mischievous, than the evil it displaced. The embargo opened the sluice-gates of social corruption. Every citizen was tempted to evade or defy the laws. At every point along the coast and frontier the civil, military, and naval services were brought in contact with corruption; while every man in private life was placed under strong motives to corrupt. Every article produced or consumed in the country became an object of speculation; every form of industry became a form of gambling. The rich could alone profit in the end; while the poor must sacrifice at any loss the little they could produce.

If war made men brutal, at least it made them strong; it called out the qualities best fitted to survive in the struggle for existence. To risk life for one's country was no mean act even when done for selfish motives; and to die that others might more happily live was the highest act of self-sacrifice to be reached by man. War, with all its horrors, could purify as well as debase; it dealt with high motives and vast interests; taught courage, discipline, and stern sense of duty. Jefferson must have asked himself in vain what lessons of heroism or duty were taught by his system of peaceable coercion, which turned every citizen into an enemy of the laws,—preaching the fear of war and of self-sacrifice, making many smugglers and traitors, but not a single hero.

If the cost of the embargo was extravagant in its effects on the Constitution, the economy, and the morals of the nation, its political cost to the party in power was ruinous. War could have worked no more violent revolution. The trial was too severe for human nature to endure. At a moment's notice, without avowing his true reasons, President Jefferson bade foreign commerce to cease. As the order was carried along the seacoast, every artisan dropped his tools, every merchant closed his doors, every ship was dismantled. American produce — wheat, timber, cotton, tobacco, rice — dropped in value or became unsalable; every imported article rose in price; wages stopped; swarms of debtors became bankrupt; thousands of sailors hung idle round the wharves trying to find employment on coasters, and escape to the West Indies or Nova Scotia. A reign of idleness began; and the men who were not already ruined felt that their ruin was only a matter of time.

The British traveller, Lambert, who visited New York in 1808, described it as resembling a place ravaged by pestilence:[1] —

> "The port indeed was full of shipping, but they were dismantled and laid up; their decks were cleared, their hatches fastened down, and scarcely a sailor was to be found on board. Not a box, bale, cask, barrel, or package was to be seen upon the wharves. Many of the counting-houses were shut up, or advertised to be let; and the few solitary merchants, clerks, porters, and laborers that were to be seen were walking about with their hands in their pockets. The coffee-houses were almost empty; the streets, near the water-side, were almost deserted; the grass had begun to grow upon the wharves."

In New England, where the struggle of existence was keenest, the embargo struck like a thunderbolt, and society for a moment thought itself at an end. Foreign commerce and shipping were the life of the people, — the ocean, as Pickering said, was their farm. The outcry of suffering interests became every day

[1] Lambert's Travels, ii. 64, 65.

more violent, as the public learned that this paralysis was not a matter of weeks, but of months or years. New Englanders as a class were a law-abiding people; but from the earliest moments of their history they had largely qualified their obedience to the law by the violence with which they abused and the ingenuity with which they evaded it. Against the embargo and Jefferson they concentrated the clamor and passion of their keen and earnest nature. Rich and poor, young and old, joined in the chorus; and one lad, barely in his teens, published what he called "The Embargo: a Satire," — a boyish libel on Jefferson, which the famous poet and Democrat would afterward have given much to recall: —

> "And thou, the scorn of every patriot name,
> Thy country's ruin, and her councils' shame.
> . . . .
> Go, wretch! Resign the Presidential chair,
> Disclose thy secret measures, foul or fair;
> Go search with curious eye for hornèd frogs
> 'Mid the wild waste of Louisiana bogs;
> Or where Ohio rolls his turbid stream
> Dig for huge bones, thy glory and thy theme."[1]

The belief that Jefferson, sold to France, wished to destroy American commerce and to strike a deadly blow at New and Old England at once, maddened the sensitive temper of the people. Immense losses, sweeping away their savings and spreading bankruptcy through every village, gave ample cause for

[1] The Embargo; or Sketches of the Times. A Satire. By William Cullen Bryant. 1808.

their complaints. Yet in truth, New England was better able to defy the embargo than she was willing to suppose. She lost nothing except profits which the belligerents had in any case confiscated; her timber would not harm for keeping, and her fish were safe in the ocean. The embargo gave her almost a monopoly of the American market for domestic manufactures; no part of the country was so well situated or so well equipped for smuggling. Above all, she could easily economize. The New Englander knew better than any other American how to cut down his expenses to the uttermost point of parsimony; and even when he became bankrupt he had but to begin anew. His energy, shrewdness, and education were a capital which the embargo could not destroy, but rather helped to improve.

The growers of wheat and live stock in the Middle States were more hardly treated. Their wheat, reduced in value from two dollars to seventy-five cents a bushel, became practically unsalable. Debarred a market for their produce at a moment when every article of common use tended to rise in cost, they were reduced to the necessity of living on the produce of their farms; but the task was not then so difficult as in later times, and the cities still furnished local markets not to be despised. The manufacturers of Pennsylvania could not but feel the stimulus of the new demand; so violent a system of protection was never applied to them before or since. Probably for that reason the embargo was not so unpopular in

Pennsylvania as elsewhere, and Jefferson had nothing to fear from political revolution in this calm and plodding community.

The true burden of the embargo fell on the Southern States, but most severely upon the great State of Virginia. Slowly decaying, but still half patriarchal, Virginia society could neither economize nor liquidate. Tobacco was worthless; but four hundred thousand negro slaves must be clothed and fed, great establishments must be kept up, the social scale of living could not be reduced, and even bankruptcy could not clear a large landed estate without creating new encumbrances in a country where land and negroes were the only forms of property on which money could be raised. Stay-laws were tried, but served only to prolong the agony. With astonishing rapidity Virginia succumbed to ruin, while continuing to support the system that was draining her strength. No episode in American history was more touching than the generous devotion with which Virginia clung to the embargo, and drained the poison which her own President held obstinately to her lips. The cotton and rice States had less to lose, and could more easily bear bankruptcy; ruin was to them — except in Charleston — a word of little meaning; but the old society of Virginia could never be restored. Amid the harsh warnings of John Randolph it saw its agonies approach; and its last representative, heir to all its honors and dignities, President Jefferson himself woke from his long dream of power only to find his own fortunes buried in the ruin he had made.

Except in a state of society verging on primitive civilization, the stoppage of all foreign intercourse could not have been attempted by peaceable means. The attempt to deprive the laborer of sugar, salt, tea, coffee, molasses, and rum; to treble the price of every yard of coarse cottons and woollens; to reduce by one half the wages of labor, and to double its burdens, — this was a trial more severe than war; and even when attempted by the whole continent of Europe, with all the resources of manufactures and wealth which the civilization of a thousand years had supplied, the experiment required the despotic power of Napoleon and the united armies of France, Austria, and Russia to carry it into effect. Even then it failed. Jefferson, Madison, and the Southern Republicans had no idea of the economical difficulties their system created, and were surprised to find American society so complex even in their own Southern States that the failure of two successive crops to find a sale threatened beggary to every rich planter from the Delaware to the Sabine. During the first few months, while ships continued to arrive from abroad and old stores were consumed at home, the full pressure of the embargo was not felt; but as the summer of 1808 passed, the outcry became violent. In the Southern States, almost by common consent debts remained unpaid, and few men ventured to oppose a political system which was peculiarly a

Southern invention; but in the Northern States, where the bankrupt laws were enforced and the habits of business were comparatively strict, the cost of the embargo was soon shown in the form of political revolution.

The relapse of Massachusetts to Federalism and the overthrow of Senator Adams in the spring of 1808 were the first signs of the political price which President Jefferson must pay for his passion of peace. In New York the prospect was little better. Governor Morgan Lewis, elected in 1804 over Aaron Burr by a combination of Clintons and Livingstons, was turned out of office in 1807 by the Clintons. Governor Daniel D. Tompkins, his successor, was supposed to be a representative of De Witt Clinton and Ambrose Spencer. To De Witt Clinton the State of New York seemed in 1807 a mere appendage,—a political property which he could control at will; and of all American politicians next to Aaron Burr none had shown such indifference to party as he. No one could predict his course, except that it would be shaped according to what seemed to be the interests of his ambition. He began by declaring himself against the embargo, and soon afterward declared himself for it. In truth, he was for or against it as the majority might decide; and in New York a majority could hardly fail to decide against the embargo. At the spring election of 1808, which took place about May 1, the Federalists made large gains in the legislature. The summer greatly increased their strength, until Madison's friends trembled for the result, and their language became despondent beyond reason. Gallatin, who knew best the difficulties created by the embargo, began to despair. June 29 he wrote: "From present appearances the Federalists will turn us out by 4th of March next." Ten days afterward he explained the reason of his fears: "I think that Vermont is lost; New Hampshire is in a bad neighborhood; and Pennsylvania is extremely doubtful." In August he thought the situation so serious that he warned the President:—

"There is almost an equal chance that if propositions from Great Britain, or other events, do not put it in our power to raise the embargo before the 1st of October, we will lose the Presidential election. I think that at this moment the Western States, Virginia, South Carolina, and perhaps Georgia are the only sound States, and that we will have a doubtful contest in every other."[1]

Two causes saved Madison. In the first place, the opposition failed to concentrate its strength. Neither George Clinton nor James Monroe could control the whole body of opponents to the embargo. After waiting till the middle of August for some arrangement to be made, leading Federalists held a conference at New York, where they found themselves obliged, by the conduct of De Witt Clinton, to give up the hope of a coalition. Clinton decided not to risk his fortunes for the sake of his uncle the Vice-President; and this decision obliged the Federalists to put a can-

[1] Adams's Gallatin, 373, 374.

didate of their own in the field. They named C. C. Pinckney of South Carolina for President, and Rufus King of New York for Vice-President, as in 1804.

From the moment his opponents divided themselves among three candidates, Madison had nothing to fear; but even without this good fortune he possessed an advantage that weighed decisively in his favor. The State legislatures had been chosen chiefly in the spring or summer, when the embargo was still comparatively popular; and in most cases, but particularly in New York, the legislature still chose Presidential electors. The people expressed no direct opinion on national politics, except in regard to Congressmen. State after State deserted to the Federalists without affecting the general election. Early in September Vermont elected a Federalist governor, but the swarm of rotten boroughs in the State secured a Republican legislature, which immediately chose electors for Madison. The revolution in Vermont surrendered all New England to the Federalists. New Hampshire chose Presidential electors by popular vote; Rhode Island did the same, — and both States, by fair majorities, rejected Madison and voted for Pinckney. In Massachusetts and Connecticut the legislatures chose Federalist electors. Thus all New England declared against the Administration; and had Vermont been counted as she voted in September, the opposition would have received forty-five electoral votes from New England, where in 1804 it had received only nine. In New York the opponents of the embargo were very strong, and the nineteen electoral votes of that State might in a popular election have been taken from Madison. In this case Pennsylvania would have decided the result. Eighty-eight electoral votes were needed for a choice. New England, New York, and Delaware represented sixty-seven. Maryland and North Carolina were so doubtful that if Pennsylvania had deserted Madison, they would probably have followed her, and would have left the Republican party a wreck.

The choice of electors by the legislatures of Vermont and New York defeated all chance of overthrowing Madison; but apart from these accidents of management the result was already decided by the people of Pennsylvania. The wave of Federalist success and political revolution stopped short in New York, and once more the Democracy of Pennsylvania steadied and saved the Administration. At the October election of 1808, — old Governor McKean having at last retired, — Simon Snyder was chosen governor by a majority of more than twenty thousand votes. The new governor was the candidate of Duane and the extreme Democrats; his triumph stopped the current of Federalist success, and enabled Madison's friends to drive hesitating Republicans back to their party. In Virginia, Monroe was obliged to retire from the contest, and his supporters dwindled in numbers until only two or three thousand went to the polls. In New York, De Witt Clinton contented himself with taking from Madison six of the nineteen electoral votes and giving them to Vice-President Clinton. Thus the result showed comparatively little sign of the true Republican loss ; yet in the electoral college where in 1804 Jefferson had received the voices of one hundred and sixty-two electors, Madison in 1808 received only one hnndred and twenty-two votes. The Federalist minority rose from fourteen to forty-seven.

In the elections to Congress the same effects were shown. The Federalists doubled their number of Congressmen, but the huge Republican majority could well bear reduction. The true character of the Eleventh Congress could not be foretold by the party vote. Many Northern Republicans chosen to Congress were as hostile to the embargo as though they had been Federalists. Elected on the issue of embargo or anti-embargo, the Congress which was to last till March 5, 1811, was sure to be factious; but whether factious or united, it could have neither policy nor leader. The election decided its own issue. The true issue thenceforward was that of war; but on this point the people had not been asked to speak, and their representatives would not dare without their encouragement to act.

The Republican party by a supreme effort kept itself in office; but no one could fail to see that if nine months of embargo had so shattered Jefferson's power, another such year would shake the Union itself. The cost of this " engine for national purposes " exceeded all calculation. Financially, it emptied the Treasury, bankrupted the mercantile and agricultural class, and ground the poor beyond endurance. Constitutionally, it overrode every specified limit on arbitrary power and made Congress despotic, while it left no bounds to the authority which might be vested by Congress in the President. Morally, it sapped the nation's vital force, lowering its courage, paralyzing its energy, corrupting its principles, and arraying all the active elements of society in factious opposition to government or in secret paths of treason. Politically, it cost Jefferson the fruits of eight years painful labor for popularity, and brought the Union to the edge of a precipice.

Finally, frightful as the cost of this engine was, as a means of coercion the embargo evidently failed. The President complained of evasion, and declared that if the measure were faithfully executed it would produce the desired effect; but the people knew better. In truth, the law was faithfully executed. The price-lists of Liverpool and London, the published returns from Jamaica and Havana, proved that American produce was no longer to be bought abroad. On the continent of Europe commerce had ceased before the embargo was laid, and its coercive effects were far exceeded by Napoleon's own restrictions; yet not a sign came from Europe to show that Napoleon meant to give way. From England came an answer to the embargo, but not such as promised its success. On all sides evidence accumulated that the embargo, as an engine of coercion, needed a long period of time to produce a decided effect. The law of physics could easily be applied to politics ; force could be converted only into its equivalent force. If the embargo — an exertion of force less violent than war — was to do the work of war, it must extend over a longer time the development of an equivalent energy. Wars lasted for many years, and the embargo must be calculated to last much longer than any war; but meanwhile the morals, courage, and political liberties of the American people must be perverted or destroyed ; agriculture and shipping must perish ; the Union itself could not be preserved.

Under the shock of these discoveries Jefferson's vast popularity vanished, and the labored fabric of his reputation fell in sudden and general ruin. America began slowly to struggle, under the consciousness of pain, toward a conviction that she must bear the common burdens of humanity, and fight with the weapons of other races in the same bloody arena; that she could not much longer delude herself with hopes of evading laws of Nature and instincts of life; and that her new statesmanship which made peace a passion could lead to no better result than had been reached by the barbarous system which made war a duty.

CHAPTER XIII.

WHILE the people of the United States waited to see the effect of the embargo on Europe, Europe watched with breathless interest the death-throes of Spain.

The Emperor Napoleon, in December, 1807, hurried in triumphal progress from one ancient city to another, through his Italian kingdom, while his armies steadily crossed the Pyrenees, and spread over every road between Bayonne and Lisbon. From Madrid, Godoy saw that the end was near. Until that moment he had counted with certainty on the devotion of the Spanish people to their old King In the last months of 1807 he learned that even Spanish loyalty could not survive the miseries of such a reign. Conspiracy appeared in the Escorial itself. Ferdinand, Prince of the Asturias, only son of Don Carlos IV., was discovered in a plot for dethroning his father by aid of Napoleon. Ferdinand was but twenty-three years old; yet even in the flower of youth he showed no social quality. Dull, obstinate, sullen, just shrewd enough to be suspicious, and with just enough passion to make him vindictive, Ferdinand was destined to become the last and worst of the Spanish Bourbon kings; yet in the year 1807 he had a strong bond of sympathy with the people, for he hated and feared his father and mother and the Prince of Peace. Public patience, exhausted by endless disaster, and outraged by the King's incompetence, the Queen's supposed amours, and Godoy's parade of royal rank and power, vanished at the news that Ferdinand shared in the popular disgust; and the Prince of Peace suddenly woke to find the old King already dethroned in his subjects' love, while the Prince of the Asturias, who was fitted only for confinement in an asylum, had become the popular ideal of virtue and reform.

Godoy stifled Ferdinand's intrigue, and took from Napoleon that pretext for interference; but he gained at most only a brief respite for King Charles. The pardon of Ferdinand was issued Nov. 5, 1807; December 23, Napoleon sent from Milan to his minister of war orders [1] to concentrate armies for occupying the whole peninsula, and to establish the magazines necessary for their support. He was almost ready to act; and his return to Paris, Jan. 3, 1808, announced to those who were in the secret that the new drama would soon begin.

Among the most interested of his audience was General Armstrong, who had longed, since 1805, for a chance to meet the Emperor with his own weapons, and who knew that Napoleon's schemes required

[1] Napoleon to General Clarke, Dec. 23, 1807; Correspondance, xvi. 212.

control of North and South America, which would warrant Jefferson in imposing rather than in receiving terms for Florida. Whatever these terms might be, Napoleon must grant them, or must yield the Americas to England's naval supremacy. The plan as Armstrong saw it was both safe and sure. Napoleon made no secret of his wants. Whatever finesse he may have used in the earlier stage of his policy was flung aside after his return to Paris, January 3. In reply to Armstrong's remonstrances against the Milan Decree, the Emperor ordered Champagny to use the language of command:[1] —

"Answer Mr. Armstrong, that I am ashamed to discuss points of which the injustice is so evident; but that in the position in which England has put the Continent, I do not doubt of the United States declaring war against her, especially on account of her decree of November 11; that however great may be the evil resulting to America from war, every man of sense will prefer it to a recognition of the monstrous principles and of the anarchy which that Government wants to establish on the seas; that in my mind I regard war as declared between England and America from the day when England published her decrees; that, for the rest, I have ordered that the American vessels should remain sequestered, to be disposed of as shall be necessary according to circumstances."

No coarser methods were known to diplomacy than those which Napoleon commonly took whenever the moment for action came. Not only did he thus hold

[1] Napoleon to Champagny, Jan. 12, 1808; Correspondance, xvi. 243.

millions of American property sequestered as a pledge for the obedience of America, but he also offered a bribe to the United States government. January 28 he gave orders [1] for the occupation of Barcelona and the Spanish frontier as far as the Ebro, and for pushing a division from Burgos to Aranda on the direct road to Madrid. These orders admitted of no disguise; they announced the annexation of Spain to France. A few days afterward, February 2, the Emperor began to dispose of Spanish territory as already his own.

"Let the American minister know verbally," he wrote to Champagny,[2] "that whenever war shall be declared between America and England, and whenever in consequence of this war the Americans shall send troops into the Floridas to help the Spaniards and repulse the English, I shall much approve of it. You will even let him perceive (*vous lui laisserez même entrevoir*) that in case America should be disposed to enter into a treaty of alliance, and make common cause with me, I shall not be unwilling (*éloigné*) to intervene with the court of Spain to obtain the cession of these same Floridas in favor of the Americans."

The next day Champagny sent for Armstrong and gave him a verbal message, which the American minister understood as follows: [3] —

[1] Napoleon to General Clarke, Jan. 28, 1808; Correspondance, xvi. 281, 282.

[2] Napoleon to Champagny, Feb. 2, 1808; Correspondance, xvi. 301.

[3] Armstrong to Madison, Feb. 15, 1808; MSS. State Department Archives.

"General, I have to communicate to you a message from the Emperor. I am instructed to say that the measure of taking the Floridas, to the exclusion of the British, meets entirely the approbation of his Majesty. I understand that you wish to purchase the Floridas. If such be your wish, I am further instructed to say that his Majesty will interest himself with Spain in such way as to obtain for you the Floridas, and, what is still more important, a convenient western boundary for Louisiana, on condition that the United States will enter into an alliance with France."

Weary of verbal and semi-official advances, Armstrong determined to put this overture on record, and in doing so, to tell the Emperor plainly the price of American friendship. February 5 he wrote to Champagny a note, embodying the message as he understood it, and promising to convey it to the President.[1]

"I should little deserve," he added, "and still less reciprocate the frankness of this declaration, were I to withhold from your Excellency my belief that the present conduct of France toward the commerce of the United States, so far from promoting the views of his Majesty, are directly calculated to contravene them. That the United States are at this moment on the eve of a war with Great Britain on account of certain outrages committed against their rights as a neutral nation is a fact abundantly and even generally known. Another fact, scarcely less known, is that under these circumstances France also has proceeded, in many instances and by

[1] Armstrong to Champagny, Feb. 5, 1808; MSS. State Department Archives.

various means, to violate these very rights. In both cases all the injunctions of public law have been equally forgotten; but between the two we cannot fail to remark a conspicuous difference. With Great Britain the United States could invoke no particular treaty providing rights supplementary to these injunctions; but such was not their situation with France. With her a treaty did exist, . . . a treaty sanctioned with the name and guaranteed by the promise of the Emperor 'that all its obligations should be inviolably preserved.'"

This was hardly the reply which the Emperor expected; but, temper for temper, Napoleon was not a man to be thus challenged by a mere diplomatist.

"You must write to the American minister," was his order to Champagny,[1] "that France has taken engagements with America, has made with her a treaty founded on the principle that the flag covers the goods, and that if this sacred principle had not been solemnly proclaimed, his Majesty would still proclaim it; that his Majesty treated with America independent, and not with America enslaved (*asservie*); that if she submits to the King of England's Decree of November 11, she renounces thereby the protection of her flag; but that if the Americans, as his Majesty cannot doubt without wounding their honor, regard this act as one of hostility, the Emperor is ready to do justice in every respect."

In forwarding these documents to Washington, Armstrong expressed in plain language his opinion of Napoleon and Champagny. "With one hand they

[1] Napoleon to Champagny, Feb. 11, 1808; Correspondance, xvi. 319.

offer us the blessings of equal alliance against Great Britain; with the other they menace us with war if we do not accept this kindness; and with both they pick our pockets with all imaginable diligence, dexterity, and impudence." Armstrong's patience was exhausted. He besought the Government to select its enemy, either France or England; but "in either case do not suspend a moment the seizure of the Floridas."[1] A week afterward he wrote to Madison that "in a council of Administration held a few days past, when it was proposed to modify the operation of the Decrees of November, 1806, and December, 1807, though the proposition was supported by the whole weight of the council, the Emperor became highly indignant, and declared that these decrees should suffer no change, and that the Americans should be compelled to take the positive character either of allies or of enemies."[2]

These letters from Armstrong, enclosing Champagny's version of Napoleon's blunt words, were despatched to Washington during the month of February; and, as the story has already shown, President Jefferson roused a storm against France by communicating to Congress the Emperor's order that the United States government should regard itself as at war with England. Turreau felt the pub-

[1] Armstrong to Madison, Feb. 15, 1808; MSS. State Department Archives.

[2] Armstrong to Madison, Feb. 22, 1808; State Papers, iii. 250.

lication as a fatal blow to his influence; but even Turreau, soldier as he was, could never appreciate the genius of his master's audacity. Napoleon knew his ground. From the moment England adopted the Orders in Council the United States were necessarily a party in the war, and no process of evasion or delay could more than disguise their position. Napoleon told Jefferson this plain truth, and offered him the Floridas as a bribe to declare himself on the side of France. These advances were made before the embargo system was fairly known or fully understood at Paris; and the policy of peaceable coercion, as applied to England, had not been considered in the Emperor's plans. Alliance or war seemed to him the necessary alternative, and from that point of view America had no reason or right to complain because he disregarded treaty stipulations which had become a dead letter.

All this while the Emperor held Spain in suspense, but February 21 he gave orders for securing the royal family. Murat was to occupy Madrid; Admiral Rosily, who commanded a French squadron at Cadiz, was to bar the way "if the Spanish Court, owing to events or a folly that can hardly be expected, should wish to renew the scene of Lisbon."[1] Godoy saw the impending blow, and ordered the Court to Cadiz, intending to carry the King even to Mexico if no other resource remained. He would

[1] Decrès to Rosily, Feb. 21, 1808; Thiers's Empire, viii. 669.

perhaps have saved the King, and Admiral Rosily himself would have been the prisoner, had not the people risen in riot on hearing of the intended flight. March 17 a sudden mob sacked Godoy's house at Aranjuez, hunting him down like a wild beast, and barely failing to take his life; while by sheer terror Don Carlos IV. was made to abdicate the throne in favor of his son Ferdinand. March 19 the ancient Spanish empire crumbled away.

Owing to the skill with which Napoleon had sucked every drop of blood from the veins, and paralyzed every nerve in the limbs of the Spanish monarchy, the throne fell without apparent touch from him, and his army entered Madrid as though called to protect Carlos IV. from violence. When the news reached Paris the Emperor, April 2, hurried to Bordeaux and Bayonne, where he remained until August, regulating his new empire. To Bayonne were brought all the familiar figures of the old Spanish *régime*,—Carlos IV., Queen Luisa, Ferdinand, the Prince of Peace, Don Pedro Cevallos, —the last remnants of picturesque Spain; and Napoleon passed them in review with the curiosity which he might have shown in regarding a collection of rococo furniture. His victims always interested him, except when, as in the case of Tousaint Louverture, they were not of noble birth. King Charles, he said,[1] looked a *bon et brave homme*.

[1] Napoleon to Talleyrand, Correspondance, xvii. 39, 49, 65.

"I do not know whether it is due to his position or to the circumstances, but he has the air of a patriarch, frank and good. The Queen carries her heart and history on her face; you need to know nothing more of her. The Prince of Peace has the air of a bull; something like Daru. He is beginning to recover his senses; he has been treated with unexampled barbarity. It is well to discharge him of every false imputation, but he must be left covered with a slight tinge of contempt."

This was a compliment to Godoy; for Napoleon made it his rule to throw contempt only upon persons—like the Queen of Prussia, or Mme. de Staël, or Toussaint—whose influence he feared. Of Ferdinand, Napoleon could make nothing, and became almost humorous in attempting to express the antipathy which this last Spanish Bourbon aroused.

"The King of Prussia is a hero in comparison with the Prince of the Asturias. He has not yet said a word to me; he is indifferent to everything; very material; eats four times a day, and has no ideas; . . . sullen and stupid."

Madrid and Aranjuez, the Escorial and La Granja were to know King Charles and his court no more. After showing themselves for a few days at Bayonne, these relics of the eighteenth century disappeared to Compiègne, to Valençay, to one refuge after another, until in 1814 unhappy Spain welcomed back the sullen and stupid Ferdinand, only to learn his true character; while old King Charles, beggared and forgotten, dragged out a melancholy existence in Italy, served to the last by Godoy with a loyalty that half excused his faults and vices. The Bourbon rubbish was swept from Madrid; Don Carlos had already abdicated; Ferdinand, entrapped and terrified, was set aside; the old palaces were garnished for new-comers; and after Lucien and Louis Bonaparte had refused the proffered throne, Napoleon sent to Naples for Joseph, who was crowned, June 15, King of Spain at Bayonne.

Meanwhile the Spanish people woke to consciousness that their ancient empire had become a province of France, and their exasperation broke into acts of wild revenge. May 2 Madrid rose in an insurrection which Murat suppressed by force. Several hundred lives on either side were lost; and although the affair itself was one of no great importance, it had results which made the day an epoch in modern history.

The gradual breaking up of the old European system of politics was marked by an anniversary among each of the Western nations. The English race dated from July 4, 1776, the beginning of a new era; the French celebrated July 14, 1789, the capture of the Bastille, as decisive of their destinies. For a time, Bonaparte's *coup d'état* of the 18th Brumaire in 1799 forced both France and England back on their steps; but the dethronement of Charles IV. began the process in a new direction. The Second of May — or as the Spaniards called it, the Dos de Maio — swept the vast Spanish empire into the vortex of dissolution. Each of the other anniversaries — that of July 4, 1776, and of July 14, 1789 — had been followed by a long and bloody convulsion which ravaged large portions of the world; and the extent and violence of the convulsion which was to ravage the Spanish empire could be measured only by the vastness of Spanish dominion. So strangely had political forces been entangled by Napoleon's hand, that the explosion at Madrid roused the most incongruous interests into active sympathy and strange companionship. The Spaniards themselves, the least progressive people in Europe, became by necessity democratic; not only the people, but even the governments of Austria and Germany felt the movement, and yielded to it; the Tories of England joined with the Whigs and Democrats in cheering a revolution which could not but shake the foundations of Tory principles; confusion became chaos, and while all Europe, except France, joined hands in active or passive support of Spanish freedom, America, the stronghold of free government, drew back and threw her weight on the opposite side. The workings of human development were never more strikingly shown than in the helplessness with which the strongest political and social forces in the world followed or resisted at haphazard the necessities of a movement which they could not control or comprehend. Spain, France, Germany, England, were swept into a vast and bloody torrent which dragged America, from Montreal to Valparaiso, slowly into its movement; while the familiar figures of famous men, — Napoleon, Alexander, Canning, Godoy, Jefferson, Madison, Talleyrand; emperors, generals, presidents, conspirators, patriots, tyrants, and martyrs by the thousand, — were borne away by the stream, struggling, gesticulating, praying, murdering, robbing; each blind to everything but a selfish interest, and all helping more or less unconsciously to reach the new level which society was obliged to seek. Half a century of disorder failed to settle the problems raised by the Dos de Maio; but from the first even a child could see that in the ruin of a world like the empire of Spain, the only nation certain to find a splendid and inexhaustible booty was the Republic of the United States. To President Jefferson the Spanish revolution opened an endless vista of democratic ambition.

Yet at first the Dos de Maio seemed only to rivet Napoleon's power, and to strengthen the reaction begun on the 18th Brumaire. The Emperor expected local resistance, and was ready to suppress it. He had dealt effectually with such popular outbreaks in France, Italy, and Germany; he had been overcome in St. Domingo not by the people, but, as he believed, by the climate. If the Germans and Italians could be made obedient to his orders, the Spaniards could certainly offer no serious resistance. During the two or three months that followed the dethronement of the Bourbons, Napoleon stood at the summit of his hopes. If the letters he then wrote were not extant to prove the plans he had in mind, common-sense would refuse to believe that schemes so unsubstantial could have found lodgment in his brain. The English navy and English commerce were to be driven from the Mediterranean Sea, the Indian Ocean, and American waters, until the ruin of England should be accomplished, and the empire of the world should be secured. Order rapidly followed order for reconstructing the navies of France, Spain, and Portugal. Great expeditions were to occupy Ceuta, Egypt, Syria, Buenos Ayres, the Isle de France, and the East Indies.

"The concurrence of these operations," he wrote May 13,[1] "will throw London into a panic. A single one of them, that of India, will do horrible damage there. England will then have no means of annoying us or of disturbing America. I am resolved on this expedition."

For this purpose the Emperor required not only the submission of Spain, but also the support of Spanish America and of the United States. He acted as though he were already master of all these countries, which were not yet within his reach Continuing to treat the United States as a dependent government, he issued April 17 a new order directing the seizure of all American vessels which should enter the ports of France, Italy, and the Hanse towns.[2] This measure, which became famous

[1] Napoleon to Decrès, May 13, 1808; Correspondance, xvii. 112.

[2] Napoleon to Gaudin, April 17, 1808; Correspondance, xvii. 16.

as the Bayonne Decree, surpassed the Decrees of Berlin and Milan in violence, and was gravely justified by Napoleon on the ground that, since the embargo, no vessel of the United States could navigate the seas without violating the law of its own government, and furnishing a presumption that it did so with false papers, on British account or in British connection. "This is very ingenious," wrote Armstrong in reporting the fact.[1] Yet it was hardly more arbitrary or unreasonable than the British "Rule of 1756," which declared that a neutral should practise no trade with a belligerent which it had not practised with the same nation during peace.

While these portentous events were passing rapidly before the eyes of Europe, no undue haste marked Madison's movements. Champagny's letter of Jan. 15, 1808, arrived and was sent to Congress toward the end of March; but although the United States quickly knew by heart Napoleon's phrase, "War exists in fact between England and the United States, and his Majesty considers it as declared from the day on which England published her decrees;" although Rose departed March 22, and the embargo was shaped into a system of coercion long before Rose's actual departure, — yet Congress waited until April 22 before authorizing the President to suspend the embargo, if he could succeed in persuading or compelling England or France to withdraw the belli-

[1] Armstrong to Madison, April 25, 1808; MSS. State Department Archives. Cf. State Papers, iii. 291.

gerent decrees; and not until May 2 — the famous Dos de Maio — did Madison send to Armstrong instructions which were to guide that minister through the dangers of Napoleonic diplomacy.

The Secretary began by noticing Champagny's letter of January 15, which had assumed to declare war for the United States government.

"That [letter]," said Madison,[1] " . . . has, as you will see by the papers herewith sent, produced all the sensations here which the spirit and style of it were calculated to excite in minds alive to the interests and honor of the nation. To present to the United States the alternative of bending to the views of France against her enemy, or of incurring a confiscation of all the property of their citizens carried into the French prize courts, implied that they were susceptible of impressions by which no independent and honorable nation can be guided; and to prejudge and pronounce for them the effect which the conduct of another nation ought to have on their councils and course of proceeding, had the air at least of an assumed authority not less irritating to the public feeling. In these lights the President makes it your duty to present to the French government the contents of Mr. Champagny's letter; taking care, as your discretion will doubtless suggest, that while you make that Government sensible of the offensive tone employed, you leave the way open for friendly and respectful explanations, if there be a disposition to offer them, and for a decision here on any reply which may be of a different character."

[1] Madison to Armstrong, May 2, 1808; State Papers, iii. 252.

While Armstrong waited for Napoleon's "friendly and respectful explanations," he was to study the Act of Congress which vested in the President an authority to suspend the embargo:—

> "The conditions on which the suspending authority is to be exercised will engage your particular attention. They appeal equally to the justice and the policy of the two great belligerent Powers now emulating each other in violations of both. The President counts on your best endeavors to give to this appeal all the effect possible with the French government. Mr. Pinkney will be doing the same with that of Great Britain."

The Florida affair remained to be discussed. The President courteously acknowledged the Emperor's wishes "for an accession of the United States to the war against England, as an inducement to which his interposition would be employed with Spain to obtain for them the Floridas." Armstrong was told to say in reply "that the United States having chosen as the basis of their policy a fair and sincere neutrality among the contending Powers, they are disposed to adhere to it as long as their essential interests will permit, and are more particularly disinclined to become a party to the complicated and general warfare which agitates another quarter of the globe, for the purpose of obtaining a separate and particular object, however interesting to them; but," Madison added, "should circumstances demand from the United States a precautionary occupation against the hostile designs of Great Britain, it will be recollected with satisfaction that the measure has received his Majesty's approbation." Finally, Armstrong's advice to seize the Floridas without delay was answered only by the singular remark that the Emperor had given no reason to suppose he would approve the step. In private Jefferson gave other explanations, but perhaps he most nearly expressed his true feeling when he added that Armstrong wrote "so much in the buskin that he cannot give a naked fact in an intelligible form." [1]

Turreau, who stood nearer than any other man to the secrets of American foreign politics, attempted to draw the President from this defensive attitude. Turreau's instructions were such as to warrant him in using strong language. In a despatch dated February 15, Champagny repeated to his minister at Washington in still plainer words the substance of what had been said to Armstrong: "Some American ships have been seized, but the Emperor contents himself for the moment with holding them in sequestration. His conduct toward the Americans will depend on the conduct of the United States toward England." As previously to Armstrong, so again to Turreau, the threat was supported by the bribe: —

"The Emperor, wishing on this occasion to establish a still more intimate union of interests between America and France, has authorized me to notify Mr. Armstrong

[1] Jefferson to Madison, Sept. 13, 1808; Writings, v. 367. Cf. Jefferson to Armstrong, March 5, 1809; Works, v. 433.

verbally that if England should make any movement against the Floridas, he would not take it ill if the United States should move troops there for defence. You will be cautious in making use of this communication, which is purely conditional, and can take effect only in case the Floridas are attacked."[1]

Not until late in the month of June did Turreau find an opportunity to talk at his ease with the President and Secretary of State; but, as usual, his account of the conversation was interesting.[2] He began with Madison; and after listening with some impatience to the Secretary's long list of complaints, he brought forward the suggestion of alliance: —

"I watched the Secretary of State, and the experience I have in dealing with him made me easily perceive that my proposal embarrassed him; so he replied in an evasive manner. At last, finding himself too hard pressed, for a third time he said to me 'that the intention of the Federal government was to observe the most exact impartiality between France and England.' 'You have departed from it,' said I, 'when you place the two Powers on the same line relatively to their conduct toward you.' . . . 'Well,' said he, 'we must wait the decision of the next Congress with regard to the embargo; doubtless it will be raised in favor of the Power which shall first recall the measures that harass our commerce.'"

[1] Champagny to Turreau, Feb. 15, 1808; Archives des Aff. Étr. MSS.

[2] Turreau to Champagny, June 28, 1808; Archives des Aff. Étr. MSS.

For three hours Turreau lectured the secretary on the iniquities of England, while the secretary doggedly repeated his phrases. Wearied but not satisfied, the French minister abandoned Madison and attacked the President. Jefferson entertained him with a long list of complaints against Spain, which Turreau had heard so often as to know them by memory. When at last the conversation had been brought to the subject of alliance against England, Jefferson took a new view of the situation, which hardly agreed with that taken by the Secretary of State.

"You have complained," replied the President, "that in consequence of our measures and of the proceedings of the last Congress, France has been put on a level with England in regard to the wrongs we allege against both Powers, while there was no kind of analogy either in the date or the gravity of their wrongs toward the Americans. I am going to prove to you generally that we never intended to admit any comparison in the conduct of these two Powers, by recalling to you the effect of the very measures you complain of. The embargo, which seems to strike at France and Great Britain equally, is in fact more prejudicial to the latter than to the former, by reason of the greater number of colonies which England possesses, and their inferiority in local resources."

After pursuing this line of argument Jefferson reverted to his own policy, and made an advance toward an understanding.

"It is possible," he said, "that Congress may repeal the embargo, the continuation of which would do us more harm than a state of war. For us in the present situation all is loss; whereas, however powerful the English may be, war would put us in a way of doing them much harm, because our people are enterprising. Yet as it is probable that Congress will favor raising the embargo if the Orders in Council are withdrawn, it would be necessary for your interests, if you are unwilling to withdraw your decrees, that at least you should promise their withdrawal on condition that the embargo be withdrawn in your favor. You will also observe that were the embargo withdrawn in favor of the English, this will not close our differences with them, because never — no, never — will there be an arrangement with them if they do not renounce the impressment of our seamen on our ships."

With this avowal, which Turreau understood as a sort of pledge that Jefferson would lean toward war with England rather than with France, the French minister was obliged to content himself; while he pressed on his Government the assurance that both the President and the secretary wished more than all else to obtain the Floridas. Such reports were little calculated to change the Emperor's course. Human ingenuity discovered but one way to break Napoleon's will, and this single method was that of showing power to break his plans.

In due time Armstrong received his instructions of May 2, and wrote June 10 to Champagny a note declining the proposed alliance, and expressing the satisfaction which his Government felt at hearing the Emperor's approval of "a cautionary occupation of the Floridas." Napoleon, who was still at Bayonne in the flush of his power, no sooner read this reply than he wrote to Champagny,[1] —

"Answer the American minister that you do not know what he means about the occupation of the Floridas; and that the Americans, being at peace with the Spaniards, cannot occupy the Floridas without the permission or the request of the King of Spain."

Armstrong, a few days afterward, was astonished by receiving from Champagny a note[2] denying positively that any suggestion had ever been made to warrant an American occupation of the Floridas without an express request from the King of Spain: "The Emperor has neither the right nor the wish to authorize an infraction of international law, contrary to the interests of an independent Power, his ally and his friend." When Napoleon chose to deny a fact, argument was thrown away; yet Armstrong could not do otherwise than recall Champagny's own words. which he did in a formal note, and there left the matter at rest, writing to his Government that the change in tone had "no doubt grown out of the new relations which the Floridas bear to this government since the abdication of Charles IV."[3]

For once Armstrong was too charitable. He might safely have assumed that Napoleon was also con-

[1] Napoleon to Champagny, June 21, 1808; Correspondance, xvii. 326.

[2] Champagny to Armstrong, June 22, 1808; MSS. State Department Archives.

[3] Armstrong to Madison, July 8, 1808; MSS. State Department Archives.

tinuing the same coarse game he had played since April, 1803, — snatching away the lure he loved to dangle before Jefferson's eyes, punishing the Americans for refusing his offer of alliance, and making them feel the constant pressure of his will. They were fortunate if he did not at once confiscate the property he had sequestered. Indeed, not only did his seizures of American property continue even more rigorously than before,[1] but such French frigates as could keep at sea actually burned and sunk American ships that came in their way. The Bayonne Decree was enforced like a declaration of war. The Emperor tolerated no remonstrance. At Bayonne, July 6, he had an interview with one of the Livingstons, who was on his way to America as bearer of despatches.

"We are obliged to embargo your ships," said the Emperor;[2] "they keep up a trade with England; they come to Holland and elsewhere with English goods; England has made them tributary to her. This I will not suffer. Tell the President from me when you see him in America that if he can make a treaty with England, preserving his maritime rights, it will be agreeable to me; but that I will make war upon the universe, should it support her unjust pretensions. I will not abate any part of my system."

Yet in one respect he made a concession. He no longer required a declaration of war from the United

[1] Napoleon to Champagny, July 11, 1808; Correspondance, xvii. 364.

[2] Armstrong to Jefferson, July 28, 1808; Jefferson MSS.

States. The embargo seemed to him, as to Jefferson, an act of hostility to England which answered the immediate wants of France. In the report on foreign relations, dated Sept. 1, 1808, Napoleon expressed publicly his approval of the embargo: —

"The Americans, — this people who placed their fortune, their prosperity, and almost their existence in commerce, — have given the example of a great and courageous sacrifice. By a general embargo they have interdicted all commerce, all exchange, rather than shamefully submit to that tribute which the English pretend to impose on the shipping of all nations."

Armstrong, finding that his advice was not even considered at home, withdrew from affairs. After obeying his instructions of May 2, and recording the conventional protest against Napoleon's uncivil tone,[1] he secluded himself, early in August, at the baths of Bourbon l'Archambault, one hundred and fifty miles from Paris, and nursed his rheumatism till autumn. Thither followed him instructions from Madison, dated July 21,[2] directing him to present the case of the burned vessels "in terms which may awaken the French government to the nature of the injury and the demands of justice;" but the limit of Armstrong's patience was reached, and he flatly refused to obey. Any new experiment made at that

[1] Armstrong to Champagny, July 4, 1808; State Papers, iii. 254.

[2] Madison to Armstrong, July 21, 1808; State Papers, iii. 254.

moment, he said, would certainly be useless and perhaps injurious: —

"This opinion, formed with the utmost circumspection, is not only a regular inference from the ill success of my past endeavors, which have hitherto produced only palliations, and which have latterly failed to produce these, but a direct consequence of the most authentic information that the Emperor does not, on this subject and at this time, exercise even the small degree of patience proper to his character." [1]

Finally Armstrong summed up the results of Jefferson's policy so far as France was concerned, in a letter [2] dated August 30, which carried candor to the point of severity: —

"We have somewhat overrated our means of coercing the two great belligerents to a course of justice. The embargo is a measure calculated above any other to keep us whole and keep us in peace; but beyond this you must not count upon it. Here it is not felt, and in England . . . it is forgotten. I hope that unless France shall do us justice we will raise the embargo, and make in its stead the experiment of an armed commerce. Should she adhere to her wicked and foolish measures, we ought not to content ourselves with doing this. There is much, very much, besides that we can do; and we ought not to omit doing all we can, because it is believed here that we cannot do much, and even that we will not do what we have the power of doing."

[1] Armstrong to Madison, Aug. 28, 1808; MSS. State Department Archives.

[2] Armstrong to Madison, Aug. 30, 1808; State Papers, iii. 256.

Fortunately for Jefferson, the answer made by Spain, May 2, to Napoleon's orders was not couched in the terms which the United States government used on the same day. Joseph Bonaparte, entering his new kingdom, found himself a king without subjects. Arriving July 20 at Madrid, Joseph heard nothing but news of rebellion and disaster. On that day some twenty thousand French troops under General Dupont, advancing on Seville and Cadiz, were surrounded in the Sierra Morena, and laid down their arms to a patriot Spanish force. A few days afterward the French fleet at Cadiz surrendered. A patriot Junta assumed the government of Spain. Quick escape from Madrid became Joseph's most pressing necessity if he were to save his life. During one July week he reigned over his gloomy capital, and fled, July 29, with all the French forces still uncaptured, to the provinces beyond the Ebro.

This disaster was quickly followed by another. Junot and his army, far beyond support at Lisbon, suddenly learned that a British force under Arthur Wellesley had landed, August 1, about one hundred miles to the north of Lisbon, and was marching on that city. Junot had no choice but to fight, and August 21 he lost the battle of Vimieiro. August 30, at Cintra, he consented to evacuate Portugal, on condition that he and his twenty-two thousand men should be conveyed by sea to France.

Never before in Napoleon's career had he received two simultaneous shocks so violent. The whole of

Spain and Portugal, from Lisbon to Saragossa, by a spasmodic effort freed itself from Bonaparte or Bourbon; but this was nothing, — a single campaign would recover the peninsula. The real blow was in the loss of Cadiz and Lisbon, of the fleets and work-shops that were to restore French power on the ocean. Most fatal stroke of all, the Spanish colonies were thenceforward beyond reach, and the dream of universal empire was already dissolved into ocean mist. Napoleon had found the limits of his range, and saw the power of England rise, more defiant than ever, over the ruin and desolation of Spain.

CHAPTER XIV.

WHEN Parliament met Jan. 21, 1808, the paroxysm of excitement which followed the "Chesapeake" affair and the attack on Copenhagen had begun to subside. War with America was less popular than it had been six months before. The "Morning Post"[1] exhorted the British public to maintain "that sublime pitch" from which all opposition was to be crushed; but the Whigs came to Parliament eager for attack, while Perceval and Canning had exhausted their energies, and were thrown back on a wearisome defensive.

The session — which lasted from January 21 to July 4 — was remarkable chiefly for an obstinate struggle over the Orders in Council. Against Perceval's commercial measures the Whigs bent the full strength of their party; and this strength, so far as intelligence was concerned, greatly outmatched that of the Ministry. New men made reputations in the conflict. In January, 1808, Alexander Baring — then about thirty-four years of age, not yet in Parliament, but second to no English merchant in standing

[1] The Morning Post, Jan. 16, 1808.

— published a pamphlet, in reply to Stephen's "War in Disguise;" and his superior knowledge and abilities gave, for the first time since 1776, solid ground of support to American influence in British politics. Side by side with Baring, a still younger man thrust himself into public notice by force of qualities which for half a century were to make him the object of mixed admiration and laughter. The new American champion, Henry Brougham, a native of Edinburgh, thirty years of age, like many other Scotch lawyers had come to seek and find at Westminster the great prize of his profession. Like Baring, Brougham was not yet in Parliament; but this obstacle — which would have seemed to most men final — could not prevent him from speaking his mind, even in presence of the House.

Lord Grenville began the attack, and Canning the defence, on the first day of the session; but not until after January 27, when news of the embargo arrived, and all immediate danger of war vanished, did the situation become clear. February 5 the debate began. The Whigs found that Perceval met their assaults on the character and policy of his orders by quotations from Lord Howick's Order, which the Whigs only twelve months before had issued and defended as an act of retaliation. Narrow as this personal rejoinder might be, it was fatal to the Whig argument. Baring and Brougham might criticise Spencer Perceval; but Lord Grenville and Lord Howick had enough to do in explaining their own words. The more vehement they became, the more obstinately their opponents persevered in holding them to this single point.

Yet the issue the Whigs wished to make was fairly met. Government showed remarkable candor in avowing the commercial object of the so-called retaliation. Admitting that even if Napoleon had issued no decrees England might have been obliged to enforce the Rule of 1756, Spencer Perceval declared that after the Berlin Decree a much stronger measure was necessary in order to protect British commerce. Lord Bathurst, Lord Hawkesbury, and Lord Castlereagh took the same tone. Their argument, carried to its ultimate conclusion, implied that Great Britain might lawfully forbid every other nation to trade with any country that imposed a prohibitive duty on British manufactures. Not even a state of war seemed essential to the soundness of the principle.

Already Lord Grenville had declared that "this principle of forcing trade into our markets would have disgraced the darkest ages of monopoly,"[1] when March 8 Lord Erskine spoke in support of a series of resolutions condemning the orders as contrary to the Constitution, the laws of the realm, and the rights of nations, and a violation of Magna Charta. With especial energy he declaimed against Perceval's favorite doctrine of retaliation as applied to the protection of British commerce. Lord Erskine, like Lord Grenville, never spared epithets.

[1] Cobbett's Debates, x. 482, 483.

"It is indeed quite astonishing," he said,[1] "to hear the word 'retaliation' twisted and perverted in a manner equally repugnant to grammar and common-sense. . . . It is a new application of the term, that if A strikes me, I may retaliate by striking B. . . . I cannot, my Lords, conceive anything more preposterous and senseless than the idea of retaliation upon a neutral on whom the decree has never been executed, because it is only by its execution on him that we can be injured."

Erskine supported his positions by a long professional argument. Lord Chancellor Eldon replied by developing international law in a direction till then unexplored.[2]

"I would beg the House to consider what is meant by the law of nations," he began. "It is formed of an accumulation of the dicta of wise men in different ages, and applying to different circumstances, but none resembling in any respect such a state of things as at present exists in the face of the world. Indeed, none of the writers upon the subject of this law appear to have such a state in their contemplation. But yet nothing is to be found in their writings which does not fully warrant the right of self-defence and retaliation. Upon that right the present ministers acted in advising those Orders in Council, and upon the same right their predecessors issued the order of the 7th of January."

The doctrine that because international law wanted the sanction of a well-defined force it was, strictly speaking, no law at all, was naturally favored by the

[1] Cobbett's Debates, x. 937, 938.

[2] Cobbett's Debates, x. 971.

school of common law; but Lord Eldon's doctrine went further, for he created a sanction of one-sided force by which international law might supersede its own principles. His brother, Sir William Scott, carried out the theory by contending in the House of Commons that "even if the French Decree was not acted upon (which rested with the other party to prove), it was nevertheless an injury, because it was an insult to the country,"[1] — a dictum which could hardly find a parallel as the foundation for an attack on the rights and property of an innocent third party.

Erskine's Resolutions were of course rejected; but meanwhile the merchants of the chief cities began to protest. As the bill for carrying the orders into effect came to its engrossment, March 7, the resistance became hot. March 11 the bill passed the House by a vote of 168 to 68; but Brougham had yet to be heard, and no ordinary power was capable of suppressing Henry Brougham. As counsel for the American merchants of Liverpool, Manchester, and London, he appeared March 18 at the bar of the House, and for the next fortnight occupied most of its time in producing testimony to prove that the orders had ruinously affected the commercial interest. April 1 he summed up the evidence in a speech of three hours, which James Stephen thought pernicious and incendiary.[2] Perceval was obliged to

[1] Cobbett's Debates, x. 1066.

[2] Brougham to Grey, April 21, 1808; Brougham's Memoirs, i. 399.

produce witnesses on the other side; and Stephen, who had been brought into Parliament for the purpose, devoted himself to the task of proving that the orders had as yet been allowed no chance to produce any effect whatever, and that the commercial distress was due to the recent enforcement of the Berlin Decree. That much distress existed no one denied; but its causes might well be matter of dispute; and Parliament left the merchants to decide the point as they pleased. Brougham's inquiry had no other effect.

Pinkney's dealings with Canning were equally fruitless. January 26, when Pinkney received official news of the embargo, he went instantly to Canning, "who received my explanations with great apparent satisfaction, and took occasion to express the most friendly disposition toward our country."[1] Pinkney used this opportunity to remonstrate against the tax imposed on American cotton by the Orders in Council. A week afterward Canning sent for him, and gravely suggested a friendly arrangement. He wished to know Pinkney's private opinion whether the United States would prefer an absolute interdict to a prohibitory duty on cotton intended for the continent.[2] The sting of this inquiry rested not so much in the alternative thus presented as in the seriousness with which Canning insisted that his overture was a concession to America. With all his wit, as Lord

[1] Pinkney to Madison, Jan. 26, 1808; State Papers, iii. 206.

[2] Pinkney to Madison, Feb. 2, 1808; State Papers, iii. 207.

Castlereagh soon had reason to learn, Canning could not quite acquire tact or understand the insults he offered. Pinkney tried, with much good temper, to make him aware that his offer was in bad taste; but nothing could stop him in the path of conciliation, and February 22 he addressed to Pinkney a note announcing that the British government meant to prohibit the export of American cotton to the continent of Europe.

"I flatter myself," he continued,[1] "that this alteration in the legislative regulations by which the Orders of Council are intended to be carried into execution, will be considered by you as a satisfactory evidence of the disposition of his Majesty's government to consult the feelings as well as the interests of the United States in any manner which may not impair the effect of that measure of commercial restriction to which the necessity of repelling the injustice of his enemies has compelled his Majesty reluctantly to have recourse."

"One object of all this is certainly to conciliate us," wrote Pinkney to Madison.[2] On the day of Canning's note Spencer Perceval carried out the promise by moving the House for leave to bring in a bill prohibiting the export of cotton, except by license. At the same time he extended the like prohibition to Jesuit's bark, or quinine. Impervious to indignation and ridicule, — caring as little for the laughter of Sydney Smith as for the wrath of Lord Grenville, —

[1] Canning to Pinkney, Feb. 22, 1808; State Papers, iii. 208.
[2] Pinkney to Madison, Feb. 23, 1808; State Papers, iii. 208.

Perceval pushed all his measures through Parliament, and by the middle of April succeeded in riveting his restrictive system on the statute-book. No power short of a new political revolution could thenceforward shake his grasp on American commerce.

Yet Perceval felt and dreaded the effects of the embargo, which threatened to paralyze the healthiest industries of England. To escape the effects of this weapon Perceval would have made every possible concession short of abandoning his great scheme of restrictive statesmanship. March 26 he submitted to his colleagues a paper containing suggestions on this point.[1] "It must be admitted," he began, "that it is extremely desirable that America should relax her embargo at least as far as respects the intercourse with this country." The Americans submitted to it with reluctance, chiefly because they feared the seizure of their vessels in case England or France should declare war. To profit by this situation Perceval proposed a new order, which should guaranty the safety of every merchant-vessel, neutral or belligerent, on a voyage to or from a British port. The advantages of this step were political as well as commercial. The British ministry was disposed to meet the wishes of the Boston Federalists. Such an order, Perceval said, "would have the appearance of a friendly act on the part of this government toward America, and would increase the embarrassment and

[1] Suggestions by S. P. for a Supplementary Order in Council, March 26, 1808; Perceval MSS.

difficulties of that government in prevailing upon their subjects to submit to the embargo."

Lord Bathurst approved the suggestion; Lord Castlereagh opposed it, for reasons best given in his own words:[1] —

"If the only object to be aimed at in conducting ourselves toward America was to force the abrogation of the embargo, I agree with Mr. Perceval that the proposed measure would make it more difficult for the American government to sustain it; but in yielding so far to the popular feeling the governing party would still retain much of their credit, and they would continue to act on all the unsettled questions between the two countries in their past spirit of hostility to Great Britain and partiality to France. I think it better to leave them with the full measure of their own difficulties to lower and degrade them in the estimation of the American people. The continuance of the embargo for some time is the best chance of their being destroyed *as a party;* and I should prefer exposing them to the disgrace of rescinding their own measure at the demand of their own people than furnish them with any creditable pretext for doing so. I look upon the embargo as operating at present more forcibly in our favor than any measure of hostility we could call forth were war actually declared, and doubt the policy of exhibiting too great an impatience on our part of its continuance, which so strong a departure from our usual practice toward neutrals would indicate."

Secretary Canning wrote to his colleague in accord with Castlereagh's views.[2]

[1] Opinion of Lord Castlereagh, March–April, 1808; Perceval MSS.

[2] Opinion of Mr. Canning, March 28, 1808; Perceval MSS.

"It is so plain upon the face of this measure," began Canning, "that however comprehensive it may be made in words, it *in fact* refers to America *only;* and the embargo in America seems to be working so well for us, without our interference, that on that ground alone I confess I could wish that no new steps should be taken, at least till we have more certain information of the real issue of the present crisis in America. I have no apprehension whatever of a war with the United States. . . . Above all things I feel that *to do nothing now*, at this precise moment, — absolutely nothing, — is the wisest, safest, and most manful policy. The battle about the Orders in Council is just fought. They are established as a system. We have reason to hope that they are working much to good, and very little to mischief. Every day may be expected to bring additional proofs of this. But whether this be true to the extent that we hope or no, their effects, whatever they are, have been produced in America. Nothing that we now do can alter those effects; but an attempt to do something will perplex the view of them which we shall otherwise have to present to the country in so short a time, and which there is so much reason to believe will be highly satisfactory."

Perceval, was less certain than Canning that the country would feel high satisfaction with the effect of the orders; and he rejoined by an argument which overthrew opposition: —

"The reason which strongly urges me to continue the circulation of this paper, after having read Mr. Canning's paper, in addition to those already stated, is the apprehension I feel of the want of provision not only for Sweden, but for the West Indies; and therefore every possible facility or encouragement which we could give to prevail upon the American people either to evade the embargo by running their produce to the West Indian Islands, or to compel their government to relax it, would in my opinion be most wise."

The order was accordingly issued. Dated April 11, 1808,[1] it directed British naval commanders to molest no neutral vessel on a voyage to the West Indies or South America, even though the vessel should have no regular clearances or papers, and "notwithstanding the present hostilities, or any future hostilities that may take place." No measure of the British government irritated Madison more keenly than this. "A more extraordinary experiment," he wrote to Pinkney,[2] "is perhaps not to be found in the annals of modern transactions." Certainly governments did not commonly invite citizens of friendly countries to violate their own laws; but one avowed object of the embargo was to distress the British people into resisting their government, and news that the negroes of Jamaica and the artisans of Yorkshire had broken into acts of lawless violence would have been grateful to the ears of Jefferson. So distinct was this object, and so real the danger, that Perceval asked Parliament[3] to restrict the consumption of grain in the distilleries in order to countervail the loss of American wheat and avert a famine.

[1] American State Papers, iii. 281.

[2] Madison to Pinkney, July 18, 1808; State Papers, iii. 224.

[3] Cobbett's Debates, xi. 536.

The price of wheat had risen from thirty-nine to seventy-two shillings a quarter, and every farmer hoped for a rise above one hundred shillings, as in 1795 and 1800. Disorders occurred; lives were lost; the embargo, as a coercive measure, pressed severely on British society; and Madison, with such a weapon in his hand, could not require Perceval to perceive the impropriety of inviting a friendly people to violate their own laws.

The exact cost of the embargo to England could not be known. The total value of British exports to America was supposed to be nearly fifty million dollars; but the Americans regularly re-exported to the West Indies merchandise to the value of ten or fifteen millions. The embargo threw this part of the trade back into British hands. The true consumption of the United States hardly exeeeded thirty-five million dollars, and was partially compensated to England by the gain of freights, the recovery of seamen, and by smuggling consequent on the embargo. Napoleon's decrees must in any case have greatly reduced the purchasing power of America, and had in fact already done so. Perhaps twenty-five million dollars might be a reasonable estimate for the value of the remaining trade which the embargo stopped; and if the British manufacturers made a profit of twenty per cent on this trade, their loss in profits did not exceed five million dollars for the year, — a sum not immediately vital to English interests at a time when the annual expenditure reached three hundred and fifty million dollars, and when, as in 1807, the value of British exports was reckoned at nearly two hundred million dollars. Indeed, according to the returns, the exports of 1808 exceeded those of 1807 by about two millions.

Doubtless the embargo caused suffering. The West Indian negroes and the artisans of Staffordshire, Lancashire, and Yorkshire were reduced to the verge of famine; but the shipowners rejoiced, and the country-gentleman and farmers were enriched. So ill balanced had the British people become in the excitement of their wars and industries that not only Cobbett but even a man so intelligent as William Spence undertook to prove[1] that foreign commerce was not a source of wealth to England, but that her prosperity and power were derived from her own resources, and would survive the annihilation of her foreign trade. James Mill replied[2] at great length to the eccentricities of Spence and Cobbett, which the common-sense of England would in ordinary times have noticed only with a laugh.

The population of England was about ten millions. Perhaps two millions were engaged in manufactures. The embargo by raising the price of grain affected them all, but it bore directly on about one tenth of them. The average sum expended on account of the poor was £4,268,000 in 1803 and 1804; it was

[1] Britain Independent of Commerce, by William Spence (London), 1808.

[2] Commerce Defended, by James Mill (London), 1808.

£5,923,000 in 1811; and in 1813, 1814, and 1815, when the restrictive system had produced its full effect, the poor-rates averaged £6,130,000. The increase was probably due to the disturbance of trade and was accompanied by a state of society bordering on chronic disorder.

Probably at least five thousand families of workingmen were reduced to pauperism by the embargo and the decrees of Napoleon; but these sufferers, who possessed not a vote among them and had been in no way party to the acts of either government, were the only real friends whom Jefferson could hope to find among the people of England; and his embargo ground them in the dust in order to fatten the squires and ship-owners who had devised the Orders in Council. If the English laborers rioted, they were shot: if the West Indian slaves could not be fed, they died. The embargo served only to lower the wages and the moral standard of the laboring classes throughout the British empire, and to prove their helplessness.

Each government thus tried to overthrow the other; but that of England was for the moment the more successful. The uneducated force of democracy seemed about to break against the strength of an aristocratic system. When Parliament rose, July 4, domestic opposition was silenced, and nothing remained but to crush the resistance of America, — a task which all advices from the United States showed to be easy; while as though to make ministers invulnerable, Spain suddenly opened her arms to England, offering new markets that promised boundless wealth. At this unexpected good fortune England went well-nigh mad; and the Spanish revolution, which was in truth a gain to democracy, seemed to strike Jefferson a mortal blow. During the month of July, 1808, Canning and his colleagues exulted over Europe and America alike, looking down on Jefferson and his embargo with the disgust and horror which they might have felt for some monster of iniquity like the famous butcher of the Marrs, who was to rouse the shudders of England during these lurid years. According to Canning, Napoleon's system was already "broken up into fragments utterly harmless and contemptible."[1] According to Henry Brougham,[2] hardly ten men could be found in London who did not believe Bonaparte utterly broken, or think him worth paying one hundred pounds a year to live in retirement at Ajaccio the rest of his life. America was still more contemptible, and equally hated. Early in August, at a great dinner given at the London Tavern to the Spanish patriots, Sir Francis Baring, of the house of Baring Brothers, — a man who for a whole generation had stood at the head of British merchants, — proposed as chairman, among the regular toasts, the health of the President of the United States, and his voice was instantly drowned in hisses and protests. Jefferson,

[1] Canning to Pinkney, Sept. 23, 1808; State Papers, iii. 231.

[2] Brougham to Grey, July 2, 1808; Brougham's Memoirs, i. 405.

thanks to the slanders of Pickering and the Federalists, stood before England in the attitude of a foiled cutthroat, at the moment when by his order the American minister in London came to the British Foreign Office with a request that the Orders in Council should be withdrawn.

"That the Orders in Council did not produce the embargo, that they were not substantially known in America when the embargo took place,"[1] was the burden of Canning's and Castlereagh's constant charge against the United States government. Canning was one of six or eight men in the world who might with truth have said that they knew the orders to have produced the embargo. He alone could have proved it by publishing Erskine's official evidence;[2] but he preferred to support Timothy Pickering and Barent Gardenier in persuading the world that Jefferson's acts were dictated from Paris, and that their only motive was the assassination of England. "Nor, sir, do I think," continued Canning before the whole House of Commons, "that the Orders in Council themselves could have produced any irritation in America. . . . Since the return of Mr. Rose no communication has been made by the American government in the form of complaint, or remonstrance, or irritation, or of any description whatever." With infinite industry the assertions of Pickering and Gar-

[1] Speech of Mr. Canning, June 24, 1808; Cobbett's Debates, xi. 1050.

[2] See pp. 175, 176.

denier, of John Randolph and of the Boston newspapers and pamphlets, were reprinted and circulated in London. "Your modesty would suffer," wrote Rose to Pickering,[1] "if you were aware of the sensation produced in this country by the publication of a letter from a senator of Massachusetts to his constituents."

Every American slander against Jefferson was welcomed in England, until Pinkney asked Madison in disgust, "Have you prohibited the exportation of all pamphlets which uphold our rights and honor?"[2] The English people could hardly be blamed if they became almost insane under the malice of these falsehoods, for no whisper of Iago was more poisonous than Canning's innuendoes. Believing Jefferson to be in secret league with Napoleon, they insisted that the United States should be punished for the treason Jefferson had planned. Joseph Marriatt, a prominent member of Parliament, in a pamphlet[3] published in August, reminded President Jefferson of the fate of the late Czar Paul. The feeling of society was so bitter that by tacit agreement America ceased to be talked about; no one ventured longer to defend her.

In June Pinkney received instructions, dated April 30,[4] authorizing him to offer a withdrawal of the em-

[1] Rose to Pickering, May 8, 1808; New England Federalism, p. 371.

[2] Wheaton's Life of Pinkney, p. 91.

[3] Hints to both Parties (London), 1808, pp. 64, 65.

[4] Madison to Pinkney, April 30, 1808; State Papers, iii. 222.

bargo on condition that England should withdraw the Orders in Council. In the situation of English feeling such an offer was almost an invitation to insult, and Pinkney would have gladly left it untouched. He tried to evade the necessity of putting it in writing; but Canning was inexorable. From week to week Pinkney postponed the unpleasant task. Not until August 23 did he write the note which should have been written in June. No moment could have been more unfortunate; for only two days before, Arthur Wellesley had defeated Junot at Vimieiro; and August 30 Junot capitulated at Cintra. The delirium of England was higher than ever before or since.

September 23 Canning replied.[1] Beginning with a refusal to admit the President's advance, his note went on to discuss its propriety. "His Majesty," it said, "cannot consent to buy off that hostility which America ought not to have extended to him, at the expense of a concession made, not to America, but to France." Canning was a master of innuendo; and every sentence of his note hinted that he believed Jefferson to be a tool of Napoleon; but in one passage he passed the bounds of official propriety: —

"The Government of the United States is not to be informed that the Berlin Decree of Nov. 21, 1806, was the practical commencement of an attempt, not merely to check or impair the prosperity of Great Britain, but utterly to annihilate her political existence through the

[1] Canning to Pinkney, Sept. 23, 1808; State Papers, iii. 231.

ruin of her commercial prosperity; that in this attempt almost all the Powers of the European continent have been compelled more or less to co-operate; and that the American embargo, though most assuredly not intended to that end, — for America can have no real interest in the subversion of the British power, and her rulers are too enlightened to act from any impulse against the real interests of their country, — but by some unfortunate concurrence of circumstances, without any hostile intention, the American embargo did come in aid of the 'blockade of the European continent' precisely at the very moment when if that blockade could have succeeded at all, this interposition of the American government would most effectually have contributed to its success."

Like his colleague Lord Castlereagh, Canning deliberately tried to "lower and degrade" the American government in the eyes of its own people. His defiance was even more emphatic than his sarcasm.

"To this universal combination," he continued, "his Majesty has opposed a temperate but a determined retaliation upon the enemy, — trusting that a firm resistance would defeat this project, but knowing that the smallest concession would infallibly encourage a perseverance in it.

"The struggle has been viewed by other Powers not without an apprehension that it might be fatal to this country. The British government has not disguised from itself that the trial of such an experiment might be arduous and long, though it has never doubted of the final issue. But if that issue, such as the British government confidently anticipated, has providentially arrived much sooner than could even have been hoped; if 'the blockade of the Continent,' as it has been triumphantly styled by the enemy, is raised even before it had been well established; and if that system, of which extent and continuity were the vital principles, is broken up into fragments utterly harmless and contemptible, — it is, nevertheless, important in the highest degree to the reputation of this country (a reputation which constitutes a great part of her power), that this disappointment of the hopes of her enemies should not have been purchased by any concession; that not a doubt should remain to distant times of her determination and of her ability to have continued her resistance; and that no step which could even mistakenly be construed into concession should be taken on her part while the smallest link of the confederacy remains undissolved, or while it can be a question whether the plan devised for her destruction has or has not either completely failed or been unequivocally abandoned."

With this sweeping assertion of British power Canning might well have stopped; but although he had said more than enough, he was not yet satisfied. His love of sarcasm dragged him on. He thought proper to disavow the wish to depress American prosperity, and his disavowal was couched in terms of condescension as galling as his irony; but in one paragraph he concentrated in peculiar force the worst faults of his character and taste: —

"His Majesty would not hesitate to contribute, in any manner in his power, to restore to the commerce of the United States its wonted activity; and if it were possible to make any sacrifice for the repeal of the embargo without appearing to deprecate it as a measure of hostility, he would gladly have facilitated its removal as a measure of inconvenient restriction upon the American people."

Earl Grey, although he approved of rejecting the American offer, wrote to Brougham that in this note Canning had outdone himself.[1] No doubt his irony betrayed too much of the cleverness which had been so greatly admired by Eton schoolboys; but it served the true purpose of satire, — it stung to the quick, and goaded Americans into life-long hatred of England. Pinkney, whose British sympathies had offered long resistance to maltreatment, fairly lost his temper over this note. "Insulting and insidious," he called it in his private correspondence with Madison.[2] He was the more annoyed because Canning wrote him an explanatory letter of the same date which gave a personal sting to the public insult.[3] "I feel that it is not such a letter as I could have persuaded myself to write in similar circumstances," he complained.[4]

Pinkney's abilities were great. In the skirmish of words in which Canning delighted, Pinkney excelled; and in his later career at the bar, of which

[1] Grey to Brougham, Jan. 3, 1809; Brougham's Memoirs, i. 397.

[2] Pinkney to Madison, Oct. 11, 1808; Wheaton's Pinkney, p. 412.

[3] Canning to Pinkney, Sept. 23, 1808; State Papers, iii. 230.

[4] Pinkney to Madison, Nov. 2, 1808; Wheaton's Pinkney, p. 416.

he was the most brilliant leader, and in the Senate, where he was heard with bated breath, he showed more than once a readiness to overbear opposition by methods too nearly resembling those of Canning; but as a diplomatist he contented himself with preserving the decorous courtesy which Canning lacked. He answered the explanatory letter of September 23 with so much skill and force that Canning was obliged to rejoin; and the rejoinder hardly raised the British secretary's reputation.[1]

With this exchange of notes, the diplomatic discussion ended for the season; and the packet set sail for America, bearing to Jefferson the news that his scheme of peaceable coercion had resulted in a double failure, which left no alternative but war or submission.

[1] Pinkney to Canning, Oct. 10, 1808; State Papers, iii. 233. Canning to Pinkney, Nov. 22, 1808; State Papers, iii. 237.

CHAPTER XV.

EARLY in August, at the time when public feeling against the embargo was beginning to turn into personal hatred of Jefferson, news of the Spanish outbreak reached America, and put a new weapon into Federalist hands. The embargo, in its effects upon Spain and her colonies was a powerful weapon to aid Napoleon in his assault on Spanish liberty and in his effort to gain mastery of the ocean. In an instant England appeared as the champion of human liberty, and America as an accomplice of despotism. Jefferson, in his pursuit of Florida, lost what was a thousand times more valuable to him than territory,— the moral leadership which belonged to the head of democracy. The New England Federalists seized their advantage, and proclaimed themselves the friends of Spain and freedom. Their press rang with denunciations of Napoleon, and of Jefferson his tool. For the first time in many years the Essex Junto stood forward as champions of popular liberty.

So deeply mired was Jefferson in the ruts of his Spanish policy and prejudices that he could not at once understand the revolution which had taken place. On hearing the earlier reports of Spanish resistance his first thought was selfish. "I am glad to see that Spain is likely to give Bonaparte employment. *Tant mieux pour nous!*"[1] To each member of his Cabinet he wrote his hopes:[2]—

"Should England make up with us, while Bonaparte continues at war with Spain, a moment may occur when we may without danger of commitment with either France or England seize to our own limits of Louisiana as of right, and the residue of the Floridas as reprisals for spoliations. It is our duty to have an eye to this in rendezvousing and stationing our new recruits and our armed vessels, so as to be ready, if Congress authorizes it, to strike in a moment."

The victories at Bailen and Vimieiro, the flight of Joseph from Madrid, the outburst of English enthusiasm for Spain, and the loud echo from New England, in the anxieties of a general election, brought the President to wider views. October 22 the Cabinet debated the subject, arriving at a new result, which Jefferson recorded in his memoranda:[3]—

"Unanimously agreed in the sentiments which should be unauthoritatively expressed by our agents to influential persons in Cuba and Mexico; to wit: 'If you remain under the dominion of the kingdom and family of Spain, we are contented; but we should be extremely unwilling to see you pass under the dominion or ascendency of

[1] Jefferson to Robert Smith, Aug. 9, 1808; Writings, v. 335.

[2] Jefferson to Dearborn, Aug. 12, 1808; Writings, v. 338. Jefferson to Gallatin, v. 338. Jefferson to R. Smith, v. 337. Jefferson to Madison, v. 339.

[3] Cabinet Memoranda; Jefferson MSS.

France or England. In the latter case, should you choose to declare independence, we cannot now commit ourselves by saying we would make common cause with you, but must reserve ourselves to act according to the then existing circumstances; but in our proceedings we shall be influenced by friendship to you, by a firm feeling that our interests are intimately connected, and by the strongest repugnance to see you under subordination to either France or England, either politically or commercially.'"

No allusion to Florida was made in this outline of a new policy, and none was needed, for Florida would obviously fall to the United States. The Spanish patriots, — who were as little disposed as Don Carlos IV. and the Prince of Peace to see their empire dismembered, and who knew as well as Godoy and Cevallos the motives that controlled the United States government, — listened with only moderate confidence to the protests which Jefferson, through various agents, made at Havana, Mexico, and New Orleans.

"The truth is that the patriots of Spain have no warmer friends than the Administration of the United States," began the President's instructions to his agents;[1] "but it is our duty to say nothing and to do nothing for or against either. If they succeed, we shall be well satisfied to see Cuba and Mexico remain in their present dependence, but very unwilling to see them in that of France or England, politically or commercially. We consider their interests and ours as the same, and that the

[1] Jefferson to Claiborne, Oct. 29, 1808; Writings, v. 381.

object of both must be to exclude all European influence from this hemisphere."

The patriotic junta at Cadiz, which represented the empire of Spain, could hardly believe in the warm friendship which admitted its object of excluding them from influence over their own colonies. In private, Jefferson avowed[1] that American interests rather required the failure of the Spanish insurrection. "Bonaparte, having Spain at his feet, will look immediately to the Spanish colonies, and think our neutrality cheaply purchased by a repeal of the illegal parts of his decrees, with perhaps the Floridas thrown into the bargain." In truth, Jefferson and the Southern interest cared nothing for Spanish patriotism; and their indifference was reflected in their press. The independence of the Spanish colonies was the chief object of American policy; and the patriots of Spain had no warmer friends than the Administration of the United States so far as they helped and hurried this great catastrophe; but beyond this purpose Jefferson did not look.

In the Eastern States the Democratic and Southern indifference toward the terrible struggle raging in Spain helped to stimulate the anger against Jefferson, which had already swept many firm Republicans into sympathy with Federalism. In their minds indifference to Spain meant submission to Napoleon and hatred of England; it proved the true motives which had induced the President to suppress Mon-

[1] Jefferson to Monroe, Jan. 28, 1809; Writings, v. 419.

roe's treaty and to impose the Non-importation Act and the embargo; it called for vehement, universal, decisive protest. The New England conscience, which had never submitted to the authority of Jefferson, rose with an outburst of fervor toward the Spaniards, and clung more energetically than ever to the cause of England, — which seemed at last, beyond the possibility of doubt, to have the sanction of freedom. Every day made Jefferson's position less defensible, and shook the confidence of his friends.

With the sanguine temper which had made him victorious in so many trials, the President hoped for another success. He still thought that England must yield under the grinding deprivations of the embargo, and he was firm in the intention to exact his own terms of repeal. Pinkney's earlier despatches offered a vague hope that Canning might withdraw the orders; and at this glimpse of sunshine Jefferson's spirits became buoyant.

"If they repeal their orders, we must repeal our embargo; if they make satisfaction for the 'Chesapeake,' we must revoke our proclamation, and generalize its application by a law; if they keep up impressments, we must adhere to non-intercourse, manufactures, and a Navigation Act."[1]

Canning was not altogether wrong in thinking that concession by Great Britain would serve only to establish on a permanent footing the system of peaceable coercion.

[1] Jefferson to Madison, Sept. 6, 1808; Writings, v. 361.

The first blow to the President's confidence came from France. Armstrong's letters gave no hope that Napoleon would withdraw or even modify his decrees.

"We must therefore look to England alone," wrote Madison September 14,[1] "for the chances of disembarrassment, — and look with the greater solicitude as it seems probable that nothing but some striking proof of the success of the embargo can arrest the successful perversion of it by its enemies, or rather the enemies of their country."

To England, accordingly, the President looked for some sign of successful coercion, — some proof that the embargo had been felt, or at least some encouragement to hold that its continuance might save him from the impending alternative of submission or war; and he had not long to wait. The "Hope," bringing Canning's letters of September 23, made so quick a voyage that Pinkney's despatches came to hand October 28, as the President was preparing his Annual Message to Congress for its special meeting November 7.

Had Canning chosen the moment when his defiance should have most effect, he would certainly have selected the instant when the elections showed that Jefferson's authority had reached its limit. Friends and enemies alike united in telling the President that his theory of statesmanship had failed, and must be thrown aside. The rapid decline of his authority

[1] Madison to Jefferson, Sept. 14, 1808; Jefferson MSS.

was measured by the private language of representative men, speaking opinions not meant for popular effect. In the whole Union no men could be found more distinctly representative than Wilson Cary Nicholas, James Monroe, John Marshall, and Rufus King. Of these, Nicholas was distinguished as being the President's warm and sympathetic friend, whose opinions had more weight, and whose relations with him were more confidential, than those of any other person not in the Cabinet; but even Nicholas thought himself required to prepare the President's mind for abandoning his favorite policy.

"If the embargo could be executed," wrote Nicholas October 20,[1] "and the people would submit to it, I have no doubt it is our wisest course; but if the complete execution of it and the support of the people cannot be counted upon, it will neither answer our purpose nor will it be practicable to retain it. Upon both these points I have the strongest doubts. . . . What the alternative ought to be, I cannot satisfy myself. I see such difficulties at every turn that I am disposed to cling to the embargo as long as there is anything to hope from it; and I am unwilling to form an opinion until I have the aid of friends upon whom I rely, and who are more in the way of information."

This admission of helplessness coming from the oldest Virginian Republicans betrayed the discouragement of all Jefferson's truest friends, and accorded with the language of Monroe, who whatever

[1] W. C. Nicholas to Jefferson, Oct. 20, 1808; Jefferson MSS.

might be his personal jealousies was still Republican in spirit. After his return from England, at the moment when his attitude toward the Administration was most threatening, both Jefferson and Madison had made efforts, not without success, to soothe Monroe's irritation; and in the month of February Jefferson had even written to him a letter of friendly remonstrance, to which Monroe replied, admitting that he had been "deeply affected" by his recall, and had freely expressed his feelings. The correspondence, though long and not unfriendly, failed to prevent Monroe from appearing as a rival candidate for the Presidency. One of his warmest supporters was Joseph H. Nicholson, to whom he wrote, September 24, a letter which in a different tone from that of Wilson Cary Nicholas betrayed the same helplessness of counsel:[1] —

"We seem now to be approaching a great crisis. Such is the state of our affairs, and such the compromitment of the Administration at home and abroad by its measures, that it seems likely that it will experience great difficulty in extricating itself. . . . We are invited with great earnestness to give the incumbents all the support we can, — by which is meant to give them our votes at the approaching election; but it is not certain that we could give effectual support to the person in whose favor it is requested, or that it would be advisable in any view to yield it. While we remain on independent ground, and give support where we think it is due,

[1] Monroe to Joseph H. Nicholson, Sept. 24, 1808; Nicholson MSS.

we preserve a resource in favor of free government within the limit of the Republican party. Compromit ourselves in the sense proposed, and that resource is gone. After what has passed, it has no right to suppose that we will, by a voluntary sacrifice, consent to bury ourselves in the same tomb with it."

If Wilson Cary Nicholas and James Monroe stood in such attitudes toward the Administration, admitting or proclaiming that its policy had failed, and that it could command no further confidence, what could be expected from the Federalists, who for eight years had foretold the failure? New England rang with cries for disunion. The Federalist leaders thought best to disavow treasonable intentions;[1] but they fell with their old bitterness on the personal character of President Jefferson, and trampled it deep in the mire. Many of the ablest and most liberal Federalist leaders had lagged behind or left the party, but the zealots of Pickering's class were stronger than ever. Pickering bent his energies to the task of proving that Jefferson was a tool of Napoleon, and that the embargo was laid in consequence of Napoleon's command. The success of this political delusion, both in England and America, was astounding. Even a mind so vigorous and a judgment so calm as that of Chief-Justice Marshall bent under this popular imposture.

[1] George Cabot to Pickering, Oct. 5, 1808; Lodge's Cabot, p. 308.

"Nothing can be more completely demonstrated," he wrote to Pickering,[1] "than the inefficacy of the embargo; yet that demonstration seems to be of no avail. I fear most seriously that the same spirit which so tenaciously maintains this measure will impel us to a war with the only power which protects any part of the civilized world from the despotism of that tyrant with whom we shall then be arranged. You have shown that the principle commonly called the Rule of 1756 is of much earlier date, and I fear have also shown to what influences the embargo is to be traced."

Chief-Justice Marshall had read Canning's insulting note of September 23 more than a month before this letter to Pickering was written; yet the idea of resenting it seemed not to enter his mind. Napoleon alone was the terror of Federalism; and this unreasoning fear exercised upon Marshall's calm judgment hardly less power than upon the imagination of Fisher Ames or the austerity of Timothy Pickering. Second only to Marshall, Rufus King was the foremost of Federalists; and the same horror of France which blinded Marshall, Ames, and Pickering to the conduct of England led King to hold the President responsible for Napoleon's violence. December 1, 1808, King wrote to Pickering a long letter containing views which in result differed little from those of Nicholas and Monroe. The Berlin Decree, he said, had violated treaty rights:[2]

[1] Marshall to Pickering, Dec. 19, 1808; Lodge's Cabot, p. 489.

[2] Rufus King to Pickering, Dec. 1, 1808; Pickering MSS.

"How dare then our Government with this document before them, to affirm and endeavor to impose upon the country so gross a misstatement as they have done in reference to this French Decree? The Berlin Decree, being an infringement of our rights, should have been resisted, as a similar decree of the Directory was resisted by the Federalists in 1798. Had we so done, there would have been no Orders in Council, no embargo, and probably before this we should have been again in peace with France. . . . We are now told that the embargo must be continued or the country disgraced. Admitting the alternative, how shameful is it — how criminal rather, might I say — that the men who have brought the country to this condition should have the effrontery to make this declaration! The Administration will be disgraced by the repeal, and they deserve to be; perhaps they merit more than disgrace. But will the continuance of the embargo save the country from disgrace? As to its effect on France and England, we have sufficient evidence of its inefficacy. The longer it is continued, the deeper our disgrace when it is raised. It is earnestly to be hoped that the Federalists will leave to the Administration and its supporters all projects by way of substitute to the embargo. Having plunged the nation into its present embarrassment, let them bear the whole responsibility for their measures. The embargo must be repealed. That simple, unqualified measure must be adopted. It is high time to discard visionary experiments. For God's sake, let the Federalists abstain from any share in them!"

King was not only the ablest of the Northern Federalists, he was also the one who knew England best; and yet even he condescended to the excuse or palliation of England's conduct, as though Jefferson could have resisted the Berlin Decree without also resisting the previous robberies, impressments, and blockades of Great Britain. So deeply diseased was American opinion that patriotism vanished, and the best men in the Union took active part with Lord Castlereagh and George Canning in lowering and degrading their own government. Not even Rufus King could see the selfishness of that Tory reaction which, without regard to Napoleon's decrees, swept Great Britain into collision with the United States, and from which no act of Jefferson could have saved American interests. Though King were admitted to be right in thinking that the system of peaceable coercion, the "visionary experiments" of President Jefferson's statesmanship, the fretfulness of Madison's diplomacy, had invited or challenged insult, yet after these experiments had evidently failed and the failure was conceded, a modest share of patriotism might consent that some policy for the future should be indicated, and that some remnant of national dignity should be saved. No such sentimental weakness showed itself in the ranks of Federalism. Jefferson's friends and enemies alike foresaw that the embargo must be repealed; but neither friend nor enemy could or would suggest a remedy for national disgrace.

No record remains to show in what temper Jefferson received the letters of Canning and the warnings of Wilson Cary Nicholas. Had he in the course of his sorely tried political life ever given way to unrestrained violence of temper, he might fairly have flamed into passion on reading Canning's notes; but he seemed rather to deprecate them,—he made even an effort to persuade Canning that his innuendoes were unjust. A long memorandum in his own handwriting recorded an interview which took place November 9 between him and Erskine, the British minister.[4]

"I told him I was going out of the Administration, and therefore might say to him things which I would not do were I to remain in. I wished to correct an error which I at first thought his Government above being led into from newspapers; but I apprehended they had adopted it. This was the supposed partiality of the Administration, and particularly myself, in favor of France and against England. I observed that when I came into the Administration there was nothing I so much desired as to be on a footing of intimate friendship with England; that I knew as long as she was our friend no enemy could hurt; that I would have sacrificed much to have effected it, and therefore wished Mr. King to have continued there as a favorable instrument; that if there had been an equal disposition on their part, I thought it might have been effected; for although the question of impressments was difficult on their side, and insuperable with us, yet had that been the sole question we might have shoved along in the hope of some compromise; . . . that he might judge

[1] Cabinet Memoranda; Jefferson MSS.

from the communications now before Congress whether there had been any partiality to France, to whom he would see we had never made the proposition to revoke the embargo immediately, which we did to England; and, again, that we had remonstrated strongly to them on the style of M. Champagny's letter, but had not to England on that of Canning, equally offensive; that the letter of Canning now reading to Congress, was written in the high ropes, and would be stinging to every American breast. . . . I told him in the course of the conversation that this country would never return to an intercourse with England while those Orders in Council were in force. In some part of it also I told him that Mr. Madison (who, it was now pretty well understood, would be my successor, to which he assented) had entertained the same cordial wishes as myself to be on a friendly footing with England."

Erskine reported this conversation to his Government;[1] and his report was worth comparing with that of Jefferson: —

"I collected from the general turn of his sentiments that he would prefer the alternative of embargo for a certain time, until the Congress should be enabled to come to some decided resolution as to the steps to be pursued. By this observation I believe he meant that he would wish to wait until March next, when the new Congress would be assembled, and the general sense of the people of the United States might be taken upon the state of their affairs. . . . He took an opportunity of observing in the course of his conversation that his Administration had been most wrongfully accused of

[1] Erskine to Canning, Nov. 10, 1808; MSS. British Archives.

partiality toward France; that for his own part he felt no scruple, as he was about to retire, to declare that he had been always highly desirous of an intimate connection with Great Britain; and that if any temporary arrangement on the subject of impressment could have been made, although he never would have consented to abandon the principle of immunity from impressment for the citizens of the United States, yet that the two countries might have shoved along (was his familiar expression) very well until some definite settlement could have taken place. He remarked also that these were, he knew, the sentiments of Mr. Madison, who would in all probability succeed him in his office. He hinted also that both had been long jealous of the ambitious views and tyrannical conduct of Bonaparte."

"These declarations," continued Erskine, "are so opposite to the general opinion of what their real sentiments have been that it is very difficult to reconcile them." In truth, the footing of intimate friendship with England so much desired by Jefferson demanded from England more concessions than she was yet ready to yield; but nothing could be truer or more characteristic than the President's remark that under his charge the two countries might have "shoved along very well," had peace depended only upon him. In this phrase lay both the defence and the criticism of his statesmanship.

In any event, nothing could be more certain than that the time for shoving along at all was past. The country had come to a stand-still; and some heroic resolution must be taken. The question pressing for an answer concerned Jefferson more directly than it concerned any one else. What did he mean to do? For eight years, in regard to foreign relations his will had been law. Except when the Senate, in 1806, with disastrous results, obliged him to send William Pinkney to negotiate a treaty with England, Congress had never crossed the President's foreign policy by wilful interference; and when this policy ended in admitted failure, his dignity and duty required him to stand by the government, and to take the responsibility that belonged to him. Yet the impression which Erskine drew from his words was correct. He had no other plan than to postpone further action until after March 4, 1809, when he should retire from control. With singular frankness he avowed this wish. After the meeting of Congress, November 7, when doubt and confusion required control, Jefferson drew himself aside, repeating without a pause the formula that embargo was the alternative to war.[1] "As yet the first seems most to prevail," he wrote,[2] a few days after his interview with Erskine; and no one doubted to which side he leaned, though as if it were a matter of course that he should quit the government before his successor was even elected, he added: "On this occasion I think it is fair to leave to those who are to act on them the decisions they

[1] Jefferson to Governor Pinckney, Nov. 8, 1808; Writings, v. 383.

[2] Jefferson to Governor Lincoln, Nov. 13, 1808; Writings, v. 387.

prefer, being to be myself but a spectator. I should not feel justified in directing measures which those who are to execute them would disapprove. Our situation is truly difficult. We have been pressed by the belligerents to the very wall, and all further retreat is impracticable."

Madison and Gallatin did not share Jefferson's notion of Executive duties, and they made an effort to bring the President back to a juster sense of what was due to himself and to the nation. November 15 Gallatin wrote a friendly letter to Jefferson, urging him to resume his functions.

"Both Mr. Madison and myself," wrote Gallatin,[1] "concur in the opinion that considering the temper of the Legislature it would be eligible to point out to them some precise and distinct course. As to what that should be we may not all perfectly agree, and perhaps the knowledge of the various feelings of the members, and of the apparent public opinion, may on consideration induce a revision of our own. I feel myself nearly as undetermined between enforcing the embargo or war as I was at our last meeting. But I think that we must, or rather you must, decide the question absolutely, so that we may point out a decisive course either way to our friends. Mr. Madison, being unwell, proposed that I should call on you, and suggest our wish that we might, with the other gentlemen, be called by you on that subject. Should you think that course proper, the sooner the better."

[1] Gallatin to Jefferson, Nov. 15, 1808; Gallatin's Writings, i. 420.

Jefferson's reply to this request was not recorded, but he persisted in considering himself as no longer responsible for the government. Although Madison could not become even President-elect before the first Wednesday in December, when the electors were to give their votes; and although the official declaration of this vote could not take place before the second Wednesday in February, — Jefferson insisted that his functions were merely formal from the moment when the name of his probable successor was known.

"I have thought it right," he wrote December 27,[1] "to take no part myself in proposing measures the execution of which will devolve on my successor. I am therefore chiefly an unmeddling listener to what others say. On the same ground, I shall make no new appointments which can be deferred till the fourth of March, thinking it fair to leave to my successor to select the agents for his own Administration. As the moment of my retirement approaches I become more anxious for its arrival, and to begin at length to pass what yet remains to me of life and health in the bosom of my family and neighbors, and in communication with my friends undisturbed by political concerns or passions."

So freely did he express this longing for escape that his enemies exulted in it as a fresh proof of their triumph. Josiah Quincy, his fear of the President vanishing into contempt, — "a dish of skim-milk curdling at the head of our nation," — writing to the man whom eight years before Jefferson had driven

[1] Jefferson to Dr. Logan, Dec. 27, 1808; Writings, v. 404.

from the White House, gave an account of the situation differing only in temper from Jefferson's description of himself:[1] —

"Fear of responsibility and love of popularity are now master-passions, and regulate all the movements. The policy is to keep things as they are, and wait for European events. It is hoped the chapter of accidents may present something favorable within the remaining three months; and if it does not, no great convulsion can happen during that period. The Presidential term will have expired, and then — away to Monticello, and let the Devil take the hindmost. I do believe that not a whit deeper project than this fills the august mind of your successor."

Had Jefferson strictly carried out his doctrine, and abstained from interference of any kind in the decision of a future policy, the confusion in Congress might have been less than it was, and the chance of agreement might have been greater; but while apparently refusing to interfere, in effect he exerted his influence to prevent change; and to prevent a change of measures was to maintain the embargo. In insisting that the whole matter should be left to the next Congress and President, Jefferson resisted the popular pressure for repeal, embarrassing his successor, distracting the Legislature, and destroying the remnants of his own popularity. Especially the Eastern Democrats, who had reason to believe that in New England the Union depended on repeal, were exas-

[1] Josiah Quincy to John Adams, Dec. 15, 1808; Quincy's Life of J. Quincy, p. 146.

perated to find Jefferson, though declaring neutrality, yet privately exerting his influence to postpone action until the meeting of another Congress. Among the Eastern members was Joseph Story, who had been elected to succeed Crowninshield, as a Republican, to represent Salem and Marblehead. Story took his seat Dec. 20, 1808, and instantly found himself in opposition to President Jefferson and the embargo: —

"I found that as a measure of retaliation the system had not only failed, but that Mr. Jefferson, from pride of opinion as well as from that visionary course of speculation which often misled his judgment, was absolutely bent upon maintaining it at all hazards. He professed a firm belief that Great Britain would abandon her Orders in Council if we persisted in the embargo; and having no other scheme to offer in case of the failure of this, he maintained in private conversation the indispensable necessity of closing the session of Congress without any attempt to limit the duration of the system."[1]

Josiah Quincy and Joseph Story were comparatively friendly in their views of Jefferson's conduct. The extreme Federalist opinion, represented by Timothy Pickering, placed the President in a light far more repulsive.

"It is scarcely conceivable," wrote Pickering[2] to Christopher Gore Jan. 8, 1809, "that Mr. Jefferson should so obstinately persevere in the odious measure of

[1] Story's Life of Story, i. 184.
[2] Pickering to C. Gore, Jan. 8, 1809; Pickering MSS.

the embargo, which he cannot but see has impaired his popularity and hazards its destruction, if he were not under secret engagements to the French Emperor, — unless you can suppose that he would run that hazard and the ruin of his country, rather than that a measure which he explicitly recommended should be pronounced unwise. . . . When we advert to the real character of Mr. Jefferson, there is no nefarious act of which we may not suppose him capable. *He would rather the United States should sink, than change the present system of measures.* This is not opinion, but history. I repeat it confidentially to you until I obtain permission to vouch it on evidence which I trust I can obtain."[1]

Pickering's hatred of Jefferson amounted to mania; but his language showed the influence which, whether intentionally or not, the President still exerted on the decisions of Congress. All accounts agreed that while refusing to act officially, the President resisted every attempt to change, during his time, the policy he had established. Canning's defiance and Napoleon's discipline reduced him to silence and helplessness; but even when prostrate and alone, he clung to the remnant of his system. Disaster upon disaster, mortification upon mortification, crowded fast upon the man whose triumphs had been so brilliant, but whose last hope was to escape a public censure more humiliating than any yet inflicted on a President of the United States. The interest attached to the history of his administration — an interest at all times

[1] Cf. Pickering to S. P. Gardner; New England Federalism, p. 379.

singularly personal — centred at last upon the single point of his personality, all eyes fixing themselves upon the desperate malice with which his ancient enemies strove to drive him from his cover, and the painful efforts with which he still sought to escape their fangs.

CHAPTER XVI.

NOVEMBER 8 President Jefferson sent to Congress his last Annual Message, and with it the correspondence of Pinkney and Armstrong. Intent as the public was upon foreign affairs alone, the Message had no further interest than as it dealt with the question of embargo; but Jefferson showed that he had lost none of his old dexterity, for he succeeded in giving to his words the appearance of conveying no opinion: —

"Under a continuance of the belligerent measures which, in defiance of laws which consecrate the rights of neutrals, overspread the ocean with danger, it will rest with the wisdom of Congress to decide on the course best adapted to such a state of things; and bringing with them as they do from every part of the Union the sentiments of our constituents, my confidence is strengthened that in forming this decision they will, with an unerring regard to the rights and interests of the nation, weigh and compare the painful alternatives out of which a choice is to be made. Nor should I do justice to the virtues which on other occasions have marked the character of our fellow-citizens, if I did not cherish an equal confidence that the alternative chosen, whatever it may be, will be maintained with all the fortitude and patriotism which the crisis ought to inspire."

The favorite assumption that Congress, not the Executive, directed the national policy served again to veil Jefferson's wishes, but in this instance with some reason; for no one was ignorant that a strong party in Congress meant if possible to take the decision out of the President's hands. Only by the phrase "painful alternatives" did he hint an opinion, for every one knew that by this phrase he aimed at narrowing the choice of Congress between embargo and war. One other paragraph suggested that his own choice would favor continued commercial restrictions: —

"The situation into which we have thus been forced has impelled us to apply a portion of our industry and capital to internal manufactures and improvements. The extent of this conversion is daily increasing, and little doubt remains that the establishments formed and forming will — under the auspices of cheaper material and subsistence, the freedom of labor from taxation with us, and of protecting duties and prohibitions — become permanent."

Not only the Message but also the language, still more emphatic, of private letters showed that Jefferson had become a convert to manufactures and protected industries. "My idea is that we should encourage home manufactures," he said,[1] "to the ex-

[1] Jefferson to Colonel Humphreys, Jan. 20, 1809; to Mr. Leiper, Jan. 21, 1809; Works, v. 415, 416.

tent of our own consumption of everything of which we raise the raw material." This avowal did much to increase the ill-will of New England, where Jefferson's hostility to foreign commerce as a New England interest was believed to be inveterate and deadly; but the anger of Massachusetts and Connecticut at the wound thus threatened to their commerce and shipping could not exceed the perplexity of Southern Republicans, who remembered that Jefferson in 1801 promised them "a wise and frugal government, which shall restrain men from injuring one another; which shall leave them otherwise free to regulate their own pursuits of industry and improvement, and shall not take from the mouth of labor the bread it has earned." Not only manufactures but also internal improvements were to become a chief object of governmental regulation to an extent which no Federalist had ever suggested. The absolute prohibition of foreign manufactures was to go hand in hand with a magnificent scheme of public works. In the actual state of public affairs, — without revenue and on the verge of war with France and England, — Jefferson exposed himself to ridicule by alluding to a surplus; years were to pass before the employment of surplus revenue was to become a practical question in American politics, and long before it rose Jefferson had reverted to his old theories of "a wise and frugal government;" but in 1808, as President, he welcomed any diversion which enabled him to avoid the need of facing the spectre of war.

"The probable accumulation of the surpluses of revenue," he said, "whenever the freedom and safety of our commerce shall be restored, merits the consideration of Congress. Shall it lie unproductive in the public vaults? Shall the revenue be reduced? Or shall it not rather be appropriated to the improvements of roads, canals, rivers, education, and other great foundations of prosperity and union, under the powers which Congress may already possess, or such amendments of the Constitution as may be approved by the States?"

The whole meaning of this paragraph was explained by other documents. March 2, 1807, the Senate adopted a Resolution calling upon the President for a plan of internal improvements. April 4, 1808, Gallatin made an elaborate Report, which sketched a great scheme of public works. Canals were to be cut through Cape Cod, New Jersey, Delaware, and from Norfolk to Albemarle Sound, — thus creating an internal water-way nearly the whole length of the coast. Four great Eastern rivers — the Susquehanna, Potomac, James, and Santee, or Savannah — were to be opened to navigation from tide-water to the highest practicable points, and thence to be connected by roads with four corresponding Western rivers, — the Alleghany, Monongahela, Kanawha, and Tennessee, — wherever permanent navigation could be depended upon. Other canals were to connect Lake Champlain and Lake Ontario with the Hudson River; to pass round Niagara and the falls of the Ohio; and to connect other important points. A turnpike road was to be established from Maine to Georgia along the coast. To carry out these schemes Congress was to pledge two million dollars of the annual surplus for ten years in advance; and the twenty millions thus spent might be partly or wholly replaced by selling to private corporations the canals and turnpikes as they should become productive; or the public money might at the outset be loaned to private corporations for purposes of construction.

A national university was intended to crown a scheme so extensive in its scope that no European monarch, except perhaps the Czar, could have equalled its scale. Jefferson cherished it as his legacy to the nation,— the tangible result of his "visionary" statesmanship. Five years afterward he still spoke of it as "the fondest wish of his heart," and declared that "so enviable a state in prospect for our country induced me to temporize and to bear with national wrongs which under no other prospect ought ever to have been unresented or unresisted."[1] Even in the close presence of bankruptcy or war he could not lay aside his hopes, or abstain from pressing his plan upon the attention of Congress at the moment when the last chance of its success had vanished.

The contrast between the President's sanguine visions and the reality was made the more striking by Gallatin's Annual Report, sent to Congress a few days later. The President spoke for the Administration that was passing away, while Gallatin repre-

[1] Jefferson to Eppes, Sept. 11, 1813; Works, vi. 194.

sented the Administration to come. That the secretary leaned toward war was notorious, and that he was Madison's chief adviser, perhaps to be the head of his Cabinet, was known or suspected by the men who stood nearest to the Secretary of State, and who studied Gallatin's Report as though it were Madison's first Annual Message. The more carefully it was studied, the more distinctly it took the character of a War Budget.

Receipts from customs had stopped, but the accrued revenue of 1807 had brought nearly eighteen million dollars into the Treasury; and sixteen millions would remain to supply the wants of Government at the close of the year 1808. Of this sum the ordinary annual appropriations would consume thirteen millions. Starting from this point, Gallatin discussed the financial effect of the alternatives which lay before Congress. The first was that of total or partial submission to the belligerents; "and as, in pursuing that humble path, means of defence will become unnecessary,— as there will be no occasion for either an army or a navy,— it is believed that there would be no difficulty in reducing the public expenditures to a rate corresponding with the fragments of impost which might still be collected." The second choice of measures was to continue the embargo without war; and in this case the government might be supported for two years with no greater effort than that of borrowing five million dollars. Finally, Congress might declare war against one or both of the belligerents, and in that event Gallatin asked only leave to contract loans. Persons familiar with the history of the Republican party, and with the career of its leaders when in opposition, could not but wonder that Gallatin should ask leave to create a new funded debt for purposes of war. To reconcile the inconsistency Gallatin once more argued that experience proved debt to be less dangerous than had ten years before been supposed: —

"The high price of public stocks and indeed of all species of stocks, the reduction of the public debt, the unimpaired credit of the general government, and the large amount of existing bank-stock in the United States leave no doubt of the practicability of obtaining the necessary loans on reasonable terms. The geographical situation of the United States, their history since the Revolution, and above all present events remove every apprehension of frequent wars. It may therefore be confidently expected that a revenue derived solely from duties on importations, though necessarily impaired by war, will always be amply sufficient during long intervals of peace not only to defray current expenses, but also to reimburse the debt contracted during the few periods of war. No internal taxes, either direct or indirect, are therefore contemplated, even in the case of hostilities carried on against the two great belligerent Powers."

Such language was an invitation to war. Gallatin carried courage as far as the President carried caution. While Jefferson talked of surpluses and deprecated "painful alternatives," his Secretary of the Treasury invited Congress to declare war against the two greatest Powers in the world, and promised to support it without imposing a single internal tax.

Madison, upon whose decision even more than on that of Congress the future policy of the Government depended, would not express an emphatic opinion. A glimpse of the chaos that prevailed in the Executive Department was given in a letter from Macon to Nicholson,[1] written December 4, after Macon had offered Resolutions in the House looking to a persistence in the system of embargo and peaceable coercion: —

"Gallatin is most decidedly for war, and I think that the Vice-President [Clinton] and W. C. Nicholas are of the same opinion. It is said that the President [Jefferson] gives no opinion as to the measures that ought to be adopted. It is not known whether he be for war or peace. It is reported that Mr. Madison is for the plan which I have submitted, with the addition of high protecting duties to encourage the manufacturers of the United States. I am as much against war as Gallatin is in favor of it. Thus I have continued in Congress till there is not one of my old fellow-laborers that agrees with me in opinion."

Indecision ruled everywhere at Washington down to the close of the year. Jefferson would say nothing at all; Madison would say nothing decisive;[2] and Gallatin struggled in vain to give a show of character

[1] Macon to Joseph H. Nicholson, Dec. 4, 1808; Adams's Gallatin, p. 384.

[2] Madison to Pinkney, Dec. 5, 1808; Madison's Writings, ii. 427.

to the Government. December 29 one of the Massachusetts representatives wrote to a correspondent the details of the secretary's plan:[1] —

"Yesterday I spent an hour with Mr. Gallatin, when he unfolded to me his plan, — a plan which he thinks will finally prevail. It is this: That we immediately pass a non-intercourse Act to take effect, say, June 1 next; and as the bill now reads, that it become null toward that Power which may relax. Send out the Act forthwith to England and to France, together with an Act raising the embargo partially, say, at the same time, and arming, or granting letters of marque, etc. These being made known to Great Britain and France, it is expected that the obstinate Emperor will not alter his course, but it is expected that Great Britain, when she finds the stand we deliberately take, — that we have no rebellion; that Madison and a majority of Democrats are chosen; and that we shall be fighting a common enemy (France) with her, — and when she finds that we intend living without dishonorable purchases of her goods, etc., will study her interest and relax."

The same day Gallatin wrote confidentially to Nicholson, describing the extreme anxieties he felt:[2] —

"Never was I so overwhelmed with public business. That would be nothing if we went right; but a great confusion and perplexity reign in Congress. Mr. Madison is, as I always knew him, slow in taking his ground, but firm when the storm arises. What I had foreseen has taken place. A majority will not adhere to the embargo

[1] Orchard Cook to J. Q. Adams, Dec. 29, 1808; Adams MSS.

[2] Gallatin to Nicholson, Dec. 29, 1808; Adams's Gallatin, p. 384.

much longer, and if war be not speedily determined on, submission will soon ensue."

Joseph Story two days afterward wrote a more exact account of the distraction which prevailed at the White House.

"The Administration are desirous of peace," wrote Story,[1] in confidence, December 31. "They believe that we must suffer much from war; they are satisfied, even now, that if the embargo could be continued for one year our rights would be acknowledged were our own citizens only true to their own interests. They deem this continuance impracticable, and therefore are of opinion that after midsummer the plan must be abandoned; and war will then ensue unless the belligerents abandon their aggressions."

The chaos prevailing in the White House was order compared with the condition of Congress; and there again Gallatin was forced to guide. After listening November 8 to the President's serene Message, the House three days later referred the paragraphs concerning foreign Powers to a committee with G. W. Campbell at its head. Campbell probably consulted Madison, and his instance doubtless caused the fruitless appeal of November 15, through Gallatin, to Jefferson. Failing to obtain guidance from the President, Gallatin wrote a Report, which was probably approved by Madison, and which Campbell presented November 22 to the House. For clearness and calm-

[1] Joseph Story to Joseph White, Dec. 31, 1808; Story's Life of Story, i. 172.

ness of statement this paper, famous in its day as "Campbell's Report,"[1] has never been surpassed in the political literature of the United States; but the rigorous logic of its conclusions terrified men who could not refute and would not accept them:—

"What course ought the United States to pursue? Your committee can perceive no other alternative but abject and degrading submission, war with both nations, or a continuance and enforcement of the present suspension of commerce.

"The first cannot require any discussion; but the pressure of the embargo, so sensibly felt, and the calamities inseparable from a state of war, naturally create a wish that some middle course might be discovered which should avoid the evils of both and not be inconsistent with national honor and independence. That illusion must be dissipated; and it is necessary that the people of the United States should fully understand the situation in which they are placed.

"There is no other alternative but war with both parties or a continuance of the present system. For war with one of the belligerents only would be submission to the edicts and will of the other; and a repeal, in whole or in part, of the embargo must necessarily be war or submission."

To Federalists these stern truths were not wholly unwelcome, since they brought to an issue the whole policy, domestic and foreign, which for eight years the Federalist party had never ceased to condemn; but to Republicans, who were equally responsible with

[1] State Papers, iii. 259.

the President for the policy which ended in Gallatin's alternative, the harshness of the choice was intolerable. They felt that the embargo must be abandoned; but they felt still more strongly that the double war was ruin. In vain Gallatin tried in his Treasury Report to persuade them that to fight the two nations was a practicable task. Congress writhed and rebelled.

Campbell's report closed by recommending three Resolutions as common ground on which all parties could take their stand, whether for war or embargo. The first declared that the United States could not, without a sacrifice of their rights, honor, and independence, submit to the edicts of Great Britain and France. The second declared the expediency of excluding from the United States the ships and the products of all Powers which maintained these edicts in force. The third recommended immediate preparations for defence.

The Federalists were eager for attack; and when, November 28, Campbell called up the first of his Resolutions for debate, Josiah Quincy fell upon it with violence not easily forgotten, and doubtless meant to strengthen the general belief that New England would control her passions no longer.

"The course advocated in that Report is in my opinion loathsome," he said; "the spirit it breathes disgraceful; the temper it is likely to inspire neither calculated to regain the rights we have lost, nor to preserve those which remain to us."

Assuming that the Report was made in the interest of embargo, and that it foreshadowed the permanence of the anti-commercial system, he met it by threats of insurrection and civil war, expressed in the same breath with which they were disavowed: —

"Good Heavens! Mr. Chairman, are men mad? Is this House touched with that insanity which is the never-failing precursor of the intention of Heaven to destroy? The people of New England, after eleven months' deprivation of the ocean, to be commanded still longer to abandon it! for an undefined period to hold their unalienable rights at the tenure of the will of Britain or of Bonaparte! . . . I am lost in astonishment, Mr. Chairman. I have not words to express the matchless absurdity of this attempt. I have no tongue to express the swift and headlong destruction which a blind perseverance in such a system must bring upon this nation. . . . This embargo must be repealed. You cannot enforce it for any important period of time longer. When I speak of your inability to enforce this law, let not gentlemen misunderstand me. I mean not to intimate insurrection or open defiance of them; although it is impossible to foresee in what acts that oppression will finally terminate which, we are told, makes wise men mad." Nature gave the ocean to New England, "and among a people thus situated, thus educated, thus numerous, laws prohibiting them from the exercise of their natural rights will have a binding effect not one moment longer than the public sentiment supports them."

Always assuming that the talk of war covered the plan of retaining the embargo, Quincy allowed himself to encourage warlike ideas much more recklessly than suited some of his party friends. He ventured to goad the majority toward a decision which of all possible results was most disliked by the Federalists of New England: —

"Take no counsel of fears. Your strength will increase with the trial, and prove greater than you are now aware. But I shall be told this may lead to war. I ask, Are we now at peace? Certainly not, unless retiring from insult be peace, unless shrinking under the lash be peace. The surest way to prevent war is not to fear it. The idea that nothing on earth is so dreadful as war is inculcated too studiously among us. Disgrace is worse. Abandonment of essential rights is worse."

Whatever Quincy might have been willing to accept, the party to which he belonged wanted no war except with France, while the Republicans were opposed to war in any shape. John Randolph did indeed hint at the use of force, but Randolph's opinion was never for two days the same. Philip Barton Key of Maryland, as vehement a Federalist as Quincy, also advised a policy which could lead only to war: —

"I would let our vessels go out armed for resistance, and if they were interfered with I would make the *dernier* appeal. We are able and willing to resist; and when the moment arrives, there will be but one heart and one hand throughout the Union."

The sentiment was patriotic; but as though expressly to prove how little it could be trusted, Barent

Gardenier rose to say, in emphatic and unqualified terms, that England was wholly in the right, and that from the first the American government had aimed at provoking war.[1] Gardenier's views were those of a majority of Federalists, and in the end were adopted by the party. Quincy's blindness to the serious danger of war cost him the confidence of more cautious conservatives.

On the opposite side, the Republicans seemed for the most part fairly cowed by the vigor with which the Federalists defied the embargo and war at once. Nothing in American history offered a more interesting illustration of the first stage of the national character than the open avowals by Congress in 1808 of motives closely akin to fear. America as a nation could run no serious military peril, even though she declared war on England and France at once. The worst military disaster that could happen would be a bombardment or temporary occupation of some seaboard city; the most terrible punishment within the range of possibility was the burning of a few small wooden towns which could be rebuilt in three months, and whose destruction implied no necessary loss of life. Neither England nor France had armies to spare for permanent conquest in America; but so thoroughly had the theory of peaceable coercion taken possession of the national character that men of courage appealed to motives such as in a private dispute they would have thought degrading.

[1] Annals of Congress, 1808–1809, p. 839.

"The gentleman talked of resistance, and resistance on sea," said Willis Alston of North Carolina, in reply to Quincy.[1] "Did any one believe that he seriously meant meeting the powerful navy of Great Britain on the sea, — of that Britain who had been emphatically styled 'the mistress of the ocean,' and who was 'fighting for the liberties of the world and of mankind'? No, sir; nothing of the kind is meant. Submission to her orders would be the inevitable consequence of the gentleman's resistance, and finally a loss of everything dear to the American character, — a loss of our liberty and independence as a free people."

As though one such admission were not enough, Alston obstinately recurred to it. "An idea of that sort of resistance is too idle to merit serious consideration." That Willis Alston was a man of no great distinction might be true; but such expressions were not confined to him. Richard M. Johnson of Kentucky, as brave a man as lived, could not face the idea of war: —

"At the most alarming crisis that ever convulsed the political world, when empires and kingdoms have changed with the season, and America, buffeted on every side, has maintained the ground of perfect neutrality, this nation should make a pause on this high eminence before they plunge into the dread conflict."

A nation which had never yet moved a muscle could hardly "make a pause;" but even if Colonel Johnson's figures had been more correct, the sentiment was in his mouth unexpected, for in Kentucky

[1] Annals of Congress, 1808–1809, p. 556.

gentlemen "buffeted on every side" were not supposed to pause. Still more remarkable was the language of Troup of Georgia — "the hot-headed Georgian," as Jefferson afterward called him, who twenty years later challenged a civil war, but who in 1808 was even more anxious than Johnson to pause on the high eminence where he was buffeted on every side.

"Permission to arm," he said,[1] "is tantamount to a declaration of war; and the people of this country want peace as long as they can preserve it with honor. And do you think, sir, we are ready to plunge into a ruinous war, naked and unarmed, to gratify a few bankrupt commercial speculators? It is easy to declare war; it is more difficult under present circumstances to maintain peace; and it is most difficult of all to wage a successful war. Sir, beware! It is the object of the gentleman from Massachusetts and his friends to lead you step by step into a war, and if he can into an unpopular war, which the moment you cease to conduct with effect you are ruined, and he and his friends are exalted; . . . and, sir, the moment this party ceases to rule, republicanism is gone, and with it the hopes of all good men forever."

Apart from the picture of American jealousies, Troup's remarks offered an interesting example of the ideas then held in regard to national honor. No one made the obvious retort that a nation which preserved peace by tolerating insults like those inflicted by Champagny and Canning had best say nothing of its honor. The fiction of pride was still kept up,

[1] Annals of Congress, 1808–1809, p. 606.

though members descended to appeals which seemed to imply physical fear. Madison's brother-in-law, John G. Jackson, admitted himself to be cowed by Canning's brutality.

"The fires lighted up in Copenhagen," said he,[1] "are scarcely extinguished; they are yet glowing before us in imagination at least. And we ought to recollect that if we do not submit, it is war; if we do submit, it is tribute; and if we have war, our towns will share the fate of fortified Copenhagen, unless we strengthen and fortify them."

On such reasoning, submission and tribute alone were possible, since fortifications which had failed to protect Copenhagen were little likely to protect Norfolk or New York. Macon joined in the same cry:

"We have enough of the necessaries of life to make us content, and there is no nation in the world at this time that enjoys more of the luxuries of Europe and of the East and West Indies than we do, — in a word, none that enjoys more of the good things of this world."

The spectacle of simple and hardy Speaker Macon in his homespun suit enjoying all the luxuries of Europe and the farthest East, while Pinkney and Armstrong paid for them in the spoils of American merchants, was quaintly humorous; but no one felt its sting of satire. Even the typical South Carolinian, David R. Williams, — a man second to none in courage and independence of character, — wished to hide behind the embargo for fear of war: —

[1] Annals of Congress, 1808–1809, p. 657.

"I see no other honorable course in which peace can be maintained. Take whatever other project has been hinted at and war inevitably results. While we can procrastinate the miseries of war, I am for procrastinating. We thereby gain the additional advantage of waiting the events in Europe. The true interests of this country can be found only in peace. Among many other important considerations, remember that the moment you go to war you may bid adieu to every prospect of discharging the national debt."[1]

The Secretary of the Treasury had only a month before officially asserted the contrary; but any excuse for avoiding war seemed to satisfy the House. From the beginning to the end of this long and ardent debate not one member from any quarter of the Union ventured to say — what every man in the United States would have said ten years later — that after the formal and fixed decisions of France and England war existed in fact and should be declared in form.

With all John Randolph's waywardness and extravagance, he alone shone among this mass of mediocrities, and like the water-snakes in Coleridge's silent ocean his every track was a flash of golden fire. At moments he struck passionately at his own favorite companions — at Macon and Williams — as he struck at Jefferson. The steady decline of public spirit stung his pride. "It was in that fatal session of 1805–1806 that the policy of yielding to anything

[1] Annals of Congress, 1808–1809, p. 797.

that might come in the shape of insult and aggression was commenced. The result was then foretold. It has happened."[1] Speaker after speaker revelled in narrating the long list of insults and outrages which America had endured in patience.

"The House will pardon me," said Randolph,[2] "if I forbear a minute recapitulation of the wrongs which we have received not only from the two great belligerents of Europe, but from the little belligerents also. I cannot, like Shylock, take a pleasure in saying, 'On such a day you called me dog; on such a day you spit upon my gabardine.'"

Yet Randolph himself fell naturally into the habits at which he sneered; and his wit alone raised him above the common level of Congressmen. However happily he might ridicule the timidity and awkwardness of others, he never advanced a positive opinion of his own without repudiating it the moment he was taken at his word. "I would scuffle for commerce," he said;[3] and the phrase was itself unworthy of a proud people like the Virginians; but when Campbell tried to force from him a pledge to stand by the Government in asserting the national rights, Randolph declined to gratify him.

Of all the speakers, George Washington Campbell — the reputed author of the Report — alone took a tone which might almost be called courageous; but

1 Annals of Congress, 1808–1809, p. 685.

2 Annals of Congress, 1808–1809, p. 595.

3 Annals of Congress, 1808–1809, pp. 687, 688.

even Campbell thought more of tactics than of dignity. He admitted that the object of his Report was to unite the party on common ground; but he dared not say whether this common ground was to be embargo or war; he did not even say — what must have been in his mind — that the Government had exhausted alternatives. His chief effort seemed rather to be directed toward making a dilemma for the Federalists: —

"Are they determined to vindicate the rights and independence of their country? If they are, we wish to know in what manner. If they are not willing to pursue the measures of resistance we propose, of a total interdiction of intercourse with those Powers, will they assume a higher ground? Will they prefer war? If they do, this is one of the alternatives presented in the Report. We wish to know what measures they are willing to adopt for the safety of the nation. The crisis is awful. The time has come to unite the people of America. We join issue with the gentlemen as to a temporizing policy. We have not, — we will not now temporize. We say there is no middle course. We are in the first place for cutting off all intercourse with those Powers who trample on our rights. If that will not prove effectual, we say take the last alternative, war, with all its calamities, rather than submission or national degradation."

The most interesting part of Campbell's speech was his awkward admission that peaceable coercion had failed. Such an admission was equivalent to avowing that the Republican party had failed, but Campbell stumbled as he best could through this mortifying confession.

"We could not foresee," he said,[1] "that the Governments of those Powers would not regard the distress and sufferings of their own people; that France would suffer her West Indian colonies to be almost desolated with famine, and to be compelled to apply to their inveterate enemy to save them from actual starvation rather than revoke her decrees; nor could we know that the Government of Great Britain would be regardless of the complaints and representations of her manufacturers and a respectable portion of her merchants; that it would lend a deaf ear to the hungry cries of the starving mechanics, and silence their just and loud complaints with the thunder of their murdering guns, and quench their hunger with a shower of balls instead of bread. We cannot be culpable for not anticipating such events."

Yet for twenty years the Federalists had wearied the country with prophecies of these disappointments which Campbell and his Republican friends said they could not be expected to foresee. Jefferson had persisted in acting on the theory that he could enforce national rights by peaceable means; had staked his reputation, after long and varied experience, on the soundness of this doctrine which his political opponents denied; and suddenly, on its failure, his followers pleaded that they could not be held culpable for failing to anticipate what their political opponents had steadily foretold. The confession of such an over-

[1] Annals of Congress, 1808–1809, p. 747.

sight was more fatal than all the sneers of Randolph and the taunts of Quincy.

There Congress for the moment stopped. The debate — which began November 28 and lasted till December 17 — ended in the adoption of Campbell's first Resolution by a vote of one hundred and eighteen to two; of the second by eighty-four to thirty; and of the third without opposition. Nothing was decided; and the year closed leaving Congress, as Gallatin told his friend Nicholson, in "great confusion and perplexity."

CHAPTER XVII.

BEHIND the scenes diplomacy was at work, actively seeking to disentangle or to embroil the plot of the culminating drama. Erskine, the British minister, sympathizing with his father Lord Erskine, in good-will to America, hurried from one to another of the officials at Washington, trying to penetrate their thoughts, — an easy task, — and to find a bond of union between them and George Canning, — a problem as difficult as any that ever diplomacy solved. Besides his interview with Jefferson, he reported conversations with the Cabinet.

"I have had several interviews with Mr. Madison since the arrival of the 'Hope,'" he wrote November 5,[1] "and have often turned the conversation upon the points above mentioned, which he did not seem willing to discuss; but I could collect from what he did say that it was his own opinion that all intercourse ought to be broken off with the belligerents, and that some steps further — to use his expression — ought to be taken. . . . I will just communicate to you the hints which were thrown out by Mr. Smith, Secretary of the Navy, in a conversation which I had with him, — of an unofficial

[1] Erskine to Canning, Nov. 5, 1808; MSS. British Archives.

kind, indeed, but in which he expressed his sentiments unequivocally, — that in addition to the steps alluded to by Mr. Madison, he would wish that their ministers should be recalled from England and France, and that preparations should be immediately made for a state of hostility. Mr. Gallatin, the Secretary of the Treasury, would have preferred taking a decided part against one or other of those Powers before the embargo was first laid, but thinks that no other course can now be adopted. The Vice-President, Mr. Clinton, was and is strongly averse to the embargo system; and though he does not openly declare himself, it is well known that he is entirely opposed to the present Administration. . . . Indeed, in conversation with me yesterday he inveighed with great force against the conduct of Bonaparte toward Spain, and expressed his astonishment that any American should have *hesitated* to express such sentiments. He alluded to the conduct of this Government in not only withholding any approbation of the noble efforts of the Spaniards to resist that usurper's tyranny over them, but to the language held by their newspapers, and in private by themselves, of regret at these events as being likely to conduce to the interest and success of England. A different tone is now assumed upon that important subject; and the President said to me a few days ago that however he might doubt the eventual success of the Spanish cause, the feelings of a *tiger* could alone lead to an attempt to subjugate them through such torrents of blood and such devastation as must ensue if followed by success."

Erskine's report was nearly exact. In regard to Robert Smith, it was confirmed by a letter written at the same moment by Smith to the President;[1] and so far as concerned Madison, Gallatin, and George Clinton, it was not far wrong. A month then passed while Congress drifted toward a decision. At last, about December 1, Erskine roused himself to an effort. Doubtless Madison and Gallatin knew his purpose,—perhaps they inspired it; but in any case, Erskine acted rather in their interests than in the spirit or policy of Canning.

December 3 the British minister wrote to his Government the first of a series of despatches calculated to bring Canning to his senses.

> "The Government and party in power," said he,[2] "unequivocally express their resolution not to remove the embargo, except by substituting war measures against both belligerents, unless either or both should relax their restrictions upon neutral commerce."

To reinforce this assertion Erskine reported an interview with Secretary Madison, who after reviewing the facts had ended by explicitly threatening a declaration of war. He said in substance—

> "That as the world must be convinced that America had in vain taken all the means in her power to obtain from Great Britain and France a just attention to their rights as a neutral Power by representations and remonstrances, that she would be fully justified in having recourse to hostilities with either belligerent, and that she

[1] R. Smith to Jefferson, Nov. 1, 1808; Jefferson MSS.

[2] Erskine to Canning, Dec. 3, 1808; Cobbett's Debates, xvii., Appendix cxxxiv.

only hesitated to do so from the difficulty of contending with both; but that she must be driven even to endeavor to maintain her rights against the two greatest Powers in the world, unless either of them should relax their restrictions upon neutral commerce, — in which case the United States would side with that Power against the other which might continue the aggression. Mr. Madison observed to me that it must be evident that the United States would enter upon measures of hostility with great reluctance, as he acknowledged that they are not at all prepared for war, much less with a Power so irresistibly strong as Great Britain; and that nothing would be thought to be too great a sacrifice to the preservation of peace, except their independence and their honor. He said that he did not believe that any Americans would be found willing to submit to (what he termed) the encroachments upon the liberty and the rights of the United States by the belligerents; and therefore the alternatives were, Embargo or War. He confessed that the people of this country were beginning to think the former alternative too passive, and would perhaps soon prefer the latter, as even less injurious to the interests, and more congenial with the spirit, of a free people."

In support of Madison's views Erskine reported December 4 [1] a long conversation with Gallatin, which connected the action of Congress with the action of diplomacy. Gallatin and Robert Smith, according to the British minister, had not approved the embargo as a measure of defence, "and had thought that it had been better to have resorted to measures

[1] Erskine to Canning, Dec. 4, 1808; Cobbett's Debates, xvii., Appendix cxxxvii.

of a more decided nature at first; but that now they had no other means left but to continue it for a short time longer, and then in the event of no change taking place in the conduct of the belligerents toward the United States, to endeavor to assert their rights against both Powers." Gallatin — acting as Madison's Secretary of State — sketched an ingenious and plausible project which Erskine was to suggest for Canning's use. His leading idea was simple. The total non-intercourse with both belligerents — the measure recommended by Campbell's Report, and about to become law — must remove two causes of dispute with England; for this non-intercourse superseded the President's "Chesapeake" proclamation and the Non-importation Act of April, 1806, against British manufactures. Henceforward England could not complain of American partiality to France, seeing that America impartially prohibited every kind of intercourse with both countries. This mode of conciliation was but a fair return for Canning's conciliatory prohibition of American cotton, and if carried one step further must end on both sides in a declaration of war in order to prove their wish for peace; but Canning could hardly object to his own style of reasoning. After thus evading two English grievances, Gallatin arrived at his third point, — that Congress meant to interdict the employment of foreign seamen on American vessels, and thus put an end to all occasion for impressment. Finally, Erskine represented Gallatin as saying that the

United States were ready to concede the Rule of 1756, and not to claim in time of war a trade prohibited in time of peace.

In the ease of private and friendly conversation the most cautious of men, even more than the most reckless, stood at the mercy of reporters. Gallatin was by temperament excessively cautious, and was evidently on his guard in talking with Erskine; but he could not prevent Erskine from misunderstanding his words, and still less from misconstruing his reserve. The British minister afterward officially explained that the Secretary of the Treasury had offered no such concession as was implied by the Rule of 1756; he proposed only to yield the American claim, never yet seriously pressed, to the direct trade between the colonies of France and their mother country;[1] but although Erskine's mistake on this point proved troublesome, it was not so embarrassing to Gallatin as the inference which the British minister drew from his reserve on a point of merely personal interest.

"I have no doubt," continued Erskine, "but these communications were made with a sincere desire that they might produce the effect of conciliation; because it is well known that Mr. Gallatin has long thought that the restrictive and jealous system of non-import laws, extra duties, and other modes of checking a free trade with Great Britain has been erroneous and highly injurious to the interests of America. He informed me

[1] Erskine to Gallatin, Aug. 15, 1809; State Papers, iii. 307.

distinctly that he had always entertained that opinion, and that he had uniformly endeavored to persuade the President to place the conduct of Great Britain and France in a fair light before the public. He seemed to check himself at the moment he was speaking upon that subject, and I could not get him to express himself more distinctly; but I could clearly collect from his manner, and from some slight insinuations, that he thought the President had acted with partiality toward France; for he turned the conversation immediately upon the character of Mr. Madison, and said that he could not be accused of having such a bias toward France, and remarked that Mr. Madison was known to be an admirer of the British Constitution, to be generally well disposed toward the nation, and to be entirely free from any enmity to its general prosperity. He appealed to me whether I had not observed that he frequently spoke with approbation of its institutions, its energy, and spirit, and that he was thoroughly well versed in its history, literature, and arts. These observations he made at that time for the purpose of contrasting the sentiments of Mr. Madison with those of the President, as he knew that I must have observed that Mr. Jefferson never spoke with approbation of anything that was British, and always took up French topics in his conversation, and always praised the people and country of France, and never lost an opportunity of showing his dislike to Great Britain."

When in course of time this despatch was printed, Gallatin felt himself obliged to make a public disavowal of Erskine's statements. That he had at first preferred measures more decided than the embargo was, he said, a mistake; and the inferences drawn in regard to President Jefferson were wholly erroneous: —

"Eight years of the most intimate intercourse, during which not an act, nor hardly a thought, respecting the foreign relations of America was concealed, enable me confidently to say that Mr. Jefferson never had in that respect any other object in view but the protection of the rights of the United States against every foreign aggression or injury, from whatever nation it proceeded, and has in every instance observed toward all the belligerents the most strict justice and the most scrupulous impartiality."[1]

This denial was hardly necessary. The despatches themselves plainly showed that Erskine, having set his heart on effecting a treaty, used every argument that could have weight with Englishmen, and dwelt particularly upon the point — which he well knew to be a dogma of British politics — that President Jefferson had French sympathies, whereas Madison's sympathies were English. If Erskine had been a Tory, he would have known better than to suppose that Perceval's acts were in any way due to Jefferson or his prejudices; but the British minister wished to employ all the arguments that could aid his purpose; and to do him justice, he used without stint that argument which his British instincts told him would be most convincing, — the single word, War.

[1] Gallatin to the National Intelligencer, April 21, 1810; Gallatin's Writings, i. 475.

"I ascertained from Mr. Madison," he wrote November 26,[1] "that . . . the Report of the Committee seemed distinctly to announce that the ULTIMATE and only effectual mode of resisting the aggressions of the belligerents would be by a *war*."

If Canning could be panic-struck by italics and capital letters, Erskine meant to excite his worst alarms. Perhaps Madison was a little the accomplice of these tactics; for at the moment when he threatened war in language the most menacing, the future President was trembling lest Congress should abjectly submit to British orders. Erskine's despatches early in December echoed the official words of Madison, Gallatin, and Robert Smith, but gave little idea of their difficulties. The same tactics marked his next letters. Jan. 1, 1809, he wrote to Canning[2] that the bill which was to carry into effect the Resolutions of Campbell's Report had been laid before the House:—

"You will observe, sir, that the provisions of this bill are exactly such as this Government informed me would be adopted, and which I detailed to you in my despatches by the last month's packet. On these measures, and a strict enforcement of the embargo, the Government and Congress have determined to rely for a short time, in the hope that some events in Europe may take place to enable them to extricate themselves from their present highly embarrassing situation. It is now universally

[1] Erskine to Canning, Nov. 26, 1808; MSS. British Archives.

[2] Erskine to Canning, Jan. 1, 1809 (No. 1); MSS. British Archives.

acknowledged that the Embargo Act must be raised by next summer; and nearly all the members of the ruling party declare that unless the belligerent Powers should remove their restrictions upon neutral commerce before that time, it will be incumbent upon the United States to adopt measures of hostility toward such of those Powers as may continue their aggressions."

War was the incessant burden of Erskine's reports; and he spared no pains to convince his Government that Madison had both the power and the will to fight. The next House, he reported, would contain ninety-five Republicans to forty-seven Federalists: "This great majority (which may vary a few votes) would of course be strong enough to carry any measures they wished; and all their declarations and their whole conduct indicate a determination to adopt the line of conduct which I have before pointed out." Only three days earlier Gallatin had privately written to Nicholson that great confusion and perplexity reigned in Congress, that Madison was slow in taking his ground, and that if war were not speedily determined submission would soon ensue; but Erskine reported little of this pacific temper, while he sent cry after cry of alarm to London. Toward the end of December Congress took up a measure for raising fifty thousand troops. Erskine asked the Secretary of State for what purpose so large a force was needed; and Madison replied that the force was no greater than the state of relations with foreign Powers required.

"He added (to my great surprise) that if the United States thought proper, they might act as if war had been declared by any or all of them, and at any rate by Great Britain and France. When I pressed him for a further explanation of his meaning, he said that such had been the conduct of both those Powers toward the United States that they would be justified in proceeding to immediate hostilities. From his manner as well as from his conversation, I could perceive that he was greatly incensed; and it appeared to me that he wished that Great Britain might take offence at the conduct of the United States and commence hostilities upon them, so as to give this Government a strong ground of appeal to the people of this country to support them in a war, — unless indeed they could be extricated from their difficulties by Great Britain giving way and withdrawing her Orders in Council."[1]

Following one letter by another, in these varied tones of menace, Erskine ended by sending, Jan. 3, 1809, a Message from the President-elect which wanted nothing except a vote of Congress to make it a formal announcement of war:[2] —

"I have the honor to inform you that I had an interview with Mr. Madison yesterday, in which he declared that he had no hesitation in assuring me that in the event of the belligerent nations continuing their restrictions upon neutral commerce, it was intended by this Government to recommend to Congress to pass a law to allow merchant-ships to arm, and also to issue letters of

[1] Erskine to Canning, Jan. 1, 1809 (No. 2); MSS. British Archives.

[2] Erskine to Canning, Jan. 3, 1809; MSS. British Archives.

marque and reprisal. The exact time when this course would be adopted, he said, might depend upon circumstances such as could not precisely be described; but he said that he was confident that if it was not taken before the expiration of the present Congress, in March, it would be one of the first measures of the new Congress, which will be held early in May next."

Erskine added that the Federalists also thought Great Britain wrong in refusing the American offers, and that they too declared war to be necessary if these offers should still be rejected. He wrote to Sir James Craig to be on guard against sudden attack from the United States. These measures taken, the British minister at Washington waited the echo of his alarm-cries, and Madison left the matter in his hands. No instructions were sent to Pinkney, no impulse was given to the press; and the public obstinately refused to believe in war. Perhaps Erskine received some assurance that no decisive step would be taken before he should have obtained from London a reply to his despatches of December; but whether or not he had any tacit understanding with Madison, his ambition to reunite the two countries and to effect the diplomatic triumph of a treaty certainly led him to exaggerate the warlike ardor of America, and to cross by a virtuous intrigue what he thought the ruinous career of his own Government.

On the other hand, General Turreau flattered himself that the diplomatic triumph would fall not to Erskine, but to himself; and the hope of war upon

England almost overcame for a sanguine moment his contempt for American character and courage. Turreau acquiesced in the embargo, since such was the Emperor's will, — but only as a choice of evils; for he knew better than Napoleon how deep a wound the embargo inflicted on Martinique and Guadeloupe. He consoled himself only by the hope that it injured Great Britain still more. "I have always considered," he said,[1] "that the embargo, rigorously executed, hurt us less than it hurt England, because our colonial interests are of small account in the balance against the colonial interests of the enemy." In his eyes a declaration of war against France was better suited than the embargo to French interests, provided it were joined with a like declaration against England; and he prepared his Government in advance for treating such a war as though it were an alliance.

"I believe that France ought not to take this declaration in its literal sense, because its apparent object would be only nominal, and not in the intention of the legislators. I know that such is now their disposition; and although it is conceded that the number of Federalists will be greater in the next Congress than in this, yet the Administration will always have a great majority in the House, and a still greater in the Senate. I am in such close relations with the greater number of senators as not to be deceived in regard to their intentions. But in this case, too, it would be necessary that France should not answer the challenge of war, and should wait until the

[1] Turreau to Champagny, Jan. 15, 1809; Archives des Aff. Étr. MSS.

first hostilities had taken place between England and the United States. Then I shall hope that the declaration against France will be immediately withdrawn. I have reason to believe that a declaration of war against France as well as against England will take place only with the intention of reaching this last Power without too much shocking public opinion, and in order to avoid the reproach of too much partiality toward the first. Your Excellency can, from this, form an idea of the weakness of Congress, and of the disposition of the American people."[1]

This despatch, written in the middle of January, completed the diplomatic manœuvres by which Madison hoped to unite his foreign with his domestic policy. The scheme was ingenious. Even if it should fail to wring concessions from Canning, hostilities would result only in a cheap warfare on the ocean, less wearisome than the embargo, — a war which, so far as concerned the continent of Europe, would rather benefit than injure commerce; but a policy like this, at once bold and delicate, required the steady support of a vigorous Congress. Neither Erskine nor Turreau told the full strength of the difficulties with which Madison and Gallatin struggled within their own party; or that while the new Administration was laboring to build up a new policy, the Federalists had already laid their hands on the material that the new policy needed for its use.

Whatever might be their differences in other re-

[1] Turreau to Champagny, Jan. 15, 1809; Archives des Aff. Étr. MSS.

spects, Jefferson, Madison, and Gallatin agreed on one common point. They held that until some decision should be reached in regard to peace or war, the embargo must be maintained and enforced. Neither the dignity nor the interests of the country permitted a sudden break with the policy which had been steadily followed during the eight years of their power. Abandonment of embargo without war was an act of submission to England and France which would certainly destroy whatever national self-respect might have survived the mortifications of the last three years; but if the embargo was to be maintained, it must be enforced, and without new legislation strict enforcement was impossible. This new legislation was demanded by Gallatin, in a letter of Nov. 24, 1808, addressed to Senator Giles of the Senate committee. December 8, Giles introduced a Bill conferring on Gallatin the "arbitrary" and "dangerous" powers he asked. The new measure answered Gallatin's description. Henceforward coasting-vessels were to give impossible bonds, to the amount of six times the value of vessel and cargo, before any cargo could even be put on board; collectors might refuse permission to load, even when such bonds were offered, "whenever in their opinion there is an intention to violate the embargo;" in suits on the bond, the defence was to be denied the right to plead capture, distress, or accident, except under conditions so stringent as to be practically useless; no ship-owner could sell a vessel without giving bond, to the amount of three hundred dollars for each ton, that such ship should not contravene any of the Embargo Acts; and by Section 9, the whole country was placed under the arbitrary will of government officials: "The collectors of all the districts of the United States shall . . . take into their custody specie or other articles of domestic growth, produce, or manufacture . . . when in vessels, carts, wagons, sleighs, or any other carriage, or in any manner apparently on their way toward the territory of a foreign nation or the vicinity thereof, or toward a place whence such articles are intended to be exported;" and after seizure the property could be recovered by the owner only on giving bonds for its transfer to some place "whence, in the opinion of the collector, there shall not be any danger of such articles being exported." The collectors not only received authority to seize at discretion all merchandise anywhere in transit, but were also declared to be not liable at law for their seizures, and were to be supported at need by the army, navy, and militia.

In vain did Giles[1] and the other stanch followers of Jefferson affirm that this bill contained no new principles of legislation; that it was but an extension of ordinary customs laws; and that its provisions were "necessary and proper" for carrying into effect the great constitutional object,—the embargo. Giles held so many opinions in the course of his public life that no Federalist cared to ask what might be his momen-

[1] Annals of Congress, 1808–1809, p. 259.

tary theory of the Constitution; but whether as a matter of law he was right or wrong, he could hardly dispute what Gallatin in private admitted, that the powers conferred by his Enforcement Act were "most arbitrary," "equally dangerous and odious." The Senate knew well the nature of the work required to be done, but twenty senators voted for the passage of the bill, December 21, while only seven voted in the negative.

In pressing this measure at a moment so critical, Gallatin may have been bold, but was certainly not discreet. If he meant to break down the embargo, he chose the best means; if he meant to enforce it, he chose the worst. The Eastern congressmen made no secret that they hoped to resist the law by force.

"This strong tone was held by many of the Eastern members in a large company where I was present," wrote the British minister to Canning Jan. 1, 1809; "and the gentlemen who so expressed themselves declared that they had no hesitation in avowing such opinions, and said that they would maintain them in their places in Congress."

They were as good as their word, and when the bill came before the House arguments and threats were closely intermingled; but the majority listened to neither, and January 5, in a night session, forced the bill to its passage by a vote of seventy-one to thirty-two. January 9 the Enforcement Act received the signature of President Jefferson.

Senator Pickering, of Massachusetts, alone profited by this audacious act of power; and his overwhelming triumph became every day more imminent, as the conservative forces of New England arrayed themselves under his lead. Since the departure of Rose, in March, he had basked in the sunshine of success and flattery. Single-handed he had driven John Quincy Adams from public life, and had won the State of Massachusetts, for the first time, to the pure principles of the Essex Junto. That he felt, in his austere way, the full delight of repaying to the son the debt which for eight years he had owed to the father was not to be doubted; but a keener pleasure came to him from beyond the ocean. If the American of that day, and especially the New England Federalist, conceived of any applause as deciding the success of his career, he thought first of London and the society of England; although the imagination could scarcely invent a means by which an American could win the favor of a British public. This impossibility Pickering accomplished. His name and that of John Randolph were as familiar in London as in Philadelphia; and Rose maintained with him a correspondence calculated to make him think his success even greater than it was.

"In Professor Adams's downfall, at which I cannot but be amused," wrote Rose from London,[1] "I see but the forerunner of catastrophes of greater mark. This prac-

[1] Rose to Pickering, Aug. 4, 1808; New England Federalism, p. 372.

tical answer of your common constituents to his reply to you was the best possible. By his retreat he admits his conviction that you were the fitter representative of the State legislature. In the conversion of Massachusetts, I see the augury of all that is of good promise with you. Let me thank you cordially for your answer to Governor Sullivan. It was an unintentional kindness on his part thus to compel you to bring to the public eye the narrative of a life so interesting, so virtuous, and honorable. Receive the assurance of how anxiously I hope that though gratitude is not the virtue of republics, the remaining years of that life may receive from yours the tribute of honor and confidence it has so many claims to. In so wishing, I wish the prosperity of your country."

Flattery like this was rare in Pickering's toilsome career; and man, almost in the full degree of his antipathy to demagogy, yearns for the popular regard he will not seek. Pickering's ambition to be President was as evident to George Rose as it had been to John Adams. "Under the simple appearance of a bald head and straight hair," wrote the ex-President,[1] "and under professions of profound republicanism, he conceals an ardent ambition, envious of every superior, and impatient of obscurity." That Timothy Pickering could become President over a Union which embraced Pennsylvania and Virginia was an idea so extravagant as to be unsuited even to coarsely flavored flattery; but that he should be the chief of a New England Confederation was not an extravagant thought, and toward a New England Con-

[1] Cunningham Letters, p. 56.

federation events were tending fast. The idea of combining the Eastern States against the embargo,—which if carried out put an end to the Union under the actual Constitution,—belonged peculiarly to Pickering; and since he first suggested it in his famous embargo letter, it had won its way until New England was ripe for the scheme.

One by one, the Federalist leaders gave their adhesion to the plan. Of all these gentlemen, the most cautious — or, as his associates thought, the most timid — was Harrison Gray Otis, President of the Massachusetts Senate. Never in the full confidence of the Essex Junto, he was always a favorite orator in Boston town-meeting, and a leader in Boston society; but he followed impulses stronger than his own will, and when he adopted an opinion his party might feel secure of popular sympathy. Dec. 15, 1808, Otis wrote from Boston to Josiah Quincy at Washington a letter which enrolled him under Pickering's command.[1]

"It would be a great misfortune for us to justify the obloquy of wishing to promote a separation of the States, and of being solitary in that pursuit. . . . On the other hand, to do nothing will seem to be a flash in the pan, and our apostate representatives will be justified in the opinions which they have doubtless inculcated of our want of union and of nerve. What then shall we do? In other words, what can Connecticut do? For we can

[1] H. G. Otis to Quincy, Dec. 15, 1808; Quincy's Life of Quincy, p. 164.

and will come up to her tone. Is she ready to declare the embargo and its supplementary chains unconstitutional; to propose to their State the appointment of delegates to meet those from the other commercial States, in convention at Hartford or elsewhere, for the purpose of providing some mode of relief that may not be inconsistent with the Union of these States, to which we should adhere as long as possible? Shall New York be invited to join; and what shall be the proposed objects of such a convention?"

In thus adopting the project of Timothy Pickering for a New England convention, Otis was not less careful than Pickering himself to suggest that the new Union should be consistent with the old one. American constitutional lawyers never wholly succeeded in devising any form of secession which might not coexist with some conceivable form of Union, such as was recognized by the Declaration of July 4, 1776; but no form of secession ever yet devised could coexist with the Union as it was settled by the Constitution of 1789; and the project of a New England convention, if carried out, dissolved that Union as effectually as though it had no other object. "No State shall, without the consent of Congress, . . . enter into an agreement or compact with another State."[1] Such was the emphatic interdict of the Constitution, and its violation must either destroy the Union or give it new shape. Doubtless the Union had existed before the Constitution, and might sur-

[1] Constitution of the United States, Art. I. sect. 10.

vive it; but a convention of the New England States could not exist under the Union of 1789.

Another Boston Federalist, second to none in standing, who unlike Otis was implicitly trusted by the Essex Junto, wrote a letter to Senator Pickering, dated five days later: —

"Our Legislature will convene on January 24," began Christopher Gore,[1] "and what will be proper for us to do under the circumstances of our times is doubtful. To ascertain the most useful course to be pursued on this occasion fills our minds with deep and anxious solicitude. . . . By conversing with our friends from the other New England States you might be able to know in what measures and to what extent they would be willing to coöperate with Massachusetts. The opposition, to be effectual of any change in our rulers, should comprehend all New England. These men, I fear, are too inflated with their own popularity to attend to any call short of this."

The action of Massachusetts was to be concerted with Connecticut; and the leading senator from Connecticut was Pickering's very intimate friend, James Hillhouse, whose amendments to the Constitution, proposed to the Senate in an elaborate speech April 12, 1808, were supposed by his enemies to be meant as the framework for a new confederacy, since they were obviously inconsistent with the actual Union. Hillhouse and Pickering stood in the most

[1] Gore to Pickering, Dec. 20, 1808; New England Federalism, p. 375.

confidential relations. From their common chamber in the "Six Buildings" they carried on their joint campaign against the embargo;[1] and with this advantage, Pickering in due time wrote his reply to Christopher Gore for the guidance of the Massachusetts General Court:—

"New England must be united in whatever great measure shall be adopted. During the approaching session of our Legislature there may be such further advances in mischief as may distinctly point out the course proper to be adopted. A convention of delegates from those States, including Vermont, seems obviously proper and necessary. Massachusetts and Connecticut can appoint their delegates with regular authority. In the other States they must be appointed by county conventions. A strong and solemn address, stating as concisely as will consist with perspicuity the evil conduct of our Administration as manifested in their measures, ought to be prepared to be laid before our Legislature when they meet, to be sent forth by their authority, to the people. But the fast, which I have repeatedly heard mentioned here, I hope will be postponed till the very crisis of our affairs, if such a crisis should be suffered to arise. To proclaim a fast sooner would, I fear, have more the appearance of management than of religion."[2]

Such action was not to be easily reconciled with the spirit of the Constitution, but Pickering attempted

[1] Pickering to Hillhouse, Dec. 16, 1814; New England Federalism, p. 414.

[2] Pickering to C. Gore, Jan. 8, 1809; New England Federalism, p. 376.

to show its accord; and in doing so he completed the revolution which for eight years had been in progress between the two political parties. He placed himself on the precise ground taken by Jefferson in the Kentucky Resolutions of 1798:—

"Pray look into the Constitution, and particularly to the tenth article of the Amendments. How are the powers reserved to the States respectively, or to the people, to be maintained, but by the respective States judging for themselves, and putting their negative on the usurpations of the general government."

That the States of Massachusetts and Connecticut meant to take the first step toward a change in the Federal compact was an open secret at Washington before the close of the year. As early as December 29 Gallatin wrote to his friend Nicholson a letter of alarm,[1] which showed that the plan was already known by the Administration:—

"I actually want time to give you more details, but I will only state that it is intended by the Essex Junto to prevail on the Massachusetts legislature, who meet in two or three weeks, to call a convention of the five New England States, to which they will try to add New York; and that something must be done to anticipate and defeat that nefarious plan."

[1] Adams's Gallatin, p. 384.

CHAPTER XVIII.

AMONG the Federalists were still a few moderate men who hoped that Jefferson might not be wholly sold to France, and who were inclined to ask for some new policy of peace or war before throwing aside the old one. Pickering's contempt for such allies echoed the old feuds of New England, and revived the root-and-branch politics of the Puritans:

"Some *cautious* men here of the Federal party discovered an inclination to wait patiently till the first of June the promised repeal of the embargo. God forbid that such timid counsels should reach the Massachusetts legislature, or a single member of it! A million of such men would not save the nation. Defeat the accursed measure now, and you not only restore commerce, agriculture, and all sorts of business to activity, but you save the country from a British war. The power of the present miserable rulers — I mean their power to do material mischief — will then be annihilated."[1]

Pickering's instructions were exactly followed; his temper infused itself through every New England town. Once more, a popular delusion approaching

[1] Pickering to S. P. Gardner; New England Federalism, p. 379.

frenzy, — a temporary insanity like the witchcraft and Quaker mania, — took possession of the mind of Massachusetts, and broke into acute expression. Not for a full century had the old Puritan prejudice shown itself in a form so unreasoning and unreasonable; but although nearly one half the people held aloof and wondered at the madness of their own society, the whole history of Massachusetts, a succession of half-forgotten disputes and rebellions, seemed to concentrate itself for the last time in a burst of expiring passions, mingled with hatred of Virginia and loathing for Jefferson, until the rest of America, perplexed at paroxysms so eccentric, wondered whether the spirit of Massachusetts liberty could ever have been sane. For the moment Timothy Pickering was its genius.

The decision reached by the Federalists at Washington, on or about December 21, when the Enforcement Bill passed the Senate, was quickly known in Massachusetts, and without further delay the crisis was begun. Hitherto the tone of remonstrance had been respectful; under cover of the Enforcement Act it rapidly became revolutionary. Dec. 27, 1808, a town-meeting at Bath, in the district of Maine, set the movement on foot by adopting Resolutions[1] which called on the general court, at its meeting January 25, to take "immediate steps for relieving the people, either by themselves alone, or in concert with other commercial States;" while at the same time the

[1] New England Palladium, Jan. 3, 1809.

town voted "that a committee of safety and correspondence be appointed, to correspond with committees of other towns, . . . and to watch over the safety of the people of this town, and to give immediate alarm so that a regular meeting may be called whenever any infringement of their rights shall be committed by any person or persons under color and pretence of authority derived from any officer of the United States." This extravagant measure, evidently intended to recall the memory of 1776, was quickly imitated by the town of Gloucester, which, January 12,[1] formally approved the Resolutions passed at Bath, voted an address to the general court, and appointed a committee of public safety. These first steps went so far that other towns could not easily keep pace with them, and were obliged to fall behind. The scheme of appointing everywhere town-committees of public safety to organize combined resistance to the national government, was laid aside, or fell to the ground; but the town-meetings went on. In the county of Hampshire, a public meeting of citizens, January 12,[2] announced "that causes are continually occurring which tend to produce a most calamitous event, — a dissolution of the Union;" and January 20, a meeting at Newburyport, in Senator Pickering's County of Essex, voted —

"That we will not aid or assist in the execution of the several embargo laws, especially the last, and that we

[1] New England Palladium, Jan. 17, 1809.

[2] New England Palladium, Jan. 20, 1809.

consider all those who do as violators of the Constitution of the United States and of this Commonwealth; and that they be considered as unworthy of the confidence and esteem of their fellow-citizens."

On the eve of the day fixed for the General Court to assemble, in the midst of town-meetings far and near, Boston called a meeting at Faneuil Hall. The town had grown to a population of more than thirty thousand, but old citizens could remember the Stamp Act and the Boston Port Bill; they had seen Samuel Adams and John Hancock defy, in Faneuil Hall, the power of Parliament; and the same town-meeting which had stood firm against King George, even to the point of armed rebellion, still existed unchanged, ready to resist the tyranny of a Virginia President. January 23 four thousand citizens swarmed to the hall famous for its Revolutionary associations; and in the minds of all, either as a hope or a terror, revolution was the absorbing thought.

Socially, nothing could be more respectable than the assembly. The names of the committee appointed to draft a petition to the general court included the best people of Boston. The list began with Thomas Handasyd Perkins, and included Samuel Dexter, John Warren, William Sullivan, Jonathan Mason, and Theodore Lyman, — members of a city aristocracy which still existed in vigor as robust as in the days when aristocracy was sustained by English example and patronage. Chief-Justice Parsons, who freely expressed his opinion that the embargo was unconstitutional, had no part in the proceedings; but on his privately given advice the meeting was to take its stand. The Essex Junto, willing to escape its own unpopularity, surrendered the apparent lead to a man who shared in few of the extreme opinions of Pickering, Parsons, and George Cabot, — a man who stood second to no Federalist in ability, but who had never sympathized with Alexander Hamilton's feuds, or with factious hostility either to Federalist or to Republican Presidents. Samuel Dexter, Secretary of War in 1800, Secretary of the Treasury in 1801, a lawyer of the highest standing, had been employed to argue against the constitutionality of the Embargo Act before Judge Davis in September, and although he lost his cause, he stoutly maintained the soundness of his argument. In truth, the question was still open; and since the trial at Salem, the Enforcement Act had greatly strengthened constitutional objections already strong. Dexter believed that his duty required him to join in protesting against such legislation, and accordingly he took an active part in drafting and defending the Resolutions and memorial reported by his committee, which appealed to the general court "for their interposition to save the people of this Commonwealth from the destructive consequences which they apprehend to their liberties and property from the continuance of the present system."

No measure reported by Samuel Dexter was likely to satisfy the hot temper of a town-meeting. The regular Resolutions were duly adopted, with little vigorous opposition, and the meeting adjourned till the next day; but when the citizens re-assembled, January 24, they passed another resolve, offered by Daniel Sargent, which startled the law-abiding public of Massachusetts by formally declaring that "we will not voluntarily aid or assist in the execution" of the Enforcement Act; and that "all those who shall so assist in enforcing upon others the arbitrary and unconstitutional provisions of this Act, ought to be considered as enemies to the Constitution of the United States and of this State, and hostile to the liberties of this people."

Alarming as was the tone of Boston, Samuel Dexter and his associates avoided taking open part with the British government against their own. Elsewhere no such reticence was shown. Not only in private, in all places, at every table, did the bitterness of New England temper and the intensity of local prejudice allow themselves the freest expression, but the numerous town-meetings also showed a spirit rather British than American. Among many examples a few are worth recalling, to show the absence of national feeling, and the difficulties and dangers which stood in the nation's way.

January 24 the town of Beverly, in Essex County, voted [1] that —

"They have witnessed with regret too strong a propensity to palliate and overlook the unjust aggressions of

[1] New England Palladium, Jan. 31, 1809.

one foreign nation, and to exaggerate and misrepresent the conduct of another; that the measures pursued are calculated and designed to force us into a war with Great Britain, — a war which would be extremely detrimental to our agriculture, fatal to our commerce, and which would probably deprive us forever of the Bank fishery, — and to unite us in alliance with France, whose embrace is death."

January 26 the town of Plymouth voted[1] —

"That by the partial and insidious management of our external relations, by a servile compliance with the views of one belligerent whose restless ambition is grasping at the subjugation of the civilized world, and by the unnecessary provocations offered to another, magnanimously contending for its own existence and the emancipation of the oppressed, our national peace is endangered, and our national dignity and good faith sacrificed on the altar of duplicity."

January 23 the town of Wells, in the district of Maine, voted[2] —

"That we deprecate that cringing sycophancy which has marked the conduct of our national government toward the tyrant of Europe, while we view with indignation and alarm its hostility toward Great Britain."

On the same day Gloucester spoke in language still more insulting to the national government:[3] —

"We see not only the purse-strings of our nation in the hands of a Frenchified Genevan, but all our naval

[1] New England Palladium, Jan. 31, 1809.

[2] New England Palladium, Feb. 3, 1809.

[3] New England Palladium, Feb. 24, 1809.

forces and all our militia placed under the control of this same foreigner, whom we cannot but think a satellite of Bonaparte. . . . In our opinion the national Cabinet has given to this country and the world the most indubitable evidence of their insincerity; that their great study has been to involve this country in a war with Great Britain, and of course to form a coalition with France, regardless of consequences. Their pledges to France of their willingness to submit to the wishes or mandates of the Corsican have been satisfactory. . . . We should deprecate a separation of the States, and would resort to every honorable means of redress before we would seek relief in a dissolution of the Union. . . . Our Administration can dissemble their real motives no longer; our dreadful forebodings prove realities; the expected blow has reached us, and by it has fled our liberty."

In quaint and pathetic phrases, the little town of Alfred, in Maine, sent to the general court a petition[1] which charged the national government with endeavoring "to provoke a ruinous and destructive war with England, to gratify the ambition and caprice, and augment the power, of the tyrant of France."

"We are the poor inhabitants of a small town," continued the Alfred petition, "rendered poorer by the wayward, inconsistent policy of the general government; but life and liberty are as dear to us as to our opulent brethren of the South, and we flatter ourselves that we have as much love of liberty and abhorrence of slavery as those who oppress us in the name of Republicanism.

[1] New England Palladium, Feb. 17, 1809.

We love liberty in principle but better in practice. We cling to a union of the States as the rock of our salvation; and nothing but a fearful looking for of despotism would induce us to wish for a severance of the band that unites us. But oppression did sever us from the British empire; and what a long and continued repetition of similar acts of the government of the United States would effect, God only knows!"

These extracts showed the temper in which the Massachusetts legislature met. The Federalist leaders had more difficulty to restrain than to excite the people, and felt themselves strong enough to assume the air of cautious and conservative men. After an exchange of opinions between the Legislature and Levi Lincoln, who had become governor on the death of Sullivan shortly before, both Houses turned their attention to national affairs. The numerous petitions on the subject of the embargo were referred to committees. Without loss of time the Senate committee, February 1, made a Report recommending an Act to secure the people of the State from "unreasonable, arbitrary, and unconstitutional searches in their dwelling-houses;" to which was added a series of four Resolutions, closing with a formal adoption of the step so long desired by Senator Pickering.

"*Resolved*, That the Legislature of this Commonwealth will zealously co-operate with any of the other States in all legal and constitutional measures for procuring such amendments to the Constitution of the United States as shall be judged necessary to obtain protection and defence for commerce, and to give to the commercial States their fair and just consideration in the government of the Union; and for affording permanent security, as well as present relief, from the oppressive measures under which they now suffer.

"*Resolved*, That the Honorable the President of the Senate, and the Honorable the Speaker of the House of Representatives, be requested to transmit a copy of this Report, and the Resolutions thereon, to the legislatures of such of our sister States as manifest a disposition to concur with us in measures to rescue our common country from impending ruin, and to preserve inviolate the union of the States."

These Resolutions proclaimed that a union of the Eastern States against the national government was the earnest wish of Massachusetts; and the advance thus made was instantly met by Connecticut, where Jonathan Trumbull, a Federalist of pure stock, who had for ten years filled the chair of governor, called a special meeting of the Legislature in pursuance of the arrangement concerted at Washington. The temper of Governor Trumbull could be judged from a letter written by him, February 4, to Secretary Dearborn, who had requested him to select militia officers on whom the collectors might call for military aid in enforcing the embargo.

"Conceiving as I do," replied Governor Trumbull, "and believing it to be the opinion of the great mass of citizens of this State, that the late law of Congress for a more rigorous enforcement of the embargo is unconstitutional in many of its provisions, interfering with the

State sovereignties, and subversive of the rights, privileges, and immunities of the citizens of the United States, . . . my mind has been led to a serious and decided determination to decline a compliance with your request, and to have no agency in the appointments which the President has been pleased to refer to me."

In calling together the legislature of Connecticut, Governor Trumbull's concert with Massachusetts was evident, and his object of resisting the embargo was avowed. So bluntly did the Federalists proclaim their purpose, that when the Connecticut legislature met, February 23, the governor in his opening speech explained his action as though it were a matter of course that he should call upon the State to nullify an Act of Congress.

"Whenever our national legislature," he said, "is led to overleap the prescribed bounds of their constitutional powers, on the State legislatures in great emergencies devolves the arduous task, — it is their right, it becomes their duty, — to interpose their protecting shield between the rights and liberties of the people and the assumed power of the general government."

If Madison was not by that time weary of his own words, — if the Resolutions of 1798 and the fatal "interpose" of Virginia had not become hateful to his ears, — he might have found some amusement in the irony with which Trumbull flung the familiar phrases of Virginia back into her face; but serious as such conduct was, the mere defiance carried less alarm than was warranted by the signs of secret concert with England which the Federalists willingly betrayed. Trumbull and Hillhouse, Pickering and Otis, were not necessarily masters of the situation, even when at the head of all New England; but when they pointed significantly at the fleets and armies of Great Britain behind them, they carried terror to the heart of the Union. So little did they hide their attitude toward the British government that their organ, the "New England Palladium," published, January 6, Canning's personal letter of Sept. 23, 1808, to Pinkney, which Madison had suppressed. How it had been obtained, no one knew. The British Foreign Office seemed to stand in direct communication with Boston, while the Boston Federalists exulted in a chance to swell what they thought the triumph of George Canning over their own Federalist friend, William Pinkney.

Tactics like these, unscrupulous though they might be, were effective. Jefferson and Madison had the best reason to know the force of such factiousness, for only ten years before, on less provocation, they had themselves led in Virginia and Kentucky a movement with a similar purpose; but although their history as leaders of an opposition implied agreement in principle with the doings of Massachusetts and Connecticut, their dignity and interest as Presidents of the United States required them to carry out the laws they had advised and approved. Whatever might be the personal wishes of a few men like Pickering, the great mass of Federalists wished at heart no more harm to the country than to overthrow and humiliate Jefferson, and to cripple Madison from the start; while the Administration, on its side, in struggling to escape a personal humiliation, was obliged to adopt any course that offered the best hope of success even though it should sacrifice the national character As the last weeks of President Jefferson's Administration approached, this personal conflict — the bitterness of sixteen years — concentrated its virulence upon a single point, but that point vital to Jefferson's fame and popularity, — the embargo.

Rarely in American history has been seen a struggle more furious or less ennobling than that which took place at Washington in the months of January and February, 1809. With a bold face, but with small confidence, Madison and Gallatin pressed their measures. After passing the Enforcement Act on the morning of January 6, Congress turned at once to a matter even more serious. January 7 a Resolution was offered in the House providing for an early meeting of the next Congress, and in the short debate that followed, a distinct line began for the first time to divide the advocates of war from the partisans of peace. The extra session was avowedly to be called for the purpose of declaring war. Simultaneously a bill was introduced to raise, arm, and equip fifty thousand volunteers to serve for the term of two years; while the Senate sent down another bill ordering all the frigates and gunboats to be "fitted out, officered, manned, and employed as soon as may be." The fourth Monday in May was the date proposed for the extra session, and Congress at last found itself face to face with the naked issue of war.

The effect of the crisis upon Congress was immediate. Doubt, defiance, dismay, and disgust took possession of the Legislature, which swayed backward and forward from day to day, as courage or fear prevailed. The old Republicans, who could not yield their faith in the embargo, begged almost piteously for delay.

"A large portion of the people, the South almost unanimously," urged David R. Williams of South Carolina, "have expressed a wish that the Government should adhere to the embargo till it produces an effect, or the capacity to produce the effect be disproved. You are like to be driven out of the embargo by war? Why, sir, look at the sensation in New England and New York, and talk about going to war when you cannot maintain an embargo! . . . If you do not adopt war before the fourth Monday in May, will the nation be ruined if you postpone it still further?"[1]

Macon declared that the embargo was still the people's choice:—

"As to the people being tired of the embargo, whenever they want war in preference to it they will send their petitions here to that effect. . . . Let each man put the question to his neighbor whether he will have war or embargo, and there is no doubt but he will answer in favor of the latter."

[1] Annals of Congress, 1808–1809, p. 1100.

Such reasoning, honest and true as it was in the mouths of men like Macon and Williams, gave a tone of weakness and irresolution to the debate, while it acted on the Federalists with the force of defiance, and drew from Josiah Quincy a speech which long remained famous, and which no Republican ever forgot or forgave.

That this strong, self-asserting Boston gentleman, gifted, ambitious, the embodiment of Massachusetts traditions and British prejudices, should feel deep contempt for the moral courage and the understanding of men whose motives were beyond the range of his sympathies and experience, was natural; for Josiah Quincy belonged to a class of Americans who cared so intensely for their own convictions that they could not care for a nation which did not represent them; and in his eyes Jefferson was a transparent fraud, his followers were dupes or ruffians, and the nation was hastening to a fatal crisis. Yet with all this to excuse him, his language still passed the bounds of license. He began by reaffirming that deception had been practised on the House when the President induced it to adopt the embargo without alluding to its coercive purpose: —

"I do not think I state my position too strongly when I say that not a man in this House deemed the embargo intended chiefly as a measure of coercion on Great Britain; that it was to be made permanent at all hazards until it had effected that object, and that nothing else effectual was to be done for the support of our maritime rights. If any individual was influenced by such motives, certainly they were not those of a majority of this House. Now, sir, on my conscience, I do believe that these were the motives and intentions of the Administration when they recommended the embargo to the adoption of this House."

So far as concerned President Jefferson this charge was true; but every one knew that Jefferson habitually threw responsibility on Congress, and after the scandal made by John Randolph in the Spanish affair of 1805, the House alone was to blame if it incurred consequences which were evident on the face of its measures. Quincy next asserted a worse and more mischievous charge: —

"Not only that embargo was resorted to as a means of coercion, but from the first it was never intended by the Administration to do anything else effectual for the support of our maritime rights. Sir, I am sick — sick to loathing — of this eternal clamor of 'war, war, war!' which has been kept up almost incessantly on this floor, now for more than two years. Sir, if I can help it, the old women of this country shall not be frightened in this way any longer. I have been a long time a close observer of what has been done and said by the majority of this House, and for one I am satisfied that no insult, however gross, offered to us by either France or Great Britain, could force this majority into the declaration of war. To use a strong but common expression, it could not be kicked into such a declaration by either nation."[1]

[1] Annals of Congress, 1808–1809, p. 1112.

Insults are pointless unless they have a foundation of truth or probability. The Parliament of Great Britain would have laughed at such a taunt; Napoleon would not have understood what it meant; but Congress drew a deep breath of dismay, for every member knew that openly and secretly, in public and in private, the single decisive argument against war had been and still was — fear. After four years of outrage such as would have made the blood of an Englishman or a Frenchman turn to fire in his veins, not an American could be found, between Canada and Texas, who avowed the wish to fight. Quincy's speech produced a momentary outbreak of passion; hot retorts were made; the chamber rang with epithets of abuse; but still no one professed to want war. The House twisted and turned like a martyr on his bed of steel, but its torture was of painful doubt, not of passion.

So far as mere words affected the public mind, Josiah Quincy's taunt, not less than the sarcasms of Canning and the arrogance of Napoleon, stung Americans beyond endurance. In one sense Quincy did good service to his country; his statesmanship, if not refined, was effective; his argument, if somewhat brutal, was strong; and within four-and-twenty hours the House met it in the only way that could preserve the dignity of Congress and the Administration, by passing the bill for an extra session with eighty votes against twenty-six. This result was reached January 20, and seemed to prove that the

Government had overcome its difficulties and mastered the situation; but nothing was further from the truth. Quincy knew what was passing behind the scenes. The Administration, so far from gaining strength, barely showed steadiness. At the moment when New England flung herself, with every sign of desperate rage, across the path of Government, faction within the Republican party struck Madison a severe blow before he had time for defence.

The first sign of Republican revolt appeared in unexpected favors lavished on the maltreated navy. Sixteen Republican senators combined with the Federalists to pass through the Senate a bill which ordered every armed vessel of the government, including gunboats, to be employed at once in active service. Gallatin saw in this measure only an intrigue of the Smiths and an attack upon the Treasury which would cost six million dollars without possible advantage to the public; but in fact the bill proved something more than an intrigue, for it showed the violence of New England reaction against the long starvation of the navy. Futile as was the scheme of manning gunboats in order to waste money which should have been spent on construction or magazines, New England was ready to join the Smiths or any other faction in any vote, however unreasonable, which promised employment for the seamen. Jefferson's system had shown its character most clearly in distrust and discouragement of the navy; and no one could wonder if the first sign of waning in his authority appeared in that department, or if Madison's first difficulties occurred in the weakest part of the old statesmanship.

Gallatin was taken by surprise, for the bill passed the Senate without serious opposition; but when it reached the House, January 10, the Treasury, through George W. Campbell, tried to strike out the clause which obliged the government to fit out and man all the vessels in the service without regard to the purpose of their employment. A number of Republican members, largely from New England, combining with the Federalists, defeated Campbell by a close vote of sixty-four to fifty-nine. In alarm at a measure which, before war was decided, threatened to take from the Treasury and throw into the ocean all the money reserved to support the first year of hostilities, Gallatin exerted himself to stop it. January 11, David R. Williams and the old Republicans came to his rescue with a motion to recommit, but they were again beaten by fifty-nine to fifty-eight. The next day John Montgomery of Maryland changed sides. By a vote of sixty-nine to fifty-three the bill was recommitted; January 13 the House in committee struck out the mandatory clause by fifty-three votes against forty-two; and January 16 the House accepted the amendment by sixty-eight votes against fifty-five. These divisions showed a considerable number of Republicans still acting with the Federalists; and in this respect the Senate was even less manageable than the House. Only after an obstinate struggle did the Senate give way so far that at last Congress agreed upon ordering four frigates to be fitted out, and as many gunboats as the public service might in the President's judgment require.

The reasons given by the Senate for persisting in its plan were proof that something remained untold; for they showed the hand and influence of the Smiths, rather than the interests of Madison's coming Administration. David R. Williams, who was a member of the Conference Committee, reported to the House that the managers for the Senate gave three reasons for insisting on their bill: —

"The first of them was that they wanted a pledge from this House that it was willing to come forward and defend the nation; another was that these [frigates] were necessary to defend the gunboats in their operations; and a third, that men could not be got to enlist for the service of the gunboats, and that to remedy this evil they might be enlisted to man the frigates, and afterwards transferred."[1]

A Navy Department which used its frigates to defend gunboats and decoy seamen was hardly fit to be trusted with unlimited credit on the Treasury. Gallatin lost his temper at finding his authority threatened with overthrow by an influence which he knew to be incompetent, and believed to be selfish and corrupt. Irritated by the vote of January 10, the Secretary of the Treasury studied the division-

[1] Annals of Congress, 1808–1809, p. 1185.

list to learn whence came the hostile influence which formed what he called[1] "the navy coalition of 1809, by whom were sacrificed forty Republican members, nine Republican States, the Republican cause itself, and the people of the United States, to a system of favoritism, extravagance, parade, and folly." He found the central point in the "Smith faction, or ruling party," of which he declared Wilson Cary Nicholas to be file-leader in the House, with six votes. With these acted six New York followers of Vice-President Clinton, and five "scared Yankees." The others were merely misled Republicans or Federalists.

"The Smith faction, or ruling party," of which Wilson Cary Nicholas was file-leader in the House, and which never failed to make its influence felt in moments of trouble, had gained in the Senate an ally whose selfishness was equal to that of General Smith, and whose nature was far more malignant. Of all the enemies with whom Madison had to deal, only one in his own party was venomous. Old George Clinton, though openly hostile, possessed strong qualities, and in any event was too old for serious effort. Samuel Smith played the game of politics somewhat too much like a game of whist, in which he allowed his trumps to fall indifferently on his partners or on his opponents, whenever he saw the chance to insure a trick to his own hand; but Smith was still a man from whom in the last resort cour-

[1] Adams's Gallatin, p. 387.

age and energy might be expected, and in whom, selfishness apart, confidence could be placed. No such redeeming quality could be truthfully attributed to William Branch Giles, the senator from Virginia, the third member of the senatorial cabal who was about to place himself in the path of the Administration, and to apply his abilities and persistence to the deliberate task of blocking the wheels of government.

Giles had served his party long and well, and thought himself entitled to higher recognition than he had as yet received. In later times a safe seat in the Senate became almost the highest prize of politics, — men sometimes preferred it to a candidacy for the Presidential office itself; but in 1809 the Cabinet stood above the Senate, and Giles looked upon himself as entitled to the Department of State, and in due time to the Presidency. Madison, with a different view of the public good and of his own comfort, betrayed the intention of appointing Gallatin his Secretary of State; and Gallatin's fitness for the post was so evident as to make his appointment the best that could be suggested; but at the first rumor of the intention, Giles united with Smith in threatening to procure the rejection of Gallatin by the Senate. To deny the President the selection of his own Secretary of State was an act of factiousness which remained without a parallel; but Giles and Smith had both the will and the power to carry their point. Even Wilson Cary Nicholas remonstrated in vain.

"From the first," was the story told by Nicholas,[1] "Mr. Giles declared his determination to vote against Gallatin. I repeatedly urged and entreated him not to do it; for several days it was an object of discussion between us; there was no way which our long and intimate friendship would justify, consistent with my respect for him, in which I did not assail him. To all my arguments he replied that his duty to his country was to him paramount to every other consideration, and that he could not justify to himself permitting Gallatin to be Secretary of State, if his vote would prevent it."

Thus Gallatin's foreign birth — the only objection alleged against him — became the pretext for Giles to declare war against the coming Administration of President Madison. With the aid of Vice-President Clinton, Senator Samuel Smith, and the Federalists, Giles could control the Senate; and every factious interest which wished to force on Madison an object of its own was sure to ally itself with these intriguers until its object should be conceded. The Senate was already a hot-bed of intrigue, where William B. Giles, Timothy Pickering, George Clinton, and Samuel Smith held control; and unless Madison by some great effort of force or skill could crush Giles, in time not only the new Administration, but also the Union itself, might find a deadly danger in the venom of his selfishness.

At the close of January, affairs at Washington were trembling on a poise. The laws required for

[1] Adams's Gallatin p. 388.

Madison's purpose were all passed save one; but the party was rent in pieces by faction. Discipline was at an end; the States of Massachusetts and Connecticut were openly adopting treasonable measures; and the great trial of strength — the decision of Congress on immediate repeal of the embargo — had not yet been reached.

CHAPTER XIX.

EARLY in January the intended policy of Madison became known. As the story has already told, Madison and Gallatin decided to retain the embargo until June, but to call the new Congress together May 22, and then to declare war, unless Erskine could make concessions. President Jefferson was chiefly interested in maintaining the embargo until after March 4, and the despotism he had so long maintained over Congress seemed still to exasperate his enemies. By common consent, attack upon the embargo was regarded as attack upon the President: and the Northern Democrats had so far lost respect for their old leader as to betray almost a passion for telling him unpleasant truths.

Joseph Story, who took the lead in this party rebellion, came to Congress determined to overthrow the embargo, and found Ezekiel Bacon — another Massachusetts member — equally determined with himself. In after years Justice Story told the tale as he remembered it:[1] —

"The whole influence of the Administration was directly brought to bear upon Mr. Ezekiel Bacon and

[1] Story's Life of Story, i. 187.

myself to seduce us from what we considered a great duty to our country, and especially to New England. We were scolded, privately consulted, and argued with by the Administration and its friends on that occasion. I knew at the time that Mr. Jefferson had no ulterior measure in view, and was determined on protracting the embargo for an indefinite period, even for years. I was well satisfied that such a course would not and could not be borne by New England, and would bring on a direct rebellion. It would be ruin to the whole country. Yet Mr. Jefferson, with his usual visionary obstinacy, was determined to maintain it; and the New England Republicans were to be made the instruments. Mr. Bacon and myself resisted; and measures were concerted by us, with the aid of Pennsylvania, to compel him to abandon his mad scheme. For this he never forgave me."

Joseph Story, with very high and amiable qualities, was quick in temper; and in regard to Jefferson he let his temper master his memory.

"One thing I did learn while I was a member of Congress," he continued, "and that was that New England was expected, so far as the Republicans were concerned, to do everything and to have nothing. They were to obey, but not to be trusted. This, in my humble judgment, was the steady policy of Mr. Jefferson at all times. We were to be kept divided, and thus used to neutralize each other."

In this spirit toward his own President Story came to Washington, and joined hands with Timothy Pickering, John Randolph, and George Canning in the attempt "to lower and degrade" Jefferson in the eyes of his own people. Jefferson asked only to be spared the indignity of signing with his own hand the unconditional repeal of the embargo; while the single point on which Story, Bacon, Pickering, and Canning were agreed was that the repeal should be the act of the man who made the law. On one side Jefferson, Madison, Gallatin, and their friends entreated Congress to stand firm; to maintain the ground already solemnly taken; to leave the embargo until June, and then to declare war if they pleased. On the other hand, Pickering, Bacon, Story, the Clintons, and the Pennsylvanians demanded immediate repeal,—partly to pacify New England, but quite as much for the reason, which Pickering urged, that immediate repeal would prevent war. That it would in fact prevent war was obvious. Repeal was submission.

Story took no part in the public struggle, for he left Washington about January 20, and the great debate began ten days afterward; but although he held his peace in public, and his friends made no open display of their anger, the temper in which they acted was notorious, and the breach between them and Jefferson was never healed. They could not forgive him: that Jefferson should ever forget the wound they inflicted, required magnanimity beyond that of any philosopher known in politics.

As soon as the naval and military bills and the extra session for May 22 were at last fairly determined and every detail decided, Wilson Cary Nicholas took the lead of the House, and January 30 called up a Resolution intended to settle the policy of embargo and war. The words of this Resolve were too serious not to have received very careful attention:

"*Resolved*, As the opinion of this House, that the United States ought not to delay beyond the ——— day of ——— to resume, maintain, and defend the navigation of the high seas; and that provision ought to be made by law for repealing on the ——— day of ——— the several embargo laws, and for authorizing at the same time letters of marque and reprisal against Great Britain and France, provided on that day their Orders or Edicts violating the lawful commerce and neutral rights of the United States shall be in force; or against either of those nations having in force such Orders or Edicts."

Nicholas agreed to divide the Resolution so that a test vote might first be taken on the repeal of the embargo; and he then moved to fill the blank with the words, "the first day of June." The House was thus asked to pledge itself that on June 1 the embargo should cease. On this question the debate began.

David R. Williams was a typical Carolinian. With something of the overbearing temper which marked his class, he had also the independence and the honesty which went far to redeem their failings. He had stood for years, with his friend Macon, proof against the influence of patronage and power; he supported the embargo, and was not ashamed to avow his dread of war; but since his favorite measure was to be thrown aside, he stood by his character, and made an appeal to the House, giving at once to the debate an air of dignity which it never wholly lost: —

"Will you drive us to a repeal of the embargo, and make no resistance? Are you ready to lie down quietly under the impositions laid upon you? You have driven us from the embargo. The excitements in the East render it necessary that we should enforce the embargo with the bayonet or repeal it. I will repeal it, — and I could weep over it more than over a lost child. If you do not resist, you are no longer a nation; you dare not call yourself so; you are the merest vassals conceivable. . . . I appeal to the minority, who hold the destinies of the nation in their grasp, — for they can enforce embargo without the bayonet, — I beg them, if they will not declare war, that they will do the best they can for their country."

No one then wondered to see South Carolina almost on her knees before Massachusetts, beseeching her, on her own terms, for her own honor, to do the best she could for the common country; but Massachusetts had no voice to respond. Dryly, in the caustic tone of Connecticut austerity, Samuel Dana replied that the days of ancient chivalry had not yet returned. When Massachusetts at last found a spokesman, she gave her answer through the mouth of Ezekiel Bacon, — a man second to none in respectability, but not one whom, in a moment of supreme crisis, the State would naturally have chosen among all her citizens to pronounce her will. Bacon had carefully collected advice from the men in his State who were most competent to give counsel;[1] but in Massachusetts affairs at Washington were little understood. Bent only on saving the Union by forcing a repeal of the embargo, and hampered by alliance with Federalists and Pennsylvanians, Bacon could not afford to show a sense of national self-respect.

He began by admitting that the discontents in New England made immediate repeal necessary: —

"It surely could not be sound policy, by adhering to this system beyond the measure of absolute necessity, to risk in the hands of any faction which might be disposed to wield it an instrument by which they may endanger the union of our country, and raise themselves to power on the ruins of liberty and the Constitution."

Such a beginning, offering a reward for threats of disunion, and conceding to traitors what would have been refused to good citizens, was an evil augury; and the rest of Bacon's speech carried out the promise. As he refused to prolong the embargo, so he refused to vote for war. "In every point of view, the policy of declaring offensive war against any nation four months in advance is to me wholly objectionable." The conclusion was as feeble as was required by the premises; but only some demon of bad taste could have inspired an orator at such a moment to use the language of Falstaff; —

[1] Cf. J. Q. Adams to Ezekiel Bacon, Nov. 17 and Dec. 21, 1808; New England Federalism, pp, 127, 131.

"We choose not to take measures any more than to give reasons 'upon compulsion,' and we will not so take them. We will, however, I trust, defend ourselves against the depredations of both [belligerents]; and if they both or either choose to persevere in the execution of their lawless aggressions, we shall, it is hoped, become more united in our determination and our efforts to vindicate our rights, if they shall continue to be assailed. At any rate, I am for leaving it to the wisdom of the ensuing Congress, which is to meet at an early day, to determine upon that position which the nation shall take in relation to such a state of things as may grow out of the course which I propose."

Between the Federalists and the Republicans of Massachusetts Congress was left under no illusions. Bacon expressed in these vacillating phrases the true sense of the country. On the evening of February 2, after four days of debate, the committee, by seventy-three votes against forty, rejected Wilson Cary Nicholas's motion to fix June 1 as the date for removing the embargo; and the next day, by an affirmative vote of seventy, with no negatives, March 4 was fixed as the term.

Immediately after this decisive division John Randolph took the floor. Discord had become his single object in public life. The Federalists at least had a purpose in their seditiousness, and were honest in preferring the British government to their own; the Republicans of all shades, however weak in will or poor in motive, were earnest in their love of country; but Randolph was neither honest nor earnest, neither American nor English nor truly Virginian. Disappointed ambition had turned him into a mere egoist; his habits had already become intemperate, and his health was broken; but he could still charge upon Jefferson all the disasters of the country, and could delight in the overwhelming ruin which had fallen upon his former chief. Randolph's speech of February 3 was stale and tedious. Except on the single point of raising the embargo he was spiritless; and his only positive idea, borrowed from the Federalists, consisted in a motion that, instead of issuing letters of marque, Government should authorize merchant-vessels to arm and defend themselves from seizure. If the scheme had a meaning, it meant submission to the British Orders, and was suggested by the Federalists for no other object; but in Randolph's mind such a plan carried no definite consequence.

On Randolph's motion the debate continued until February 7. The Republicans, disconcerted and disheartened by the conduct of their friends from New England and New York, made little show of energy, and left to David R. Williams the task of expressing the whole ignominy of their defeat. Williams struggled manfully. Randolph's fears for the Constitution were answered by the South Carolinian in a few words, which condensed into a single paragraph the results of his party theories: —

"If the Constitution is made of such brittle stuff as not to stand a single war; if it is only to be preserved by submission to foreign taxation, — I shall very soon lose all solicitude for its preservation."

With more than Federalist bitterness he taunted the hesitation of the Democrats, — "contemptible cowardice," he called it. "It is time we should *assume*, if it is not in our natures, nerve enough to decide whether we will go to war or submit." The House replied by striking out the recommendation of reprisals, by a vote of fifty-seven to thirty-nine.

These two votes rendered the Administration for the moment powerless to make head against the sweeping Federalist victory. Josiah Quincy, who watched every symptom of democratic disaster, wrote as early as February 2, before the first defeat of the Administration:[1] "There is dreadful distraction in the enemy's camp on the subject of removing the embargo. Jefferson and his friends are obstinate. Bacon and the Northern Democrats are equally determined that it shall be raised in March." The next day Quincy added: "Jefferson is a host; and if the wand of that magician is not broken, he will yet defeat the attempt."

The contest had become personal; to break the "wand of the magician" was as much the object of Democrats as of Federalists, and neither Madison nor Gallatin could restore discipline. February 4 the Secretary of the Treasury wrote:[2] "As far as my information goes, everything grows more quiet in

[1] Quincy's Life of Quincy, p. 185.

[2] Adams's Gallatin, p. 386.

Massachusetts and Maine. All would be well if our friends remained firm here."

The attempt to hold the friends of the Administration firm brought only greater disaster. The vote in committee refusing to recommend reprisals took place February 7; and the next day Quincy wrote again: "Great caucusing is the order of the day and the night here. The Administration is determined to rally its friends, and postpone the removal of the embargo till May. But I think they cannot succeed. Bacon, I am told, stands firm and obstinate against all their solicitations and even almost denunciations. However, they had another caucus last night. The event is unknown. Jefferson has prevailed."

February 9 the result of the caucus was shown by a vote of the House discharging the Committee of the Whole, and referring the subject to the Committee of Foreign Relations, whose chairman was G. W. Campbell, — which amounted to a public admission that Madison's plan had failed, and that some new expedient for uniting the party must be invented. Ezekiel Bacon refused to obey the caucus, and voted with the Federalists against the reference.

President Jefferson, though his name was still a terror to his enemies, accepted whatever decision his Cabinet advised. Till the day of his death he never forgot the violence of these last weeks of his administration, or the outcry of the New England towns. "How powerfully did we feel the energy of this organization in the case of the embargo," he wrote long afterward.[1] "I felt the foundations of the government shaken under my feet by the New England townships." He showed the same lack of interest in February which had marked his conduct in November; not even the certainty of his own overthrow called out the familiar phrases of vexation. February 7 he wrote to his son-in-law, Thomas Mann Randolph,[2] —

"I thought Congress had taken their ground firmly for continuing their embargo till June, and then war. But a sudden and unaccountable revolution of opinion took place the last week, chiefly among the New England and New York members, and in a kind of panic they voted the 4th of March for removing the embargo, and by such a majority as gave all reason to believe they would not agree either to war or non-intercourse. This, too, was after we had become satisfied that the Essex Junto had found their expectation desperate, of inducing the people there either to separation or forcible opposition. The majority of Congress, however, has now rallied to the removing the embargo on the 4th March, non-intercourse with France and Great Britain, trade everywhere else, and continuing war preparations. The further details are not yet settled, but I believe it is perfectly certain that the embargo will be taken off the 4th of March."

As the President became more subdued, Senator Pickering became more vehement; his hatred for Jefferson resembled the hatred of Cotton Mather for

[1] Jefferson to J. C. Cabell, Feb. 2, 1816; Works, vi. 540.
[2] Works, v. 424.

a witch. February 4 he wrote to his nephew in Boston:[1] —

"I entertain no doubt that Jefferson stands pledged to Bonaparte to maintain the embargo until a non-intercourse or war shall succeed; and he dreads the explosion justly to be apprehended by him from the disappointment and passion of Bonaparte, should the embargo be removed without a substitute as well or better comporting with his views. Upon this aspect of things it behooves our State legislature to advance with a firm step in defence of the rights of our citizens and of the Constitution. The palatines tremble at their posts. The least relaxation or wavering in the councils of New England would give them fresh courage, and hazard the most disastrous consequences."

Another observer wrote comments, serious in a different sense. Erskine watched with extreme interest every detail of this complicated struggle, and reported to Canning both facts and speculations which could not fail to affect the British government. Aware that Canning had won a brilliant success, Erskine labored to profit by his triumph, and to turn it in the interests of peace. A vast majority of Americans, he said,[2] wanted only some plausible excuse to justify them in resenting Napoleon's conduct; but "they naturally wish to be saved the complete humiliation of being obliged avowedly to recant all their violent declarations of their determination never

[1] Pickering to T. Williams, Feb. 4, 1809; Pickering MSS.
[2] Erskine to Canning, Feb. 9, 1809; MSS. British Archives.

to submit to the Orders in Council of Great Britain." He speculated "how far it might be possible still further to bend the spirit of that part of the people of the United States until they should be forced to single out France to be resisted as the original aggressors while his Majesty's Orders in Council continued to be enforced." After the repeal of the embargo and the refusal to make war, but one remnant of American protest against British aggressions remained. The Republican caucus, February 7, decided in favor of returning to Jefferson's pacific non-intercourse, — the system which had been, by common consent, thrown aside as insufficient even before the embargo. February 10 Erskine gave an account of the new measure, and of its probable effect on American politics: —

"It is true that a non-intercourse law may be considered by the Eastern States very objectionable; but as it would be rather a nominal prohibition than a rigorous enforcement, a resistance to it would be less likely to be made, and of less importance if it should take place. The ultimate consequences of such differences and jealousies arising between the Southern and Eastern States would inevitably tend to a dissolution of the Union, which has been for some time talked of, and has of late, as I have heard, been seriously contemplated by many of the leading people in the Eastern division."

The Non-intercourse Bill, which Erskine described February 10 as likely to be no more than a nominal prohibition of commerce, was reported February 11 to the House from the Committee of Foreign Relations. The bill excluded all public and private vessels of France and England from American waters; forbade under severe penalties the importation of British or French goods; repealed the embargo laws, "except so far as they relate to Great Britain or France or their colonies or dependencies, or places in the actual possession of either;" and gave the President authority to reopen by proclamation the trade with France or England in case either of these countries should cease to violate neutral rights. That the proposed non-intercourse was in truth submission to the Orders in Council, no one denied.

"I conceive that great advantages may be reaped from it by England," wrote Erskine,[1] "as she has the command of the seas, and can procure through neutrals any of the produce of this country, besides the immense quantity which will be brought direct to Great Britain under various pretences; whereas France will obtain but little, at a great expense and risk."

Such a non-intercourse merely sanctioned smuggling, and was intended for no other purpose. Gallatin in his disgust flung open the doors to illicit commerce. When Erskine went to him to ask what was meant by "France, England, and their dependencies," Gallatin replied that only places in actual possession of England and France were intended; that it was impossible to say what nations had decrees in force infringing neutral rights, but that

[1] Erskine to Canning, Feb. 10, 1809; MSS. British Archives.

even Holland would be considered an independent country.[1]

"The intention of this indefinite description," continued Erskine, "is undoubtedly to leave open as many places for their commerce as they can, consistently with keeping up an appearance of resistance to the belligerent restrictions; but it is thoroughly understood that the whole measure is a mere subterfuge to extricate themselves from the embarrassments of the embargo system, and is never intended to be enforced."

When this bill came before the House, another long debate arose. Hardly a trace of national pride remained. No one approved the bill, but no one struggled longer against submission. Josiah Quincy and many of the Federalists held that the surrender was not yet complete enough, and that total submission to Great Britain must precede the return of Massachusetts to harmony with the Union, or to a share in measures of government. His words were worth noting: —

"He wished peace if possible; if war, union in that war. For this reason he wished a negotiation to be opened, unshackled with those impediments to it which now existed. As long as they remained, the people in the portion of country whence he came would not deem an unsuccessful attempt at negotiation to be cause for war. If they were removed, and an earnest attempt at negotiation was made, unimpeded with these restrictions, and should not meet with success, they would join heartily in a war."

[1] Erskine to Canning, Feb. 13, 1809; MSS. British Archives.

Doubtless Quincy believed the truth of what he said; but as though to prove him mistaken in claiming even the modest amount of patriotism which he asserted for his party, Barent Gardenier immediately followed with a declaration that Great Britain was wholly in the right, and that America should not only submit to the Orders in Council, but should take pride in submission: —

"I do not say that the orders were lawful, or that they were not infringements of our rights as a neutral nation, — as it might offend the prejudices of the House. But I may be permitted to say that if they were unlawful, I have proved that they are not hurtful; that the British Orders in Council only supplied to that which our sense of honor would lead us to do, their sanction."[1]

Gardenier's views roused no longer much outward irritation. The war Republicans liked honest avowals better than sham patriotism; but John Randolph, unwilling to be embarrassed with allies so candid, rated Gardenier sharply: —

"I looked at the gentleman from New York at that moment with the sort of sensation which we feel in beholding a sprightly child meddling with edged tools, — every moment expecting, what actually happened, that he will cut his fingers. . . . The gentleman's friends, if any he have, — and I have no right to presume that he has none, but the contrary, — will do well to keep such dangerous implements out of his way for the future."

Randolph himself persisted in the scheme of withdrawing all restrictions on commerce, and allowing

[1] Annals of Congress, 1808–1809, p. 1460.

merchant-vessels to arm, — a measure which had the advantage of being warlike or pacific, according as he should prefer in the future to represent it. David R. Williams hit upon an idea more sensible, and likely to prove more effective. "If the embargo is to be taken off, and war not to be substituted, — if the nation is to submit, — I wish to do it profitably." He proposed to shut out the shipping of England and France, but to admit their manufactures, under a duty of fifty per cent when imported in American vessels. A number of Southern Republicans approved this plan.

Much the strongest speech against the bill was that of George W. Campbell, who made no attempt to hide his mortification at seeing the House desert him, its leader, and turn its back upon the pledge it had solemnly given in accepting his Report only two months before: —

"At the very time when your own people are rallying round the standard of their government; when they are about to shake off that timidity, that alarm, that restless disposition, which the first pressure occasioned by the suspension of commerce naturally produced; when they are, in almost every quarter of the Union, declaring their determination and solemnly pledging themselves to support your measures, to maintain the embargo, or go to war if necessary, — to do anything but submit: at that very moment, instead of being invited by a similar patriotic enthusiasm to throw yourselves in front, and to lead them on to the honorable contest, you abandon the ground you have already occupied, you check their generous enthusiasm, and leave them the mortification of seeing their country disgraced by a timid, temporizing policy that must, if persevered in, ruin the nation."

Although events had already proved that no appeal to self-respect called out a response from this Congress, Campbell might reasonably suppose that arguments of self-interest would be heard; and he pressed one objection to the bill which, in theory, should have been decisive:—

"The non-intercourse would press most severely on the Southern and Western States, who depend chiefly on the immediate exchange of their productions for foreign goods, and would throw almost the whole commerce of the nation into the hands of the Eastern States, without competition, and also add a premium on their manufactures at the expense of the agricultural interest to the South and West. Foreign goods being excluded, the manufacturing States would furnish the rest of the Union with their manufactured goods at their own prices."

A moment's reflection must have satisfied the Republicans that this argument against the bill was fatal. Non-intercourse must ruin the South, in order to offer an immense bribe to the shipping and manufactures of New England as an inducement for New England to remain in the Union. The manufacturing interests never ventured to ask such extravagant protection as was thrust upon them in 1809 by the fears of the agricultural States; the greed of corporate capital never suggested the monopoly created for Eastern ships and factories by a measure which shut from America all ships and manufactures but theirs. Even if but partially enforced, such legislation was ruinous to agriculture.

Entreaty and argument were thrown away. The House lost discipline, self-respect, and party character. No one felt responsible for any result, no majority approved any suggestion. As the last days of the session drew near, the machinery of legislation broke down, and Congress became helpless. So strange and humiliating a spectacle had not before been seen. The nation seemed sinking into the weakness of dissolution.

The paralysis came in a form that could not be disguised. While the House disputed over one Non-intercourse Bill, the Senate passed another; and February 22 the House laid aside its own measure in order to take up that of the Senate, which contained the disputed clause authorizing letters of marque and reprisal against nations that should continue their unlawful edicts after repeal of the embargo. In pursuance of its vote of February 7, the House in committee promptly struck out the reprisal clause. Next it rejected David R. Williams's motion for discriminating duties. Ezekiel Bacon, perhaps somewhat scandalized at the legislation he had chiefly caused, suggested the Federalist plan of authorizing merchant-vessels to resist seizure; and February 25 a struggle occurred on the question of permitting forcible resistance by merchant-vessels. The minority was deeply agitated as the act of complete submission became imminent. David R. Williams cried that if the House could so abandon national rights, they deserved to be scoffed by all the world; John W. Eppes declared himself compelled to believe Josiah Quincy's assertion that the majority could not be kicked into a war; even the peaceable Macon moved a warlike amendment. Vote after vote was taken; again and again the ayes and noes were called on dilatory motions of adjournment; but every motion looking toward war was steadily voted down, and in the end, February 27, the Non-intercourse Bill in its most unresisting shape received the approval of the House. Not a speaker defended it; at the last moment the charge was freely made that the bill had not a single friend. The members who voted for it declared in doing so that the measure was a weak and wretched expedient, that they detested it, and took it merely as a choice of evils; but eighty-one members voted in its favor, and only forty in the negative. More extraordinary still, this non-intercourse, which bound the South to the feet of New England, was supported by forty-one Southern members, while but twelve New England representatives recorded their names in its favor.

Three months afterward, at a moment when the danger of war seemed to have vanished, John Randolph recalled the memory of this confused struggle, and claimed for President Jefferson and himself the credit for having prevented a declaration of war. He had voted against the non-intercourse, he said, because he had believed that he could get rid of the embargo on still better terms; others had voted against it because they thought it absolute disgrace:[1] —

"The fact is that nobody would advocate it; that though it was carried by a majority of two to one, those who finally voted for it condemned it, and all parties seemed ashamed of it; and that . . . all the high-toned men and high-toned presses in this country denounced the majority of this House for passing that law, as having utterly disgraced themselves. . . . If the great leaders could have been gratified, according to their own showing they would have dragged this country into a war with Great Britain. . . . Now to be sure, sir, those persons who undertook to stop their wild career were composed of heterogeneous materials; . . . there were minority men, caucus men, protesters, — in fact, sir, all parties, Catholics, Protestants, Seceders, — and all were united in the effort to prevent the leaders of both Houses from plunging the nation into a war with one Power and knuckling to the other; from riveting the chains of French influence, perhaps of French alliance upon us. Thank God that their designs were proclaimed to the nation, that the President did not give his consent, which would have made us kick the beam. Yes, sir! Federalists, minority men, protesters, and all would have kicked the beam if it had ever emanated from the Cabinet that the President was for war."

If Randolph was right, the "wand of the magician" had not been broken; and other observers besides Randolph held the same opinion. "Jefferson

[1] Annals of Congress, 1809–1810; part i. 149, 150.

has triumphed," wrote Josiah Quincy, February 27, immediately after the repeal; "his intrigues have prevailed."[1]

In a spirit widely different from that of Randolph and Quincy, Nathaniel Macon, February 28, wrote to his friend Nicholson, —

"Otis, the Secretary of the Senate, has this moment informed the House of Representatives that the Senate have agreed to the amendments made by the House to the Bill to repeal the embargo.

"The Lord, the mighty Lord, must come to our assistance, or I fear we are undone as a nation!"[2]

[1] Quincy's Life of Quincy, p. 185.

[2] Macon to Nicholson, Feb. 28, 1809; Nicholson MSS.

CHAPTER XX.

THE repeal of the embargo, which received the President's signature March 1, closed the long reign of President Jefferson; and with but one exception the remark of John Randolph was destined to remain true, that "never has there been any Administration which went out of office and left the nation in a state so deplorable and calamitous." That the blame for this failure rested wholly upon Jefferson might be doubted; but no one felt more keenly than he the disappointment under which his old hopes and ambitions were crushed.

Loss of popularity was his bitterest trial. He who longed like a sensitive child for sympathy and love left office as strongly and almost as generally disliked as the least popular President who preceded or followed him. He had undertaken to create a government which should interfere in no way with private action, and he had created one which interfered directly in the concerns of every private citizen in the land. He had come into power as the champion of State-rights, and had driven States to the verge of armed resistance. He had begun by claiming credit for stern economy, and ended by exceeding the expenditure of his predecessors. He had invented a policy of peace, and his invention resulted in the necessity of fighting at once the two greatest Powers in the world.

The feelings of the New England Democrats have been described in their own words. Angry as Ezekiel Bacon and Joseph Story were, their bitterness against Jefferson was hardly so great as that of the Clintonians in New York; but the same irritation extended even into the compact democracy of Pennsylvania. In the preceding summer, before the Presidential election, A. J. Dallas said to Gallatin:[1] "I verily believe one year more of writing, speaking, and appointing would render Mr. Jefferson a more odious President, even to the Democrats, than John Adams." So far as could be judged from the conduct of the party, the prophecy became truth. The Southern Republicans, always loyal to a Southern President, would not openly turn against their old leader, but the Northern Democrats made no disguise of their aversion.

Not even in 1798 had factiousness been so violent as in the last month of President Jefferson's power; in 1800 the country in comparison had been contented. Feb. 23, 1809, nearly three weeks after the disastrous overthrow of the embargo in Congress, the Connecticut legislature met in special session to "interpose" between the people and the national government. In a Report echoing the words of Governor Trumbull's speech, the House instantly approved his refusal to aid

1 Dallas to Gallatin, July 30, 1808; Adams's Gallatin, p. 372.

in carrying out the "unconstitutional and despotic" Enforcement Act, and pledged itself to join the legislature of Massachusetts in the measures proposed "to give to the commercial States their fair and just consideration in the Union."[1] The spirit in which Massachusetts meant to act was shown in a formal Address to the People issued by her Legislature March 1, bearing the official signatures of Harrison Gray Otis, President of the Senate, and Timothy Bigelow, Speaker of the House.

"Protesting in the sight of God the sincerity of their attachment to the Union of the States, and their determination to cherish and preserve it at every hazard until it shall fail to secure to them those blessings which alone give value to any form of government," the Massachusetts legislature laid before the people of the State certain Reports and measures adopted for the purpose of impeding the embargo laws, and apologized for having done no more, on the ground that more could not have been done "without authorizing a forcible resistance to Acts of Congress,—an ultimate resource so deeply to be deprecated that the cases which might justify it should not be trusted even to the imagination until they actually happen." Less than forty years before, Massachusetts had used much the same language in regard to Acts of Parliament, and the world knew what then followed; but even in the bitterest controversies

[1] Report and Resolutions, National Intelligencer, March 10, 1809.

over Stamp Act or Port Bill, the General Court of Massachusetts had never insulted King George as they insulted President Jefferson. The Address at great length asserted that his Government was laboring under "an habitual and impolitic predilection for France;" and even in making this assertion it apologized for England in terms which echoed the words of Canning and Castlereagh: —

"Without pretending to compare and adjust the respective injuries sustained from the two nations, it cannot be disguised that in some instances our nation has received from Great Britain compensation; in others offers of atonement, and in all the language of conciliation and respect."

On the other hand, war with England must lead to alliance with France; and that a connection with France "must be forever fatal to the liberty and independence of the nation is obvious to all who are not blinded by partiality and passion."

Such reasoning had the merits of its emphasis. The case of forcible resistance which could not be trusted to the imagination until it happened pointed designedly to a war with England, which, being equivalent to a connection with France, must be forever fatal to the liberty and independence of the United States. The dogma that a British war must dissolve the Union had become more than ever an article of Federalist faith. Even Rufus King, writing to Pickering, January 31, said:[1] "The embargo, as we are

[1] King to Pickering, Jan. 31, 1809; Pickering MSS.

now told, is to give way to war. If the project be to unite with France against England, the Union cannot be preserved." To prevent war with England was to prevent a dissolution of the Union; and the legislature of Massachusetts, acting on that idea, closed what it called its "Patriotick Proceedings," by declaring to the people of the Commonwealth the measures by which alone the Union could be saved: —

"As the malady is deep, you will still be deceived by trusting to any temporary relief. You must realize and comprehend the nature of your peculiar interests, and by steady, persevering, and well-concerted efforts rise into an attitude to promote and preserve them. The farmer must remember that his prosperity is inseparable from that of the merchant; and that there is little affinity between his condition and habits and those of a Southern planter. The interests of New England must be defined, understood, and firmly represented. A perfect intelligence must be cultivated among those States, and a united effort must be made and continued to acquire their just influence in the national government. For this purpose the Constitution should be amended, and the provision which gives to holders of slaves a representation equal to that of six hundred thousand free citizens should be abolished. Experience proves the injustice, and time will increase the inequality, of this principle, the original reason for which has entirely failed. Other amendments to secure commerce and navigation from a repetition of destructive and insidious theories are indispensable."

Such were the conditions on which Massachusetts must insist: —

"The Legislature are aware that their measures and sentiments will encourage their opponents in propagating the foul imputation of a design to dismember the Union. But when did party malice want a theme to excite popular prejudice? When did it have recourse to one more absurd and unfounded?"

The object of the Federalist majority was to strengthen the Union, — so they protested and so they doubtless believed; but in truth they insisted upon creating a new Union as a condition of their remaining in the old. The fatal word "must" ran through all their demands: —

"If the Southern States are disposed to avail themselves of the advantages resulting from our strength and resources for common defence, they must be willing to patronize the interests of navigation and commerce without which our strength will be weakness. If they wish to appropriate a portion of the public revenue toward roads, canals, or for the purchase of arms and the improvement of their militia, they must consent that you who purchase your own arms, and have already roads, canals, and militia in most excellent order, shall have another portion of it devoted to naval protection. If they in the spirit of chivalry are ready to rush into an unnecessary and ruinous war with one nation, they must suffer you to pause before you bid an eternal adieu to your independence by an alliance with another."

Union of New England against the national Union — an idea hitherto confined to the brain of Timothy Pickering — had become the avowed object of the Massachusetts and Connecticut legislatures. "Nothing less than a perfect union and intelligence among the Eastern States" could answer the objects of Pickering; but side by side with the perfect union of the Eastern States went a perfect intelligence between those States and the British government. On one side, Pickering maintained relations with Rose; on the other, Sir James Craig kept a secret agent at Boston. January 26, at the moment when the crisis of war or peace was about to be decided at Washington, Mr. Ryland at Quebec, on behalf of the Governor-General of Canada, sent for John Henry to undertake another winter journey through New England.[1] His instructions, dated February 6 and signed by Sir James Craig himself, enjoined the utmost secrecy, and restricted Henry to the task of ascertaining how far, in case of war, the Federalists of the Eastern States would look to England for assistance, or be disposed to enter into a connection with the British government.[2] Only in case the Federalist leaders should express a wish to that effect was Henry cautiously to avow his official character, and to receive any communication for transmittal. February 10 Henry started on this errand, but before he reached Boston the news that Congress had decided to repeal the embargo without declaring war left him little to do. He remained quietly in Boston, in familiar relations

[1] Ryland to John Henry, Jan. 26, 1809; State Papers, iii. 546.

[2] Sir James Craig to John Henry, Feb. 6, 1809; State Papers, iii. 546.

with the Federalist leaders,[1] without betraying his errand; and the substance of his reports to the governor-general amounted only to a decided opinion that the Federalists were not yet ready to act: "I can assure you that at this moment they do not freely entertain the project of withdrawing the Eastern States from the Union, finding it a very unpopular topic."[2] Until midsummer, when the last fear of war vanished, this accredited agent of the governor-general waited at Boston for events. "His manners being gentlemanly and his letters of introduction good," said Josiah Quincy, "he was admitted freely into society and heard the conversation at private tables."

Had Jefferson known that a British emissary was secretly waiting at Boston to profit by the result of eight years' Republican policy, he could not but have felt deep personal mortification mingled with his sense of wrong. Of all Jefferson's hopes, perhaps the warmest had been that of overthrowing the power of his New England enemies, — those whom he had once called the monarchical Federalists, — the clergy and the Essex Junto. Instead of overthrowing them he had given them, for the first time in their lives, unlimited power for mischief; he had overthrown only the moderate Federalists, who when forced to choose between treason and embargo submitted to the embargo and hated its author. The Essex

[1] Quincy's Life of Quincy, p. 250.

[2] Henry to Sir J. Craig, March 7, 1809; State Papers, iii. 549.

Junto became supreme in New England; and behind it stood the power of Great Britain, ready to interpose, if necessary, for its defence.

Jefferson submitted in silence, and even with an air of approval, to the abrupt abandonment of his favorite measure. He admitted that the embargo had failed; he even exaggerated its evils, and described it as more costly than war. His language implied that the failure of peaceable coercion was no longer a matter of doubt in his mind.

"The belligerent edicts," he wrote to Armstrong,[1] "rendered our embargo necessary to call home our ships, our seamen, and property. We expected some effect, too, from the coercion of interest. Some it has had, but much less on account of evasions and domestic opposition to it. After fifteen months' continuance, it is now discontinued because, losing fifty million dollars of exports annually by it, it costs more than war, which might be carried on for a third of that, besides what might be got by reprisal."

To Dupont de Nemours Jefferson wrote in the same strain.[2] He signed without the betrayal of a protest the bill repealing the embargo, and talked of war as a necessary evil. Not until more than a year afterward did he admit the bitterness of his disappointment and mortification; but July 16, 1810, he wrote to his old Secretary of War a letter which expressed,

[1] Jefferson to Armstrong, March 5, 1809; Works, v. 433.

[2] Jefferson to Dupont de Nemours, March 2, 1809; Works, v. 432.

in his familiar note of irritability, the feelings he had pent up:[1] —

"The Federalists during their short-lived ascendency have nevertheless, by forcing us from the embargo, inflicted a wound on our interests which can never be cured, and on our affections which will require time to cicatrize. I ascribe all this to one pseudo-Republican, — Story. He came on in place of Crowninshield, I believe, and stayed only a few days, — long enough, however, to get complete hold of Bacon, who, giving in to his representations, became panic-struck, and communicated the panic to his colleagues, and they to a majority of the sound members of Congress. They believed in the alternative of repeal or civil war, and produced the fatal measure of repeal. . . . I have ever been anxious to avoid a war with England unless forced by a situation more losing than war itself; but I did believe we could coerce her to justice by peaceable means; and the embargo, evaded as it was, proved it would have coerced her had it been honestly executed. The proof she exhibited on that occasion that she can exercise such an influence in this country as to control the will of its government and three fourths of its people is to me the most mortifying circumstance which has occurred since the establishment of our government."

In truth, the disaster was appalling; and Jefferson described it in moderate terms by admitting that the policy of peaceable coercion brought upon him mortification such as no other President ever suffered. So complete was his overthrow that his popular influence

[1] Jefferson to Dearborn, July 15, 1810; Works, v. 529.

declined even in the South. Twenty years elapsed before his political authority recovered power over the Northern people; for not until the embargo and its memories faded from men's minds did the mighty shadow of Jefferson's Revolutionary name efface the ruin of his Presidency. Yet he clung with more and more tenacity to the faith that his theory of peaceable coercion was sound; and when within a few months of his death he alluded for the last time to the embargo, he spoke of it as "a measure which, persevered in a little longer, we had subsequent and satisfactory assurance would have effected its object completely." [1]

A discomfiture so conspicuous could not fail to bring in its train a swarm of petty humiliations which for the moment were more painful than the great misfortune. Jefferson had hoped to make his country forever pure and free; to abolish war, with its train of debt, extravagance, corruption, and tyranny; to build up a government devoted only to useful and moral objects; to bring upon earth a new era of peace and good-will among men. Throughout the twistings and windings of his course as President he clung to this main idea; or if he seemed for a moment to forget it, he never failed to return and to persist with almost heroic obstinacy in enforcing its lessons. By repealing the embargo, Congress avowedly and even maliciously rejected and trampled upon the only part of Jefferson's statesmanship which claimed originality,

[1] Jefferson to W. B. Giles, Dec. 25, 1825; Works, vii. 424.

or which in his own opinion entitled him to rank as a philosophic legislator. The mortification he felt was natural and extreme, but such as every great statesman might expect, and such as most of them experienced. The supreme bitterness of the moment lay rather in the sudden loss of respect and consideration which at all times marked the decline of power, but became most painful when the surrender of office followed a political defeat at the hands of supposed friends.

The last days of his authority were embittered by a personal slight which wounded him deeply. After the peace of Tilsit the Emperor Alexander of Russia expressed a wish to exchange ministers with the United States government. In every point of view America must gain by winning the friendship of Russia; and much as Jefferson disliked multiplying diplomatic offices, he could not but feel that at a time when his ministers were likely at any moment to be driven from France and England, nothing could be more useful than to secure a foothold at St. Petersburg. Without loss of time he created the mission, and appointed his old personal friend William Short to the new post. In August, 1808, during the recess of Congress, he sent Short to Europe, with orders to stop at Paris until the Senate should confirm his appointment. For political reasons Jefferson waited till the close of the session, and then, February 24, made this appointment the subject of his last Message to the Senate, explaining the motives which had induced him to create a diplomatic agency at St. Petersburg, and announcing that Short had received his commission and had gone to Europe six months before on this errand.

No sooner had the Senate, on receiving this Message, gone into executive session than Senator Bradley of Vermont offered a Resolution that any intercourse with Russia, such as the President suggested, might "be carried on with equal facility and effect by other public agents of the United States without the expense of a permanent minister plenipotentiary;" or in case of sudden negotiations for peace in Europe, "the permanent minister at any of the Courts thereof may be instructed to attend on the same;" and that for these reasons the proposed appointment was at present inexpedient and unnecessary. After much secret debate, Senator Bradley, February 27, withdrew his motion, and the Senate then abruptly and unanimously rejected Short's nomination.

The discourtesy was flagrant. As a matter of policy the new mission might fairly be subject for argument; and the Senate had a right, if it chose, to follow its own opinions on such a subject. Unreasonable as was the idea of sending hither and thither the American ministers "at any of the Courts of Europe," when every senator knew that on the continent of Europe America had but one minister, and even he was on the verge of dismissal or recall; ill-judged as was the assertion that a consular agent could carry on "with equal facility and effect" at a

Court like that of St. Petersburg a diplomatic intercourse which would need every resource of public and private influence; narrow as was the policy of refusing "the expense of a permanent minister plenipotentiary" to the only nation in the world which offered her friendship at a moment when England and France were doing their utmost to spare America the expense of legations at London and Paris,—yet these objections to Jefferson's wish were such as the Senate might naturally make, for they were the established creed of the Republican party, and no one had done more than Jefferson himself to erect them into a party dogma. Dislike of diplomacy was a relic of the old colonial status when America had been dependent on Europe,—a prejudice rising chiefly from an uneasy sense of social disadvantage. Whenever America should become strong and self-confident, these petty jealousies were sure to disappear, and her relations with other Powers would be controlled solely by her wants; but meanwhile the Senate in every emergency might be expected to embarrass the relations of the Executive with foreign governments, and to give untenable reasons for its conduct. That the Senate should object, could have been no surprise to Jefferson; but that it should without even a private explanation reject abruptly and unanimously the last personal favor asked by a President for whom every Republican senator professed friendship, and from whom most had received innumerable favors, seemed an unpardonable insult. So Jefferson felt it. He wrote to Short in accents of undisguised mortification: —

"It is with much concern I inform you that the Senate has negatived your appointment. We thought it best to keep back the nomination to the close of the session, that the mission might remain secret as long as possible, which you know was our purpose from the beginning. It was then sent in with an explanation of its object and motives. We took for granted, if any hesitation should arise, that the Senate would take time, and that our friends in that body would make inquiries of us and give us the opportunity of explaining and removing objections; but to our great surprise and with an unexampled precipitancy they rejected it at once. This reception of the last of my official communications to them could not be unfelt."[1]

Senators attempted explanations: Short had been too long in the diplomatic service or resident abroad; the diplomatic connections of the United States with Europe were already too extensive, and rather than send more ministers those actually abroad should be recalled; "riveted to the system of unentanglement with Europe," the Senate, though sensible of "the great virtues, the high character, the powerful influence, and valuable friendship of the Emperor," declined the honor of relations with him. Yet these reasons showed only that the Senate felt as little regard for Jefferson's opinions and feelings as for those of the Czar. The manner of the rejection, even more

[1] Jefferson to W. Short, March 8, 1809; Works, v. 435.

than the rejection itself, proved the willingness of the President's oldest friends to inflict what they knew to be a painful wound on the self-respect of a fallen leader.

These mortifications, which rapidly followed each other in the last days of February, were endured by Jefferson with dignity and in silence. Perhaps senators would have better understood and might have more respected a vigorous burst of anger, even at some cost of dignity, than they did the self-restraint of the sensitive gentleman who had no longer a wish but to escape from Washington and seek peace in the calm of Monticello. He could with only a pang of mortified pride write his excuses to the Emperor Alexander and to William Short, and dismiss the matter forever from his mind. Public annoyances were for him nearly at an end, and could never recur; but unfortunately these public trials came upon him at a moment when his private anxieties were extreme.

In his style of life as President, Jefferson had indulged in such easy and liberal expenses as suited the place he held. Far from showing extravagance, the White House and its surroundings had in his time the outward look of a Virginia plantation. The President was required to pay the expenses of the house and grounds. In consequence, the grounds were uncared for, the palings broken or wanting, the paths undefined, and the place a waste, running imperceptibly into the barren fields about it. Within, the house was as simple as without, after the usual style of Virginia houses, where the scale was often extravagant but the details plain. Only in his table did Jefferson spend an unusual amount of money with excellent results for his political influence, for no President ever understood better than Jefferson the art of entertaining; yet his table cost him no excessive sums. For the best champagne he paid less than a dollar a bottle; for the best Bordeaux he paid a dollar; and the Madeira which was drunk in pipes at the White House cost between fifty and sixty cents a bottle. His French cook and cook's assistant were paid about four hundred dollars a year. On such a scale his salary of twenty-five thousand dollars was equivalent to fully sixty thousand dollars of modern money; and his accounts showed that for the first and probably the most expensive year of his Presidency he spent only $16,800 which could properly be charged to his public and official character.[1] A mode of life so simple and so easily controlled should in a village like Washington have left no opening for arrears of debt; but when Jefferson, about to quit the White House forever, attempted to settle his accounts, he discovered that he had exceeded his income. Not his expenses as President, but his expenses as planter dragged him down. At first he thought that his debts would reach seven or eight thousand dollars, which must be discharged from a private estate hardly

[1] Jefferson's Financial Diary. Harper's Magazine, March, 1885, pp. 534–542.

exceeding two hundred thousand dollars in value at the best of times, and rendered almost worthless by neglect and by the embargo. The sudden demand for this sum of money, coming at the moment of his political mortifications, wrung from him cries of genuine distress such as no public disaster had called out. He wrote to his commission-merchant entreating him to borrow the money: —

"Since I have become sensible of this deficit I have been under an agony of mortification, and therefore must solicit as much urgency in the negotiation as the case will admit. My intervening nights will be almost sleepless, as nothing could be more distressing to me than to leave debts here unpaid, if indeed I should be permitted to depart with them unpaid, of which I am by no means certain."[1]

Large as it was, this estimate of the debt fell far short of the reality. The arrears amounted in truth to twenty thousand dollars.[2] Nothing but immediate and rigid economy could restore the loss, and even with every advantage Jefferson could never hope to live again upon his old scale without incurring bankruptcy; he must cease to be a *grand seigneur*, or drag his family into the ruin which seemed to be the fate of every Virginian.

Under the weight of these troubles, public and private, Jefferson's longing to escape became intense; and his letters repeated, in accents more and more earnest, the single wish that filled his mind.

[1] Domestic Life of Thomas Jefferson, p. 400.

[2] Randall's Jefferson, iii. 326.

"I shall within a few days," he wrote February 25,[1] "divest myself of the anxieties and the labors with which I have been oppressed, and retire with inexpressible delight to my family, my friends, my farms, and books. There I may indulge at length in that tranquillity and those pursuits from which I have been divorced by the character of the times in which I have lived, and which have forced me into the line of political life under a sense of duty and against a great and constant aversion to it."

March 2 he wrote to Dupont de Nemours,[2] in stronger terms of weariness and disgust: "Never did a prisoner released from his chains feel such relief as I shall on shaking off the shackles of power. Nature intended me for the tranquil pursuits of science by rendering them my supreme delight." March 4 he rode once more on horseback to the Capitol, and stood by the side of Madison while John Marshall administered the oath of office. The weight of administration was at last removed, but the longing for home became only the greater. March 5 he wrote to Armstrong:[3] "Within two or three days I retire from scenes of difficulty, anxiety, and of contending passions, to the elysium of domestic affections and the irresponsible direction of my own affairs." A week afterward Jefferson quitted Washington forever. On horseback, over roads impassable to wheels,

[1] Jefferson to Warden, Feb. 25, 1809; Jefferson MSS.

[2] Jefferson to Dupont de Nemours, March 2, 1809; Works, v. 432.

[3] Jefferson to Armstrong, March 5, 1809; Works, v. 434.

through snow and storm, he hurried back to Monticello to recover in the quiet of home the peace of mind he had lost in the disappointments of his statesmanship. He arrived at Monticello March 15, and never again passed beyond the bounds of a few adjacent counties.

With a sigh of relief which seemed as sincere and deep as his own, the Northern people saw him turn his back on the White House and disappear from the arena in which he had for sixteen years challenged every comer. In the Northern States few regrets were wasted upon his departure, for every mind was intent on profiting by the overthrow of his system; but Virginia was still loyal to him, and the citizens of his own county of Albemarle welcomed with an affectionate address his final return. His reply, dignified and full of grateful feeling, seemed intended as an answer to the attacks of partisan grossness and a challenge to the judgment of mankind: —

"The anxieties you express to administer to my happiness do of themselves confer that happiness; and the measure will be complete if my endeavors to fulfil my duties in the several public stations to which I have been called have obtained for me the approbation of my country. The part which I have acted on the theatre of public life has been before them, and to their sentence I submit it; but the testimony of my native county, of the individuals who have known me in private life, to my conduct in its various duties and relations is the more grateful as proceeding from eye-witnesses and observers, from triers of the vicinage. Of you, then, my neighbors,

I may ask in the face of the world, 'Whose ox have I taken, or whom have I defrauded? Whom have I oppressed, or of whose hand have I received a bribe to blind mine eyes therewith?' On your verdict I rest with conscious security."

INDEX TO VOLS. I. AND II.

END OF VOL. II.